100 most beautiful national parks in the world

100 most beautiful national parks in the world

100 most
beautiful national parks in the world

A journey across five continents

REBO
PUBLISHERS

Foreword

Dear Reader,

Virtually every landscape on earth has its own special appeal and its own distinct geological features and climatic conditions which produce an individual array of flora and fauna. Seasons too impose their own changes on the landscape and the variations in light conditions or time of day can also lend a distinctly different atmosphere to each place.

For eons, the earth was left largely to its own devices. It was not until the emergence of modern civilization that nature's balance was disrupted. The Romans deforested vast areas of Italy and by the twentieth century, virtually every region on earth, apart from a tiny handful of remote areas, had been settled and, in some cases, over-populated by man. Primeval forests have been turned into farmland, high-alpine slopes transformed into ski pistes, most of the upland peat bogs drained, great rivers straightened and their vast floodplains restricted by dikes and embankments. Consequently, animals have been deprived of their natural habitats in many areas to allow man to exploit the landscape for his own gain. Occasionally, however, where man lives and works in harmony with nature, a number of species have adapted to occupy new niches in the ecosystem and have produced some distinctly individual natural landscapes. The decline in eco-friendly agricultural methods, nevertheless, means that even these areas now find themselves threatened.

Halfway through the nineteenth century, naturalists and biologists became aware of the seriousness of these threats to nature and this realization marked the start of efforts to preserve endangered natural landscapes. The first nature reserve was created in Canada during the 1870s and, since the beginning of the twentieth century, nature conservation areas, biosphere reserves, natural monuments and even national parks have been set up in nearly every country in the world. Many of these have since become

The most beautiful
waterfalls in the world:
the rolling waters
of the Iguazu
on the border between
Argentina and Brazil.

popular tourist destinations, but they have also suceeded in becoming the last sanctuaries for a large
number of animals teetering on the brink of extinction. Without these reserves, there would be no pandas
left in the wild, the giant monitor lizards of Southeast Asia would have vanished long ago and the last
few bison would not have survived in Canada. Some of the world's greatest natural wonders, such as the
Grand Canyon and the Iguazu waterfalls with their specialized flora, would have been sacrificed to mass
tourism.

It would be presumptuous to try and list these beautiful natural landscapes according to preference.
It was difficult to objectively narrow down our enormous range of choices and while we did concentrate
on the factors contributing to the uniqueness of an individual landscape, at the end of the day the choice
was bound to be subjective. Although UNESCO has conferred world heritage site status on many of these
national parks, some decisions were probably governed by political expediencies. Several thousand
nature reserves now exist throughout the world and each year sees fresh additions to this number.

Our book hopes to take you on a journey to some of the most breathtakingly beautiful areas of our
planet. It is wonderful to imagine that nature, with its unique and sometimes rare flora and fauna, might
some day be allowed to develop undisturbed, at least in a few places in the world. These national parks
are protecting and preserving our last opportunity to experience true adventure and natural beauty
on the planet.

The Publisher

Contents

Among Alaska's mountain giants

DENALI NATIONAL PARK around Mount McKinley is one of the largest nature reserves in the world

Denali
National Park

PACIFIC   USA

GETTING THERE:
Alaska Route 3 (George Parks Highway) passes the National Park. Alaska Railroad train station at the entrance to the Park. Airports in Anchorage and Fairbanks. The National Park's single road is only open to private vehicles within a 10 mile radius. Thereafter one must continue in one of the Park's own tourist buses, or else on foot or bicycle

WHERE TO STAY:
Choice of seven campsites. Maximum of 14 days' visit per year

CLIMATE:
January: -4° to +14° F (-20° to -10° C); July: between 43° and 64° F (6° and 18° C)

MAIN ATTRACTIONS:
Hiking; bird and wildlife watching; white water trips on the Nenana River; Wonder Lake and Chilchukabena Lake

SPECIAL TIPS:
Special permits required for trails through the heart of the Park. Anyone wishing to climb Mount McKinley or Mount Foraker must book 60 days in advance. A fee will be charged for the permit.

Denali National Park in Alaska is a vast conservation area and biosphere reserve covering more than 9,300 square miles (24,000km²). It is home to North America's highest mountain, Mount McKinley, a steep-sided colossus rising 15,750ft (4,800m) below its snow and ice-covered summit. This imposing mountain, almost 20,350ft (6,200m) in height, crowns the 620 mile (1,000km) long Alaska Range, a crescent-shaped chain of mountains that acts as a buffer against the damp sea air blowing in from the Gulf of Alaska.

Gleaming white glacier tongues descend toward the valley from awe-inspiring mountain peaks. Their melted ice water feeds the multitude of dark, glacial rivers flowing through the broad valleys. Meanwhile, crystal-clear rivers and streams tumble down from the low, tundra-covered hills in the north of the Park, emptying into the mighty Yukon River or the Susitna River in the south. This tundra landscape is dotted with hundreds of sparkling lakes and tarns.

Granite grows faster

Deep within the earth, geological forces are still at work below the Alaska Range. More than 600 earthquakes per year testify to the fact that this mountain range is still being thrust upwards. Not only is the Mount McKinley granite massif increasingly resistant to erosion, but it grows three-hundredths of an inch each year. While Mount McKinley has only been rising for the past 65 million years or so, most of the other major mountains in the range, composed of softer sandstones and limestone, were formed 200 to 400 million years ago when Alaska was at the bottom of an ocean. They are consequently unable to keep pace with Mount McKinley' growth rate, as their comparatively soft rock, under constant attack from frost, thaws, and glaciers, is gradually being eroded.

Visitors to the Park remain oblivious to most of the earthquakes, which usually occur directly underneath Mount McKinley. Generally speaking, these are relatively minor tremors occurring no more than 10 miles below the earth's surface. Only occasionally does the earthquake violently enough for visitors and buildings to feel tremors, which happens when the epicenter is at least 55–75 miles (89–120km) beneath Mount McKinley.

How the land bridge was formed

The pristine plant life preserved in Denali National Park is a unique combination of Asiatic and North American species. For most of the past two million years, Alaska was, after all, joined to Asia. Again and again, the land was separated from the southern part of North America by continental ice shields, thousands of feet deep. During the major Ice Ages, the bed of the Bering Sea also rose, forming a land bridge between Asia and America and providing yet another corridor for an

exchange of flora and fauna. Denali National Park is consequently home to numerous species of plants that do not occur in the more southerly regions of North America.

Only plants that can withstand the long, bitterly cold winters and manage with just a short summer growing season survive in this harsh landscape. Biologists have nevertheless identified more than 650 plant species and numerous varieties of mosses, lichens, fungi, and algae. Only a handful of tree species are able to survive in such extreme conditions. They are mostly found along the rivers, where the south-facing slopes support white and black spruce, paper birch, and quaking aspen. Many open areas are covered with heath vegetation and mosses. The north-facing slopes are underlain by deep beds of permafrost, but the thin layer of topsoil that manages to thaw each summer is enough to support forests of black spruce.

Cotton grass and dwarf vegetation

Apart from the heathers and mosses that populate the terrain, the region also contains sedges and grasses. The moist tundra slopes found at the foot of the mountains are covered with extensive meadows of cotton grass, interspersed with occasional dwarf shrubs, particularly alder and birch. The dry tundra area is carpeted by mats of mountain avens, grasses, and sedges. The National

Park is home to 39 species of mammal, but most visitors are content to see the "Big Five," which can usually be spotted from the single road running through the park. These include the massive moose, weighing in at 1,100lbs and often seen feeding on willows. Groups of caribou can sometimes be seen on the snow fields, trying to escape from the swarms of insects. Dall sheep peer down over the edge of precipitous cliffs, wolves roam the scant tundra vegetation and grizzly bears search the blueberry bushes for semi-ripe fruit.

One of the most unusual animals found in the Park is an inconspicuous little frog, measuring from just half an inch to three inches in size. This tiny wood frog is the only amphibian found in Alaska. With the advent of winter and the first frosts, the frog's liver produces glucose, a natural anti-freeze that protects the body cells from damage. It then freezes solid into a small chunk of ice; it ceases to breathe and its heart stops beating. In this way, it is able to survive even laboratory temperatures of 10º F (-12º C).

At 20,335ft, snow and ice-covered Mount McKinley is North America's highest mountain. It was first climbed in 1913 (above)

Autumn in Riley Creek, one of the main valleys in Mount McKinley region (above, left)

Deep, blue lakes present a picturesque contrast to the white, ice-covered slopes of the mountains (below, left)

The Alaskan moose is famed for its massive muzzle and hefty size (below, right)

Geysers and hot springs in the southern Rocky Mountains

YELLOWSTONE PARK, one of the last refuges for the American bison, provides a glimpse of what the earth looked like in prehistoric times

Long ago, 630,000 million years to be precise, a massive magma chamber exploded beneath this region. The area involved surrounds the point of contact of what are now the three North American states of Wyoming, Montana, and Idaho. The pressure building up under the earth's crust was finally released in a sudden eruption, creating a crater, measuring 45 kilometers in width and 75 kilometers in length. This crater, now forms the heart of Yellowstone National Park.

Subterranean activity began pushing the southern segment of the Rocky Mountains upward 65 million years ago and fresh lava flows were still spilling out over the landscape as recently as 40 million years ago. Entire forests were buried by falling ash which petrified over the course of millions of years and now provides the visitor with a glimpse of what the world looked like in its infancy.

Yellowstone is located above a so-called "Hot Spot," an area where the layer of the earth's crust above the molten earth's mantle is only a few kilometers thick. Surface water seeps down through the cracks and fissures, becoming super-heated until it either erupts as a geyser, blasting a jet of water several feet into the air, bubbles up out of the ground as a hot spring, or else is ejected in the form of fumaroles, plumes of hot steam from deep within the earth with temperatures heated to 280° F (138° C). Yellowstone harbors the most intense of natural geothermal activity anywhere in the world. There are some 10,000 or so of these hot springs in Yellowstone and more than 300 geysers spouting columns of water into the air.

When Old Faithful blows

The most famous of the geysers is Old Faithful. Since time immemorial, it has been blasting jets of hot water 100ft (30m) into the air at regular intervals of 35 to 120 minutes. These eruptions can last anything between 90 seconds and 5 minutes. The longer an eruption lasts, the longer it will be before the next one. Old Faithful's neighbor, the Giantess, on the other hand, takes six to eight months to recover between eruptions.

The shallow lake formed by the Grand Prismatic Hot Springs shimmers with every conceivable hue. An assortment of brightly-colored bacteria and algae have established themselves on its bottom, surviving on the substances that hot spring water brings to the surface from the depths of the earth. Biologists are still puzzled as to how these organisms manage to survive in such super-heated temperatures.

Mammoth Hot Springs produces water with an extremely high calcium concentrate that has built up, over the course of thousands of years, unusual terraces of sinter, which have spread like soft vanilla ice cream.

Yellowstone Lake was hollowed out by glacial movement during the last Ice Age. Its waters have carved out Yellowstone's own version of the Grand Canyon in the form of a gorge measuring 800–1,220ft (240–370m) in depth and exposing a colorful range of rock strata within the steep walls.

This huge witch's cauldron of bubbling activity has long been a source of fascination to Americans, so much so that the whole area, stretching across an area of 3,500 square miles (9,000km²), was designated a National Park as long ago as 1872, becoming the first official conservation park of its kind in the world.

Haven for deer

Apart from providing an opportunity to observe these stunning spectacles of geothermal activity, the Park also supports one of the richest concentrations of plant and animal life anywhere in the United States and is a designated biosphere reserve. Unfortunately, Yellowstone is one of a long list of North American national parks that number among the world's most endangered nature conservation areas. Outside the Park's boundaries, various enterprises are poised to pounce on its reserves of mineral resources, such as gold and oil, or are waiting for an opportunity to tap this natural source of heat for use in power stations.

Eighty percent of the National Park is covered by pristine pine forest and is home to more than one thousand, often insignificant, species of plant, such as the Agrostis rossae, a genus of grass that is found only in Yellowstone Park.

Surrounded by giant peaks soaring to heights of up to 13,200ft (4,000m), Yellowstone is the only place left where herds of wild bison are once again free to roam. These animals, which were hunted to the verge of extinction towards the end of the nineteenth century, have now recovered in number to around 2,000. The animal population of Yellowstone includes examples of every species of wildlife found in the Rocky Mountains. As well as the wolves, coyotes, and mountain cats, the individual varieties of white-tailed mule and wapiti deer, not to mention the bighorn sheep, cannot fail to draw the attention of an observant watcher. Nothing can beat the experience of catching a glimpse of a black bear among the trees or observing one of the Park's 200 grizzlies devouring its meal.

GETTING THERE:
Interstate Highway 90; at Livingstone, go south on Highway 89 for about 50 miles (80km). Airports at Cody and Jackson; Bozeman and Billings; Idaho Falls. From June to September, also at West Yellowstone to and from Salt Lake City. Buses from Bozeman

WHERE TO STAY:
Historic hotels; Wild West style lodges; cabins; camping sites within and outside the Park

CLIMATE:
Mountain climate: Average January temperature 10° F (-12° C); average July temperature 55° F (13° C)

MAIN ATTRACTIONS:
Old Faithful; Grand Prismatic Spring; Mammoth Hot Springs; Yellowstone Grand Canyon; Norris Geyser Basin; Madison Museum

SPECIAL TIPS:
Snowmobiles available in winter

Paradise for nature and animals alike: The sinter terraces of Mammoth Hot Springs (opposite, above left)

Bison and Wapiti deer are two of the animal species found in Yellowstone National Park (opposite, below left and above right)

Grand Prismatic Springs owes its shimmering colors to the presence of bacteria and algae (opposite, below right)

The eruption of a geyser is always a fascinating sight (this page)

11

The mists clear slowly in the valleys

SMOKY MOUNTAINS National Park is a haven for many animals and plants

USA
Washington●
Great
Smoky
PACIFIC
ATLANTIC

A delicate blue mist fills the valleys intersecting the 6,600ft (2,000m) high mountains and cloaking the dense forests in a mysterious veil. It takes the morning sun a long time to disperse these mists, which give the Great Smoky Mountains its name. This National Park, measuring 815 square miles (2,110km²), is situated along the border between North Carolina and Tennessee. It is an internationally designated biosphere reserve and world heritage site established to protect the central part of what is, geologically speaking, one of the oldest mountain ranges in the world with an ecosystem which owes its unique diversity to the last Ice Age.

Great Smoky Mountains National Park encompasses some of the highest peaks in the Appalachian Chain: Clingmans Dome, Mount Guyot, Collins, LeConte, and Keohart. None of these is lower than 5,900ft (1,800m). The best view over these incredibly beautiful, dark green mountains and steep, dark valleys is from the observation tower on Clingmans Dome. This is also the best spot for observing the amazing sunsets. Clingmans Dome rises 6,645ft (2,025m) in height and is the highest mountain in the Park.

The Appalachian Chain, which stretches some 1,600 miles (2,570km) southwest from the Gaspé Peninsula in Quebec, Canada to the Gulf coastal plain in Alabama, was formed 200 to 300 million years ago when two continental plates collided. Over the millions of years, rain, wind, frost and rivers sculpted the round, softly sloping mountains we see today out of once rugged peaks.

Five different types of forest

The vast ice shield that covered North America during the Ice Age did not manage to get past this mighty chain of mountains. The Appalachians were the last refuge for plants and animals whose original habitat was much further north. The resulting combination of species from both northern and southern regions has produced and preserved a unique a diversity of flora and fauna in this area.

The Smoky Mountains support a variety of habitats whose varied elevations determine a whole range of climatic zones. Several areas that experience heavy precipitation classify as rainforest.

All these factors have contributed to an astonishing diversity of undisturbed flora and fauna within the Park. A total of 1,500 flowering plants, including 130 species of trees, as well as an estimated 2,200 spore-producing plants, such as ferns, mosses, lichen, and algae, form the basis of a complex food chain.

The valleys and mountain slopes support five different types of forest. Campbell Overlook, a couple of miles beyond Sugarlands Visitor Center, provides the visitor with an incredible panoramic view of all five.

Stunning display of colors

At elevations of more than 4,600ft (1,400m), the forest resembles woodland in the northern North American state of Maine or near Quebec in Canada. Forests of red spruce, at its colorful best above 5,250ft (1,600m), cap the highest peaks in the Park, while the middle elevations around 3,300ft (1,000m) are dominated by various northern hardwoods, such as sugar maple, beech, and yellow birch, which resemble those species found throughout New England. In autumn, these forests are ablaze with color, producing a sensational display of brilliant reds, browns, and oranges, thrown into relief by occasional fir trees.

The drier ridges and peripheral areas around the Park tend to be populated by pine and oak. These areas often dry out because the ground is unable to retain water despite plentiful rainfall. Forest fires are consequently regarded as an inevitable part of the environment and, in their own way, play an integral part in the regeneration of this type of woodland. Forest management now includes controlled burning of selected areas in order to prevent unintentional forest fires from threatening lives and destroying property.

The harsher environment surrounding the river banks in these mist-covered valleys supports hemlock forest, while the warmer valleys sustain a diverse mix of lush woodland, including poplars, maple, birch, and dogwood, which remain green even when the forests higher up the mountains are aflame with their festive autumn colors.

The wildlife here is as abundant as the plant life. Early morning and late evening are the best times for viewing wildlife in the numerous open spaces within the forest.

Unpopular wild boar

The National Park is home to altogether 65 species of mammal. Some of these, like the coyote and bobcat, are very shy. Red deer are fairly common, as are black bears, red and gray foxes, possums, raccoons, gray squirrels, and southern flying squirrels. Widespread damage is caused by wild boar, a species of mammal introduced from Europe, which has successfully resisted all attempts to exterminate it.

GETTING THERE:
Nearest airports: Charlotte, North Carolina, and Knoxville, Tennessee. Interstate Highways 40 and 75

WHERE TO STAY:
All categories of hotel available outside the Park; caravan parks; camping sites; Le Conte Lodge, a mountain cabin (open to the public March-November)

CLIMATE:
Fairly unsettled weather with warm, humid summers and mild winters

MAIN ATTRACTIONS:
Clingmans Dome, Charlie's Bunion viewpoint, Mountain Farm Museum, Roaring Fork Motor Nature Trail

Indian Summer in the Smoky Mountains: The sensational colors of the mixed woodland in all its autumn glory are one of the National Park's unforgettable sights (left)

View of the peaks in the Appalachian Chain. The landscape owes its name to the fine mists clinging to the valleys (below)

Waterfalls accompany the rivers on their way down into the valley (right)

El Capitan stands guard

YOSEMITE NATIONAL PARK is the world's oldest protected granite mountain landscape

The charming landscape of Yosemite Valley lies in the Sierra Nevada, approximately 160 miles (250km) from San Francisco. The valley is encircled by vertical rock walls of bare granite and huge mountains and its entrance is guarded by two mighty granite monoliths, El Capitan and Cathedral Rock, each rising to an impressive 6,600ft (2,000m). Winding its way like a silver ribbon through this gently sloping valley, carved out during the Ice Age to a depth of 3,000ft (914m), is the crystal-clear Merced Mountain River. Lying roughly in the middle of this 8 mile (13km) long valley is the largest waterfall in the United States, plunging over 2,400ft (730m) over three cascades.

Yosemite National Park abounds in waterfalls, although some of the most spectacular are often only accessible on foot, such as the magnificent 330ft (100m) high Vernal Falls and the 600ft (180m) high Nevada Falls. If you follow the one-and-a-half mile (two and a half kilometer) long Sierra Point trail from Happy Isles to Sierra Point, you will encounter three more waterfalls: the Illilouette and the Upper and Lower Yosemite Falls.

Formed in the Ice Age

One of the most impressive peaks here is the distinctive semi-circular peak of Half Dome Mountain. Its steep slopes provide an ideal summer training area where mountain climbers from all over the world can practice their skills. The most scenic view of this mountain is undoubtedly from Glacier Point, a 7,200ft (2,200m) high promontory, which juts out into the southeastern end of the valley. It is almost certainly the Park's most breathtaking viewpoint, providing an outstanding panorama of the high peaks of the Sierra Nevada and the valley more than 3,300ft (1,000m) below.

Yosemite National Park has the largest concentration of forests and lakes in the whole Sierra Nevada, encompassing 1,200 square miles (3,000km²) of spectacular granite mountain scenery shaped by the Ice Age. The area was placed under protection in 1864 and thus enjoys the status of being the oldest protected conservation area on earth, even though it was not inaugurated as an official National Park until 1890, 18 years after Yellowstone Park.

A grove of giant trees

This magnificent mountain scenery with its gentle valleys, tranquil mountain lakes, and rushing streams represents a unique environment. There are three sites where ancient giant sequoias have survived. In the southern part of the Park, Mariposa Grove alone boasts a group of 500 of these awesome giants, the oldest of which is nicknamed "Grizzly Giant." It has been growing on this spot for 2,700 years, during which time its girth has grown to 31ft (9.4m).

The dramatic differences in elevation within the Park, starting at around 1,300ft (395m) and rising to some 13,200ft (4,000m) above sea level, have created a diversity of 27 different habitats for plant and animal life, ranging from a chaparral-type scrub zone in the low-lying areas through meadow habitats and pine forests to, finally, barren alpine terrain at 12,900ft (3,900m). Biologists have so far identified 1,400 species of plant.

The emblem of the United States of America

The diversity of vegetation is equally matched by the variety of animal species. The Park is home to 74 types of mammal, the most common of which are little gray squirrels, marmots and guinea-pig sized pikas. Californian bighorn sheep are also sometimes visible on the crags, their horns crashing together in combat. By 1914, these had completely disappeared from the Park, but were successfully reintroduced in the middle of the 1980s. If you are very lucky, you might catch sight of a black bear or mountain lion on the fringes of the forest and if you are very patient, you might be rewarded with a glimpse of a pine marten or fisher, but these animals are notoriously shy.

High above the gray, granite cliffs, the majestic peregrine falcons circle effortlessly on the updrafts and forests echo with the frantic drumming of woodpeckers hollowing out their nest sites. The Park is also one of the last breeding refuges for the rare bald-headed eagle, the distinctive emblem of the United States of America. Altogether, 230 species of bird have been recorded in Yosemite National Park. Some of these are resident, while others stop off here on their migration.

Yosemite • Washington USA

PACIFIC   ATLANTIC

GETTING THERE:
By car from Fresno; Merced; Modesto and Manteca; Lee Vining over the Tioga Pass. Airports: Fresno-Yosemite; San Francisco; Oakland; Sacramento. Bus links. Shuttle service within the Park

WHERE TO STAY:
Various categories of hotel in Yosemite Valley; cabins; camping near the Merced River

CLIMATE:
From 25°–54° F (-4°–12° C) around 8,600ft (2,600m) and 46°–90° F (8°–32° C) under 5,000ft (1,525m)

MAIN ATTRACTIONS:
Yosemite Valley and waterfall; Nevada and Vernal Falls; Mariposa Grove (giant sequoia)

Olmstead Point offers panoramic views of Yosemite's granite mountains (above)

The vertical rock face of Half Dome is a challenge that climbers find hard to resist (below, left)

There are numerous waterfalls throughout the Park (below, center)

The ground squirrel is a rarity in the Park (below, right)

Stone Age canyons

The exposed cliff faces of the **GRAND CANYON** provide a unique record of the earth's history

Grand Canyon USA Washington
PACIFIC ATLANTIC

GETTING THERE:
By car from the south on Interstate Highways 17 and 40, then via minor roads. Bus connections from Las Vegas, Phoenix, and Grand Canyon airports. Bus services throughout the National Park

WHERE TO STAY:
Wide choice of hotels, lodges, and camping sites

CLIMATE:
June-August: around 100° F (38° C) within the canyon; on the South Rim 50°-68° F (10°-20° C); North Rim cooler. November to February: snow with drifting on the South Rim; North Rim closed

MAIN ATTRACTIONS
South Rim; North Rim (less popular); Lake Powell on Glen Canyon Dam; Indian reservations; round trip flights; cycling and hiking tours; river rafting

SPECIAL TIPS:
Advisable to take a guide if undertaking trips into the inner canyon because it is easy get lost

The Colorado River in northern Arizona has carved an immense chasm a mile deep through a plateau that has gradually been thrust upward until it now sits 7,000–8,000ft (2,134–2,438m) above sea level. Over the past five to six million years, the relentless flow of water has cut one of the world's most spectacular gorges through these rocks. The Grand Canyon, which stretches for almost 310 miles (500km), is an impressive sight even from space.

Each year, around five million visitors make their way to this great rift in the earth's surface to view the incredible, often bizarre rock formations, which rise up from the bottom of the canyon. The rocks provide an illustrative record of how this deep valley, a mere 1,640ft (500m) across in some places, broadening out to 20 miles (30km) in others, was originally formed. The different strata visible in the sheer, exposed walls on either side of the Grand Canyon reflect the history of previous geological eras. The predominantly red-colored rock can change color depending on atmospheric conditions, glowing in a variety of reddish tones and even taking on a green or bluish hue in places. The ancient rocks at the bottom of the gorge were formed around 2,000 million years ago during the Pre-Cambrian period, early in the earth's history. Above this, each succeeding period has deposited its own stratum, some of which once rested at the bottom of the sea while others were

covered in primeval forest. The higher the layer, the greater the likelihood of animal fossils being found. Primitive plant fossils can be found in the lower strata of the late Pre-Cambrian period, which ended more than 500 million years ago. The climate here is almost as remarkable as the canyon. Summer temperatures on the Grand Canyon's South Rim are a very pleasant 50°–68° F (10°–20° C), but the nights can be cool and it snows in winter.

Scorching heat on the canyon floor

The North Rim is a good 985ft (300m) higher, enough to ensure a covering of snow for most of the year. In winter, this side of the canyon is usually closed due to adverse weather conditions.

An entirely different situation prevails at the bottom of the canyon where the Colorado River glistens like a silver ribbon one mile, or one and a half kilo-

meters, below. Viewed at closer quarters, it proves to be a mighty surging torrent and temperatures down here can rise to 122º F (50º C) in summer, although 100º F (38º C) is considered the norm.

The rims of this high plateau are covered with forests of grayish-green firs with scattered stands of hardy juniper bushes. The view from here spans five vegetation zones including desert conditions. The only vegetation at the bottom of the gorge, in the form of willow and tamarisk, is found immediately adjacent to the Colorado River and its tributaries. An ecosystem exposed to such extremes of heat and cold, where drought, rain, storm, and snow can follow hot on each other's heels, has resulted in a most unusual habitat to which an abundant variety of plant and animal life has adapted. This is one of the reasons why this National Park has been accorded world heritage status.

Around 1,500 varieties of plant have been identified in the five different vegetation zones, eleven of which are on the endangered list.

The region is also home to 76 species of mammal, 50 different reptiles and amphibians, and over 300 types of bird. The most common animal is the mule, which is frequently encountered trotting along the narrow mountain trails. The remote slopes of the inner canyon provide a refuge for bighorn sheep, although they too occasionally venture out onto the trails. Only the rare kaibab squirrel seems to prefer the less hospitable northern side without ever venturing across to the southern side.

Prehistoric ruins

Lynx and coyote roam all over the National Park and canyon, constantly on the hunt for deer, pronghorn antelope, or wapiti. The area is even home to a small population of mountain lions.

Many species of lizard are found here, as well as numerous tortoises and snakes, including the pink rattlesnake.

Not only does the National Park try to safeguard nature, but it also preserves evidence of the canyon's early inhabitants. More than 2,600 prehistoric sites have been found within the park. The only gap in its history seems to have occurred between 1200–1300, after which it was settled by Hulapai and Havasupai Indians who still inhabit small, impoverished reservations on the Park's boundaries.

The opening of Glen Canyon Dam in 1963 caused a great deal of environmental damage. Most worryingly, it caused some fairly dramatic changes in the river. Not only does less water now flow through the gorge, but it also carries fewer sediments, which are irregularly deposited, causing the river constantly to change course.

Viewpoint above the Colorado River valley offering a spectacular panoramic view of the depths of the Grand Canyon and the rock formations along the rim of the plateau (above)

This photo (bottom, left) shows the incredible extent of the Grand Canyon

River of grass

The EVERGLADES' landscape is a combination of mud flats, coastal prairie, and swampland

GETTING THERE:
Nearest airports: Miami, Ft Lauderdale, and Ft Myers. The main entrance for motorists at Flamingo is well marked

WHERE TO STAY:
Three lodges, three camp sites, one camping ground out in the wilderness, accessible only by boat

CLIMATE:
Rainy season from May to October with temperatures around 90° F (32° C). Hurricane season from June to November

MAIN ATTRACTIONS:
Boat (or canoe) trip from Flamingo, cable car trip from Shark Valley, hiking, visit to one of the interesting information centers

SPECIAL TIPS:
Good access and facilities for the disabled and wheelchair users

Dense areas of saw grass grow in the swamps and flood lands (above)

An alligator (below, center) and two ibis (below, right) in search of food

A view across the wide expanse of arid coastal prairie (below, left)

The Indian name for the vast expanse of swamp known as the Everglades is "river of grass," an area where the waterways are filled with huge expanses of saw grass stretching as far as the eye can see. Flowing through this area of southern Florida, and unlikely to be noticed by any visitor, is one of the most unusual rivers on earth. It is 50–60 miles (80–100km) wide, but even during the summer rainy season measures no more than 12–36in (30–90cm) in depth.

The first spring thunderstorms signal the start of the rainy season in May and rainwater begins collecting in Lake Okeechobee in central Florida. This lake averages a depth of just 12ft (3.7m), yet covers an area of 730 square miles (1,900km²). After just a few days of rain, it overflows its banks, saturating the broad expanse of flood plains. In October, when the amount of rainfall decreases, the water level drops and during the dry months, the lake splits into numerous smaller lakes. The rhythm of the seasons and vast expanse of flood land have created several unique, yet extremely sensitive, habitats that the Everglades National Park in southern Florida, comprising an area of over 2,300 square miles (6,000km²), struggles to protect. However, as the National Park is not an island, immune from environmental influences, preservation is increasingly difficult. Fifty percent of the Everglades, an area that once covered the whole of southern Florida, has dried up, yet the burgeoning cities in the area are constantly increasing their demands for water. Flood protection systems installed on the tributaries feeding the National Park are intended to channel the river, yet it remains one of the most endangered natural oases on earth.

A variety of habitats

The Everglades are not simply a monotonous landscape of water and swamp that dries up for a couple of months each year. A range of totally different habitats co-exist here side by side, and yet are heavily dependent on one another. The water discharged by the "Sea of Grass" into Florida Bay, for example, is saline, producing an environment in which saw grass cannot grow. Instead, the seabed is carpeted with dense areas of seaweed, an essential nutrient in this part of the ecosystem. The tidal waters of the coastal lagoons and tributaries, however, are a combination of salt and freshwater, creating an ideal environment for dense thickets of red, black, and white mangroves. Their root systems provide nurseries for a variety of crabs and fish. Huge flocks of wading birds can also be seen on the mud flats at low water, searching for food.

Saline coastal prairie

Situated between the wading areas and the higher hinterland is the coastal prairie, a bone-dry area supporting plants that are capable of tolerating saline soil conditions. Only a few specialized desert plants thrive in the face of the extreme conditions here.

The saw grass has its main domain in the central section of this broad waterway, where the swamps are somewhat deeper and the water flows more quickly, if only at the rate of around 100ft (30m) a day.

The area is dotted with numerous islands, rising just one or two feet above the broad expanse of water, which support small areas of woodland including mahogany, swamp cypresses, royal palms, maple and fig trees and evergreen oaks. Further up, where the humidity level is higher beneath the dense tree canopy, there is a thriving population of ferns, orchids, and epiphytic plants.

The indigenous animal world rivals that of the plants in its variety and abundance. The Everglades National Park is the only place on earth where crocodiles and 20ft (6m) long alligators live side by side in peaceful harmony. Both of these creatures are number among the thirty-six endangered species in the Park.

The Park's main priority is to protect the West Indian sea cow, or manatee, from extinction. These gentle creatures are suffering greatly from the loss of their habitat and changes in water flow in the wetlands, as a result of construction work outside the park boundaries. These large, heavy and slow-moving herbivores are nevertheless totally trusting of humans. They were once considered "stupid" because they failed to get out of the way of boats at the sound of engine noise. However, their hearing is not tuned to the same frequency range and they simply do not hear boats approaching.

An ocean spewing lava

HAWAII'S active volcanoes are constantly changing the landscape, creating new islands in the ocean

Hawaii is one of the earth's "hot spots." Beneath the island, huge bubbles of molten rock rise upward from a depth of 9,500ft (2,900m) below the earth's mantle like gas bubbles in a glass of fizzy soda. These so-called "plumes" blast upward through the earth's crust and ocean floor, forming mighty, towering volcanoes.

The "hot spot" beneath Hawaii is generally recognized as the hottest on the planet. These volcanoes began erupting around 70 million years ago and their peaks now form the islands of the Hawaiian archipelago. Hawaii itself is almost as high as the Himalayas: Mauna Loa rises an incredible 30,000ft (9,200m) out of an otherwise flat ocean floor.

Along this submarine ridge is the Pacific tectonic plate. It is moving in a northwesterly direction at the rate of about 4in (10cm) a year across the fissure where these fountains of lava are constantly erupting. The 130 islands of the Hawaiian archipelago are strung out in a 1,500 mile (2,400km) chain and were all formed above the Hawaiian "hot spot." Over the course of millions of years, they have drifted northwest along with the ocean floor and are now gradually collapsing and sinking so that in a few millions years' time they will have also become part of the extensive chain of submarine mountains leading all the way to Kampchatka in Siberia.

Land of lava

Hawaii's volcanic National Park, extending over an area of 350 square miles (900km²) in the southeast of the island, includes what are arguably two of the world's most spectacular volcanoes. Over the past 20 years alone, their lava masses have created nearly one square mile of new landmass along Hawaii's southeast coast. Occasional tremors from Loihi, a submarine volcano, are a perpetual reminder of its existence. It has already reached a height of 13,000ft (4000m) above the seabed and in a few thousand years, will emerge above the water, creating another new island.

Mauna Loa, the largest volcano in the world, accounts for 50 percent of the island's landmass, with an area measuring 74 by 64 miles (120 by 103km). Its lava flows cover an area of over 2,000 square miles (5,200km²). Its caldera, the bubbling, steaming crater of this shield volcano, is 2–3 miles (3–5km) in diameter and nearly 600ft (180m) deep. Despite the heat within, the rim of the crater is permanently crowned with snow.

To the east of Mauna Loa rises the elongated form of Kilauea, the youngest of Hawaii's volcanoes and regarded as the most active volcano on earth. It is usually seen spewing flame and lava, which bubbles up from the Halemaumau crater within the caldera. In 1990, a sedate stream of lava flowed down from the volcano's slopes, quietly burying the entire historic settlement of Kalapana. Halemaumau is home to the legendary fire goddess worshipped by local inhabitants.

Remote archipelago

The northern part of the island is dominated by three older, dormant volcanoes. Mauna Kea, measuring 13,800ft (4,206m), tops Mauna Loa by just 120ft (37m), while Kohala in the far north is in the advanced stages of collapse and is now just 5,600ft (1,700m) high. The 8,300ft (2,523m) high summit of Hualalai dominates the east coast. The Hawaiian archipelago's remote location, far away from its nearest neighbor, together with the sea winds, ocean, and constant changes wrought on the landscape by lava and ash, have all helped to shape the indigenous plant and animal life. It is precisely this volcanic activity which facilitates the rich diversity of different species. Ninety percent of all the plants found in the National Park are endemic to Hawaii. For this reason, it has been designated a world heritage site and — together with Haleakala National Park on nearby Maui — is classed as an international biosphere reserve.

The first plants to establish themselves on freshly cooled lava are lichens and mosses, followed by ferns, which grow into giant tree ferns in the dense rainforests covering the humid volcanic slopes. The island's hot, rain-free southwest flank, where the lava has created a smooth landscape devoid of plant life, is a uniquely beautiful, black wilderness.

PACIFIC · USA · Hawaii

GETTING THERE:
Airports at Hilo and Kailua-Kona. Head south by car on Highway 11

WHERE TO STAY:
Luxury accommodation in the Park itself at the historic Volcano House Hotel. Large choice of places to stay in Volcano Village

CLIMATE:
Weather can change very abruptly. Temperatures around 72° F (22° C) at sea level to around 45° F (7° C) at elevations of 11,150ft (3,400m)

MAIN ATTRACTIONS:
Mauna Loa crater; Mauna Loa rainforest trail; Kau desert; Volcano art center

Glowing lava flows down a volcano's flanks and sinks into the ocean (above)

Lava swallowed up an entire settlement on the shore of Kalapana (below, center)

Weathered lava landscapes support an abundance of undemanding vegetation (below, left)

View into Kilauea crater (right)

A haven for whooping cranes and buffalo

Canada's **WOOD BUFFALO NATIONAL PARK** is home to several species of animal that once teetered on the brink of extinction

CANADA

Wood Buffalo
National Park   Ottawa

PACIFIC   ATLANTIC

Endless expanses of tundra

In 1830, around 40 to 60 million bison still roamed the plains of North America. That was before the great slaughter, a tactic employed by the American Army to quell the Indian uprisings, began. Hunters, hired to kill the buffalo, not only benefited from the sale of buffalo meat, but also received a cash reward for each buffalo killed. By 1898, less than 1,000 of these ancient animals remained, some in Yellowstone Park and Northern Alberta, as well as 709 on a farm in Montana. Robbed of their main source of food, many Indian tribes also starved to death as a direct consequence of the buffalo's disappearance.

In 1906, the Canadian government purchased a breeding herd of buffalo in Montana and successfully returned them to the wild in Alberta, the area where Wood Buffalo National Park is now located. There, they interbred with some indigenous wood buffalo that had managed to survive, with the result that there are no longer any pure-bred animals of either buffalo species. These crossbreeds continue to be rather susceptible to disease. During the 1960s, however, a small, pure-bred herd of wood bison was discovered in a remote part of the Park and transported to Elk Island, where their numbers are gradually increasing.

Unique natural saline meadows

Wood Buffalo National Park, established in 1922 specifically to protect the buffalo, covers an area of 17,500 square miles (45,000km²). Today, 5,000 bison, the largest bison herd in the world, are once more roaming freely across the tundra.

This vast Park is so remotely situated that very few visitors make their way here. It spans three different landscapes, each with its own individual natural wonders.

Along its southern and western boundaries are the Caribou and Birch high plateaus, lying 1,650ft (500m) above sea level, in which numerous rivers have carved long, deep ravines out of the soft substrata. An abundance of fossils, the petrified remains of long extinct plant and animal life, has been exposed on the edges of the escarpment. These elevated plains are covered with typical polar tundra, consisting of firs and lichen.

The largest section of the National Park is the Alberta Plateau, part of the Canadian Shield, which terminates at the Slave River and continues as a vast, lowland plain. Springs, which surface where the lowlands run up against the edge of the Shield, are rich in mineral salts. During the dry season these are deposited over a salt pan of almost 100 square miles (250km²). These natural saline meadows, an unusual feature in North America, are home to numerous salt-tolerating plants, which are otherwise found exclusively in coastal regions.

Freshwater from Lake Claire

The plateau is an extensive wilderness of innumerable woods and mighty, meandering rivers, countless lakes and endless marshes. It is a karst landscape, peppered with numerous subterranean rivers which have hollowed out huge underground caves. When the roof of one of these caves collapses, great sinkholes are created, often with a small lake shimmering at the bottom of it. The fish that live in these lakes make their way here via subterranean streams, which connect with the rivers.

Situated in the southeast of the Park surrounding Lake Claire is the world's largest inland freshwater delta

where the rivers Peace, Athabasca, Slave, and Birch converge. The mud deposited by these rivers has created a wetland area extending over 1,700 square miles (4,500km²), comprising marshes, grasslands, and forest. The delta forms a vast nesting area and refuge for millions of water birds, as well as a spawning ground for fish. It is also one of the last breeding grounds for the endangered whooping crane. Standing 5 ft (1.5m) tall, these are the largest birds in North America. Their plumage is snowy white, with jet-black wingtips and a black head and legs. In 1941, the population of whooping cranes numbered just 15, but today around 200 of these majestic birds breed in the National Park. They often feed off the salt plains in the northern part of the Park where they can be viewed from a lookout point. In winter, they migrate 2,500 miles (4,000km) south to the coast of Texas, a long and hazardous flight which many do not survive.

Numerous flint tools have been discovered here, indicating that the region was already inhabited by man 9,000 years ago. Peace Point, a typical native settlement within the Park, is still occupied by five families who have retained a traditional lifestyle, living by fishing, hunting and trapping.

GETTING THERE:
Highway 5 between Hay River, Pine Point, and Fort Smith leads through the northeastern corner of the Park. Airports at Hay River, Pine Point, and Fort Smith

WHERE TO STAY:
Camping grounds and hotels in Hay River and Fort Smith

CLIMATE:
January: -13° F (-25° C), July: 61° F (16° C). An average of 40 thunderstorms each summer

MAIN ATTRACTIONS:
Wildlife watching; canoeing trips; numerous hiking trails; Peace Point; Northern Lights in winter

SPECIAL TIPS:
Roads in the National Park closed from November to April

Surrounded by a seemingly endless expanse of forest, two rivers converge in the Peace-Athabasca delta (above, left)

To the south, numerous tributaries empty into a huge wetland area (below, left)

Pelicans nest on islands in Slave River (center, right)

Arrow grass is found in northern sections of the Park (below, center)

More than 5,000 bison roam the land freely once more (below, right)

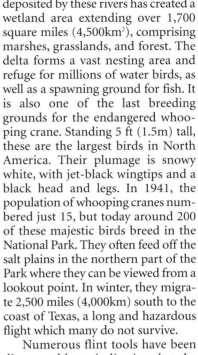

Canada's alpine wilderness

JASPER NATIONAL PARK in the Rocky Mountains spans several vegetation zones

Yellowhead Highway between Edmonton and Prince George runs through the heart of Jasper National Park, Canada's largest mountain park. It extends over an area of 385 square miles (1,000km²) and together with Banff, Kootenay, Yoho and several other smaller parks, forms a world heritage site protecting around 8,900 square miles (23,000km²) of unique Rocky Mountain scenery.

Snow-covered, jagged peaks tower majestically 9,900ft (3,000m) above broad valleys while glistening tongues of glaciers separate the summits. Dark, untouched forests cloak the mountainsides up to the tree line, while tranquil ribbons of lake line the valleys fed by the rushing waters of sparkling silver streams.

Jasper, the small tourist resort at the center of the park, is the starting point for visitors. It is here that the Icefields Parkway branches off to the south. This panoramic road, punctuated with numerous viewpoints, was to enable visitors to appreciate the Park in all its glory.

Traversing Wilcox Pass in the south of Jasper National Park and crossing into Banff National Park, the road runs past the tongue of the Athabasca Glacier, which measures 3 ¹/₂ miles (5.5km) in length and over half a mile (1km) across. It is the largest tongue of ice in the entire 125 square miles (325km²) of the Columbia Icefield, which is itself the biggest glacier area in the Rocky Mountains. The compacted ice of the Columbia Icefield stretches up to 1,150ft (350m) thick in places. Five of Canada's highest peaks, including Mount Columbia, surround this snowy expanse. Mount Columbia is the Park's highest mountain at 12,295ft (3,747m).

Rivers feeding two oceans

In addition to the Athabasca Glacier, seven other glaciers, including Dome, Kitchener, and Stutfield, descend from the Columbia Icefield. These feed three of the largest river systems in North America: the Mackenzie, which discharges into the North Polar Sea; the Nelson, which flows into Hudson Bay and thence into the Atlantic; and the Columbia, which empties in the Pacific. The Columbia Icefield has been receding since the eighteenth century, but its retreat seems to have slowed somewhat in recent times. To the east of the

central mountain chain, a narrower road, running parallel to the Icefields Parkway, weaves its way through the spectacular Maligne Canyon. Overshadowed by steep, vertical cliffs, it winds past Medicine Lake with its many legends until it reaches the 14 mile (22km) long Maligne Lake.

Every autumn, a curious natural phenomenon occurs at Medicine Lake. When its main tributary, the Maligne River, turns to ice, the lake vanishes, its waters seeping away through the porous limestone bedrock which forms a singular subterranean drainage system.

When the road terminates, the visitor is greeted by the breathtaking sight of Canada's largest mountain lake, Maligne Lake, nestling against a backdrop of majestic, snowy, glacier-covered mountains. The sparkling

water, plunging to a depth of 320ft (97m), is an unbelievable and almost impossible shade of shimmering turquoise.

The Rocky Mountains were formed 135 million years ago following the collision of two continental plates which pushed up a mountain chain stretching 2,800 miles (4,500km) along the western seaboard from Alaska to New Mexico with peaks rising to 13,125ft (4,000m) in places. Their upward movement ceased 65 million years ago, but hot springs still testify to powerful forces slumbering beneath this mighty fault zone.

High alpine fauna

Jasper National Park supports an incredible diversity of plant and animal life. The different habitats found in the various lower, sub-alpine, and

alpine zones are populated by well over 1,200 species of plant and around 56 types of mammal. The most abundantly populated habitat is the sub-alpine region situated between 5,900–6,900ft (1,800–2,100m) in altitude. Dense forests consisting of Douglas firs, arolla, and lodgepole pine cover the slopes and high valleys, providing shelter for elk, moose, mule deer, white-tailed deer and mountain caribou as well as their predators in the shape of hungry wolves, grizzly and black bears, wolverines, Canadian lynx, and puma.

The Park's most delicate region is the alpine zone above 6,900ft (2,100m). The main vegetation here consists of hardy sedges, grasses, and small polar willows, which provide fodder for mountain goats, bighorn sheep, pikas, and marmots.

The Maligne Canyon leads to the turquoise-colored Maligne Lake, surrounded by rugged rock formations (above)

The black bear is one of the mammals found within the National Park (below, right)

Ruined city of the Mayas amidst the rainforest

TIKAL NATIONAL PARK in Guatemala includes remnants of Mayan civilization, surrounded by the largest area of tropical rain forest in Central America

Towering above the dense green tree canopy of the tropical rain forest, the largest of its kind in Central America, are the gray stone peaks of the pyramids, mysterious remnants of a civilization which suddenly collapsed a thousand years ago. Tikal was the center of Mayan culture, which evolved here around 900 B.C. and reached its peak between 700 and 800 A.D. Indiscriminate exploitation of the environment led to an ecological crisis, as a result of which man disappeared and the rainforest emerged triumphant, burying the last traces of his madness under its green canopy.

Today, these ruins form an integral part of this fascinating rain forest and one of the main attractions for the visitor. In the thousand years that have elapsed since the collapse of the Maya civilization, an unparalleled ecosystem has developed in this area. Tikal National Park, which covers an area of 358 miles (576km²) is both a natural and cultural world heritage site. It is also the core area of the Maya Biosphere Reserve, which covers 6,214 miles (10,000km²) and also includes the San Miguel La Palotada wetlands, an area of almost 311 miles (500km²). Altogether, this conservation area comprises around 137 miles (200km²) of continuous tropical rain forest – the largest of its kind in Central America.

Over 300 species of trees

Tikal's Temple IV, known as the "Temple of the Two-Headed Snake," is 213ft (65m) high and the view from its summit provides an unforgettable panoramic view over the forest canopy, dotted here and there with the pointed tips of the gray stone pyramids peeping through the trees. If you can get here early enough, the sight of the blood-red morning sun rising slowly in the tropical sky is a breathtaking experience. Far below, in the quiet of the jungle, the visitor is enveloped in a blanket of wet humidity. It generally rains for approximately 150 days of the year, but the porous limestone floor does not retain the water. Instead, it constantly circulates within the delicate equilibrium of this rainforest ecosystem between the thin layer of humus on the forest floor and the canopy formed by the giant trees.

Three hundred different species of trees have been identified so far, including cedar, mahogany, palm, strangler fig and ceiba, Guatemala's national tree, also known as the kapok tree. Because of its spreading crown, which can extend 164ft (50m) across, the Mayas often planted it in the squares between the temple buildings to provide a source of shade. In the rainforest, it supports a little ecosystem all of its own. The crevices in its grayish-pink bark and branches are home to numerous orchids, ferns, cacti and bromeliads. Iguanas and other reptiles rest on its branches soaking up the few rays of sun which manage to filter through the leaf canopy.

Monkeys chatter noisily among the trees

The National Park is home to 54 species of mammal, an opportunity for the visitor to enjoy a close encounter with life in the jungle. The tapirs, white-tailed deer, armadillos, giant and lesser anteaters and three-toed sloths, dangling lazily from the branches, are stalked by predators such as pumas, ocelots and jaguars. And the ubiquitous monkeys, mainly howler and spider monkeys, are everywhere, chattering and leaping about in the tree-tops.

Small American crocodiles lie in wait for prey along the banks of the numerous rivers. Six genera of turtles rustle about in the riverbank vegetation, as do 38 different varieties of snakes, including the poisonous coral snake.

Tikal also boasts a stunning variety of birds. Turkeys, toucans, all kinds of different parrots, including the Aztec parrot, and parakeets flutter from tree to tree under the shelter of the leaf canopy, eyeing the human visitors suspiciously as they wander along winding paths on the forest floor, often following embankments dating back to Mayan civilization.

In the early morning, when the jungle is exuding the previous night's moisture and warm mists drift through the trees, the noise can be truly deafening as the birds warm up to their dawn chorus. But nothing compares to the complicated, entertaining song of the Montezuma oropendula. This chestnut-brown bird with its black head and bright yellow tail feathers performs such acrobatics during its song that it threatens to fall off its perch on the branch.

GETTING THERE:
Daily flights and bus connections from Guatemala City, Cancun and Belize. Shuttle buses to the park

WHERE TO STAY:
3 hotels and one campsite in the grounds around the Tikal ruins, as well as a wide selection of sites in El Remate, Flores and Santa Elena

CLIMATE:
Humid and warm all year round, with temperatures around 25° C. Dry season between November and May

MAIN ATTRACTIONS:
Hikes along jungle trails following ancient Maya paths, Tikal ruins, panoramic views from Temple IV

SPECIAL TIPS:
It is advisable to visit the National Park in groups and only in the company of a guide

Ruins of a Maya temple, rearing up through the rainforest canopy in Tikal National Park (left)

The ruins of the Maya temple complex of "Acropolis" (above, right)

Two crumbling temple towers peep through the wide expanse of rainforest canopy (below, right)

A gondola ride through the rainforest canopy

BRAULIO CARRILLO is Costa Rica's largest National Park – its jungle environment is home to the legendary quetzal birds

About 12 miles (20km) from San José along Highway 32 in the direction of Limón, just beyond the Zurquí tunnel, civilization comes to an abrupt end. This busy highway cuts through the middle of a wild volcanic mountain landscape and is surrounded on either side by untouched rainforest wreathed in mists.

Braulio Carrillo National Park, the largest in Costa Rica, is situated a mere 30-minute car journey from the heart of the nation's capital and is consequently the country's most easily accessible nature paradise. This does not mean, however, that you are likely to encounter other visitors and hikers at every step.

Extending over an area of some 180 square miles (470km²), the Park is, in fact, so vast that there are frequent cases of visitors, native Costa Ricans and tourists alike, losing themselves amidst the dense forest and rugged, mountainous terrain.

The entire Park is really a vast jumble of massive, often heavily eroded volcanoes, which have lain extinct for many centuries. Over the years, an impenetrable, and so far untouched, primary forest has established itself over the area. The dramatic differences in altitude, the multitude of rivers running through narrow gorges, and the numerous rushing waterfalls have created a complex and varied environmental system. The often precipitous mountainous slopes are clothed in dense, emerald-green, tropical rainforest, consisting of tree ferns, numerous species of palms, lianas, and plants that have entwined themselves in the branches of trees beneath the forest canopy. Colorful orchids and heliconias provide bright splashes of color amid the depths of the forest. Like most jungle environments, Braulio Carrillo is first and foremost a haven for birds. All 400-500 species of birds indigenous to Costa Rica are found here, including large numbers of humming-birds as well as quetzals, the sacred bird of the ancient Mayas, with their iridescent plumage. The females of the species, shimmering in shades of bright red, sapphire blue, and emerald green, measure only 13in (35 cm) while the male birds with their resplendent long tails can be over 39in (1m) long. Despite their vivid coloring, they are so well adapted to their jungle environment that it requires a well-trained eye to spot them among the profusion of plants. Their call song is unmistakable, however. Killing a quetzal was strictly

forbidden by the Mayas and these birds are still regarded as a symbol of freedom and independence throughout present-day Central America. From the three ranger stations, there are numerous trails leading off into the mountain and jungle regions. Even during the dry season from the end of December to April, these trails are usually wet and slippery. Each of them allows viewing of the tree canopy high above, thickly festooned with its colonies of plants as well as glimpses of crystal clear mountain streams, cascading over water falls into deep gorges below.

Starting from Guápiles

The Barva volcano rises majestically in the northwestern corner of the National Park. A road, as well as a hiking trail, leads from Puesto Barva station to the small lake, situated at an altitude of approximately 9,500ft (2,900m) in the crater of the volcano.

One particular attraction is a trip on the aerial tramway, which carries you up through the different levels of the rainforest. It runs along the eastern boundary of the Park, not far from the village of Guápiles. The ride in an open gondola ascends through

two levels of the tree canopy, first crossing over a valley and then climbing a small mountain. During the outward part of the trip, you are transported just a few yards above the ground through the sparse vegetation that survives in the half light of the lower tree canopy. On the return trip, the open gondolas travel at a height of 165ft (50m) above the ground through the tree canopy itself, which is home to around 60 percent of all rainforest species. Experienced guides accompany the visitors, explaining the features peculiar to the different levels of rainforest and pointing out animals, such as monkeys, snakes, leaf-cutter ants and numerous species of tropical birds.

When the government announced plans to build a new highway to the coastal town of Limón in 1973, cutting through pristine rainforest, local environmental activists managed to persuade the authorities to declare the region a conservation area. Since 1978, the National Park has served to remind visitors how Costa Rica looked like 50 years ago when three-quarters of the country was still covered by jungle ecosystems of this kind.

GETTING THERE:
From San José follow the Guápiles Highway No. 32 towards Limón, 12 miles (20km) to the main ranger station at Zurquí or 26 miles (42km) to the Puesto Carrillo station. Various bus connections from San José along these routes to Guápiles, Siquirres, or Limón

WHERE TO STAY:
A full range of accommodation is available in San José. Camping is permitted within the National Park, but it is recommended that you consult a ranger.

CLIMATE:
The weather does not vary a great deal. March and April tend to be a little drier, but showers can be expected in the afternoon. Depending on altitude, the temperatures range from 79° F (26° C) to 32° F (0° C).

MAIN ATTRACTIONS:
Barva volcano and its crater lake (accessible on foot or in a four-wheel drive vehicle); walk from the Barva crater to La Selva biological station (4 days); trip on the "Rainforest Aerial Tram"

SPECIAL TIPS:
Water from rivers or lakes in the Park should be sterilized

The National Park provides a protected area for around 195 square miles (500km²) of rainforest. Fifty years ago, jungle still covered 75 percent of the country.

Aerial view over the rainforest (left)

Looking up into the tree canopy (right)

Jungle overlooks the coast

Backing onto the beaches of Costa Rica is **MANUEL ANTONIO** National Park, an area abounding in wildlife

Covering an area of just two-and-three-quarter square miles (seven square kilometers), Manuel Antonio National Park is the country's smallest and most popular National Park. This is hardly surprising, considering its unique location right on the shores of the Pacific next to some of Costa Rica-'s most beautiful beaches, just over 4 miles (7km) south of Quepos and a mere stone's throw from the resort hotels, beach bars, and nightclubs. It is such a popular destination for tourists staying at the nearby resorts that the park authorities restrict the number of visitors to 600 per day to avoid disturbing the animals.

Surrounded by fields and pasture-land, the National Park represents an oasis of natural green wilderness and peaceful tranquility which sustains a fast-growing tourist industry. The mountains overlooking the ocean form a backdrop to the perfect, white sandy beaches of Espadilla Sur, Manuel Antonio, Escondido, and Playita. The National Park also encompasses 12 small islands, lying off the coast. Although most of these islands have little vegetation, they are important nesting sites for seabirds, such as the rare white-bellied booby.

Punta Catedral, whose densely forested cliffs rise to 236ft (72m), was once an off-shore island itself. Ocean currents gradually deposited enough sand between the island and the coast to form a narrow land-bridge, linking it to the sandy crescent beaches of Espadilla Sur and Manuel Antonio, two of the National Park's most popular beaches.

Monkeys cavort in the tree canopy

To enter the Park, one has to wade across the mouth of a shallow creek. Normally, the water is only ankle-deep, but during the rainy season the water level can rise to 5ft (1.5m). Beyond the stream, numerous hiking trails meander through the cool, shady forest. From the hills, there are spectacular views through the jungle greenery to the turquoise expanse of the Pacific Ocean, where migrating dolphins and whales can sometimes be spotted.

The main attraction of this National Park, however, is its abundance and variety of wildlife, which visitors can experience at close quarters. The animals have become so accustomed to humans that they permit close-up encounters.

The most conspicuous inhabitants of the park are undoubtedly its butterflies, its wealth of bird life, and the large, colorful land crabs. There are 109 species of mammals and 184 varieties of birds jostling for space in the Park's three main habitats: primary forest, secondary forest, and the mangroves. The tidal basins off the coast are home to 10 types of sponge, 19 species of coral, 24 types of crustaceans, 17 different algae, and 78 species of fish. During the dry season, when the seawater is at its clearest, this underwater world is best explored by snorkeling off the cliffs separating the two main beaches, or in the tidal basins just off-shore.

High up in the forest canopy above the hiking trails are large numbers of monkeys, chattering noisily and performing their acrobatics. Most common are the capuchin and howler monkeys, but troops of up to 30 red-backed squirrel monkeys can also be seen swinging through the branches in search of insects and fruits. Manuel Antonio National Park is one of just two areas in Costa Rica where this endangered species still survives. The red-backed squirrel monkey is the smallest of the four species of monkey indigenous to Costa Rica and the only one with a non-prehensile tail.

Sanctuary for sloths

Every so often, you will come across three-toed sloths draped over tree branches, doing full justice to their name. These animals too have become relatively rare everywhere else. These fascinating creatures move very slowly and eat exclusively plants. The low energy content of their leafy diet is the reason for their slow metabolism. Although their diet includes the leaves of more than 100 different trees and creepers, they have a particular preference for the foliage of the cecropia tree, a type of mulberry tree. The cecropia tree is a distant relative of the cannabis plant and

breadfruit tree. It is a pioneer species in secondary tropical forests, easily identifiable by its large, palm-shaped leaves and smooth trunk characterized by distinctive bark rings.

The area's designation as a National Park was regarded as a conservation victory by the local population along this stretch of the coast. Although the land had long been under private ownership, local residents had always enjoyed free access to the beaches. A North American purchased the land in 1968 and proceeded, violating all local regulations, to fence off the whole area, even erecting heavy gates. The local population retaliated with vandalism. After the local legislative authority finally won and insisted that the path to the beach be kept open, the property passed into the hands of a Frenchman, who planned to turn the region into a tourist center. Before he could do so, however, the land was appropriated by the government in 1972 and declared a National Park.

Enclosed by lush jungle vegetation, the sand banks of Espadilla Beach connect an off-shore island with the mainland (above)

Twelve off-shore islands also form part of the National Park (below)

Caracas
Canaima
VENEZUELA
PACIFIC
ATLANTIC

Venezuela's table mountains

Many areas of **CANAIMA NATIONAL PARK** remain unexplored

GETTING THERE:
By air from Caracas, Bolívar, Puerto Ordaz, Porlamar, or Santa Elena to Canaima. Highway from Bolívar to Brasil bisects the southeastern corner of the National Park, with a turnoff to Kavanayen

WHERE TO STAY:
Several lodges in a range of price categories in Camp Canaima; good accommodation available at several mission stations; simple inns along the road from Bolívar

CLIMATE:
Warm year-round temperatures of about 77º F (25º C). Dry season in the northwest section of the Park from December to April

MAIN ATTRACTIONS:
Camp Canaima with lagoon; Angel Waterfall; Roraima; Isla de la Orquídea (Orchid Island); Kamarata and Kavac (mission stations)

SPECIAL TIPS:
Any sites or attractions not directly on the road from Bolívar are only accessible by plane or helicopter, including Camp Canaima. No park management

In Venezuela's southeastern corner, the landscape is punctuated by gigantic table mountains (Tepui). Between 3,300ft–6,600ft (1,000m–2,000m) in height, their sheer rock walls rise dramatically from the plains of an endless expanse of tropical savannah. Innumerable waterfalls cascade over their precipices, plunging down to the steep, forested slopes far below, where millions of years of erosion debris have accumulated. Numerous rivers and streams have carved their way through the towering cliffs and cut a channel across the plains to the great Caroni River, which forms the western boundary of Canaima National Park. Its total area of 11,600 square miles (30,000km²) earns it a place among the ten largest national parks in the world.

It stretches from the uplands of La Gran Sabana and the eastern table mountains of the Roraima range to the mighty sandstone plateau of Chimantá and Auyántepui in the west, with the flat plains of the northwestern Canaima lowlands rolling away into the distance. The main settlement of Canaima is also situated in this western sector, on the shores of an enchanting lagoon. It is the main departure point for most of the excursions into the largely impenetrable wilderness. Even the idyllic hiking trails around the immediate vicinity of the Park's center are soon swallowed up in the overwhelming solitude and vastness of this incredible landscape. The curtain of water at the Sapo waterfall, for example, conceals a hidden trail. A small group of Pemón, a tribe native to the area, with a population of 10,000 live within the National Park.

The Guayana shield was formed during the Pre-Cambrian period, somewhere between 1.5 million and 2,000 million [Ed note: check these figures with author?] years ago. At that time, America and Africa were still part of what is though to have been the supercontinent of Gondwana, worn away by millions of years of wind and rain and eventually split into two sections, forming this uniquely spectacular landscape.

Solitude on the Tepui summits

The table mountains, or Tepui, as they are known, are composed of horizontal layers of colored sandstone, interspersed with seams of glittering quartz and agglomerates. The flat Tepui summits rise to heights of 6,600ft–8,900ft (2,000–2,700m) above sea-level. Their surfaces are scarred by

gullies, narrow canyons, and sinkholes, some of which are several hundred yards deep. Some of these summits have almost certainly never been explored by man. One of the most picturesque of these table mountains, the heart-shaped Auyán-Tepui Massif, encircled by the Carrao and Akanán rivers, is in the north of the region. During the 1930s, an American bush pilot, James Crawford Angel, discovered a waterfall, nestled deep within a north-facing cleft in the rocks. This waterfall, which proved to be the highest in the world, was named after him. Angel Falls plunges a good 3,300ft (1km), creating a rainbow-colored cloud of spray visible for miles around in front of the cliff wall. This spot is only accessible by aircraft — or by a two-day boat trip or ten-day hike.

Moss and lichen reign supreme

The endless, green savannah with its groves of Mauritia palms and impenetrable shrub lands is the result of centuries of forest burning by the indigenous people. Forested areas are really only found along rivers, in lateral valleys, gullies, and on the gentler slopes at the foot of the Tepui Mountains. Even in the less densely wooded bands of riverine forest, the trees are still in fierce competition with the large population of epiphytic plants and lianas.

The flat plateaus are at such high elevations and subject to such a harsh climate that, by and large, algae, ferns, mosses and lichen are the only species of vegetation which flourish here. Nevertheless, biologists have estimated that algae and ferns alone account for 3,000 to 5,000 separate species. Higher forms of plant life grow in more sheltered places. The region has a particularly high proportion of endemic plants, some 10 percent of which are exclusive to this massif and not found anywhere else on earth. Carnivorous plants and orchids in particular seem to thrive here and the Park is home to around 500 different varieties of orchid.

Although not particularly abundant, the wildlife is relatively diverse. The number of recorded species does, after all, amount to a healthy total of 72 reptiles and 55 amphibians, not to mention 550 species of birds, 30 percent of which are indigenous. Canaima is also the sole habitat for one small species of rodent. Six other mammals, the great anteater, giant armadillo, giant otter, bush dog, little spotted cat, and the margay are regarded as endangered species and are on a special protection list.

Lagoon and waterfall
in the La Gran Sabana,
with the table
mountains or "Tepui,"
as the natives call
them, in the distance
(above)

Aerial view of a valley
in the tropical
rainforests
of Guayana
Mountains
(below, left)

The land of ancient lizards

Ten million years ago, a unique ecosystem of primeval fauna evolved in the **GALAPAGOS** archipelago and it has remained intact to this day

Galapagos
• Quito
ECUADOR

PACIFIC

ATLANTIC

GETTING THERE:
Daily flights from Quito and Guayaquil to Baltra, less frequently to San Cristobál

WHERE TO STAY:
On cruise ships, all categories of hotel available on San Cristobál and Santa Cruz

CLIMATE:
daytime temperatures around 86° F (30° C) from January to May, otherwise around 82° F (28° C)

MAIN ATTRACTIONS:
All trails offer spectacular views of the archipelago's wildlife

SPECIAL TIPS:
Ban on any imports of fresh food

Lonesome George is the sole surviving member of his species. Around 80 years old and weighing 200lb (90kg), he is in the prime of his life. When he dies, it will mark the end of the line for his race, leaving only 11 of the original 14 species of tortoise that were once endemic to the Galapagos Islands. He was discovered quite unexpectedly in 1971 on Pinta Island and currently enjoys the protection of the Charles Darwin Research Station on Santa Cruz Island. It is from giant land tortoises like George that this archipelago, situated in the middle of the Pacific and straddling the equator 620 miles (1000km) off the coast of Ecuador, derives its name. Far removed from the nearest continent, these barren and rugged lava islands that are dotted with numerous shield volcanoes rising over 5,500ft

(1,700m) in height have developed a unique ecosystem of flora and fauna over the course of millions of years. The entire archipelago belongs to Ecuador and, as a designated National Park, is a protected area.

Just one single pregnant tortoise, which turned up here 10 million years ago, was enough to start a unique evolutionary process.

The volcanic island on which the original tortoise was washed up has long since sunk back into the ocean. The Galapagos Islands lie directly over a so-called "hot spot," a hole in the earth's crust from which hot lava bubbles up from the earth's core. It erupts through the plate, forming volcanic cones. While the ocean floor has been shifting toward South America over millions of years, the old islands have been sinking into the sea, with

fresh ones constantly forming over the hot spot.

Española in the eastern part of the archipelago, dating back 3,300,000 years, is the oldest island, while the islands of Fernandina and Isabela to the west are a mere 700,000 years old and still volcanically active.

Tortoises and finches

Around the same time that the pregnant tortoise came ashore on these distant islands, a storm must have also carried a flock of finches to the same area. These birds have evolved into the famous Darwin Finches, which can be grouped into 13 subspecies. Each group has its own specific niche in the food chain.

The ground finch with its stout, strong beak can crush tough seeds, while the warbler finch's pincer-like

View across the rocky Isla Bartolomé to James Island beyond (above, left)

Two individual forms of the same species, adapted to different living conditions: Marine iguanas (above, right)

Land iguanas (left)

The brilliant plumage of the frigate bird (right)

beak is designed for catching insects. The woodpecker finch even uses a tool: it probes insect larvae out of tree bark with a cactus spine. The most unusual species, however, must surely be the vampire finch, which pecks open the flesh on the heads of seabirds and dines on their blood. The victims do not seem unduly concerned by this procedure.

Large predators never found their way to the Galapagos, with the result that the indigenous animals know no fear of each other. Even the numerous sea lions and fur seals show little concern when curious snorkellers swim around them in the crystal-clear waters of the Pacific. Nor do the hundreds of prehistoric-looking miniature dragons — land lizards and marine iguanas —sunbathing on the bare, black lava rocks seem to notice when their larger neighbors enjoy a friendly nibble at their long tails. They are unafraid of humans as well as seabirds, thousands of which colonize the rugged cliffs that drop steeply away to the sea. The seabird population includes flamingos, blue-footed boobies, frigate birds, flightless cormorants and even small penguins,

which like to cool off in damp, lava caves.

Treeless crater landscape

The central lowlands are arid and barren, the only vegetation being thorn bushes and cacti growing on turf. A transition zone at higher elevations is covered by forest consisting mainly of guava trees and pisonnia, a "four o'clock" plant with white or yellow, and occasionally red or pink-tinged, flowers which do not open until late afternoon. The forest above this transition zone is very damp and often shrouded in mist. The vegetation here, consisting predominantly of $6^1/_2$–13ft (2–4m) high trees, is much lusher, with dense undergrowth. Finally, the treeless upland zone around the crater supports only lichen and mosses.

These islands were probably first discovered in the 15th century by the Inca ruler Tupac Yupanqui. The first documented discovery, however, was by the Bishop of Panama, Tomás de Berlanga, whose ship ended up here in 1535 after being blown off course during a storm.

When Charles Darwin, the famous naturalist, visited these islands in 1835

at the age of 26, they provided him with inspiration for the ground-breaking ideas that later revolutionized existing biological theories on the origin of the species. During his visit, he also came across signs of early permanent settlements on Santa Maria, one of the islands in the southern part of the archipelago.

A small population of red marine iguanas, the last of their kind, has survived on the Galapagos Islands

Volcanic panorama

The National Park surrounding **COTOPAXI** in Ecuador provides a habitat for many alpine flowers verging on extinction

Quito • Cotopaxi
ECUADOR

PACIFIC

ATLANTIC

GETTING THERE:
By road or bus from Quito to Machachi; railway station at Aloag

WHERE TO STAY:
Camping; José Ribas mountain cabin

CLIMATE:
Daytime temperatures around 45° F (7° C), falling to 32° F (0° C) at night. Permafrost on the summits

MAIN ATTRACTIONS:
Hiking; mountain climbing; bird and wildlife-watching; El Boliche; stone ruins of pre-Columbian cultures and Inca civilization

SPECIAL TIPS:
Very little tourist infrastructure. Local guide mandatory for climbing Cotopaxi

The sight of the clouds above Cotopaxi glowing red at night, reflecting the fire within the volcanic crater, is a truly breathtaking spectacle. The conical summit of this perfectly shaped volcano, the most active in the world, is almost invariably hidden behind clouds. Its textbook symmetry is marred only by another, smaller cone, known as the Cabeza del Inca.

The volcano, which rises to a height of 19,350ft (5,897m), has a long history of destruction. It has seldom remained dormant for longer than 15 years at a stretch. It caused the greatest disaster in 1877 when an eruption dislodged masses of ice and snow from its summit, triggering an avalanche that wiped the town of Latacunga off the map.

The vast expanse of open grassland from which the volcano dramatically rises has frequently been devastated by earthquakes or buried under layers of ash and lava. The entire cone consists of alternating layers of dark lava flows and paler layers of ash. At the bottom of its crater, which is 1,200ft (366m) deep, is a cauldron of boiling, bubbling lava which periodically emits huge plumes of steam and gasses.

Cotopaxi's outer, older crater rim stretches about 2,300ft (700m) from north to south and more than 1,640ft (500m) from west to east. Its external flanks are covered with a deep layer of snow.

For a very long time, this mountain refused to be conquered. The first person to attempt its ascent was Alexander von Humboldt in 1802. He failed, as did many others who followed him. It was not until 28 November 1872 that Wilhelm Reiss, a German scientist and explorer, finally succeeded in reaching the summit.

Nowadays, Cotopaxi, situated just 37 miles (60km) from Quito, is a popular destination for mountain climbing expeditions, accompanied by experienced local guides. The José Ribas cabin, located at an altitude of around 15,750ft (4,800m) on the volcano's northeastern flank, provides climbers with overnight accommodation and an opportunity to become acclimatized to the thinner air at these high altitudes. From this high vantage point, there are absolutely stunning views stretching from the glittering lake in Limpiopungo valley to the magnificent and awe-inspiring volcanic scenery of the Andes mountains beyond.

Picturesque lakes

The 14 mile (23km) base of Mount Cotopaxi is situated at the heart of the 130 square miles (334km²) of Cotopaxi National Park. The Park also incorporates Mount Ruminahui, 15,460ft (4,712m) in height, and the smaller volcanoes of Pasochoa and Sincholagua. This delightful nature park, dotted with lakes and criss-crossed with rivers of melted ice, is Ecuador's most popular conservation area.

Even so, human beings, other than vistors, are relatively scarce and any that are encountered are most likely to be Quichua Indians, the native inhabitants of this region and direct descendants of the Incas.

The Park's broad valleys, all at least 11,200ft (3,400m) above sea level, support vegetation typical of barren high-alpine terrain, including a variety of grasses, romerillo, a plant resembling St. John's Wort, Quichuar lilac and heather. This high-altitude region is also an ideal habitat for the extremely rare and heavily protected Chuquiragua, a prickly, orange-flowering species of aster. The native Indians used this plant as a cure for stomach and intestinal problems. There are also a few dwindling areas of woodland, which still support populations of gnarled quinoa trees. The forested areas on the southwest flank of Mount Rumiñahui are also home to the Andean alchemilla, a type of lady's mantle.

Llamas

Blue and white miniature lupins bloom at higher altitudes and patches of gentians and club moss peep from between bare boulders and grow on scree beds. Sometimes, a waft of heavily scented valerian or loricaria may be carried on the breeze. From the recreation area at El Boliche, a network of hiking trails leads through a unique pine forest that was planted as an experiment in 1928 and has blended successfully into the rest of this mountain environment.

Occasionally, one may catch a glimpse of a white-tailed deer among the bushes, while wild horses graze on the gentle valley slopes. Llamas of course are everywhere. For many animals, such as Paramo rabbits and wolves, spectacled bears, Ecuador possum mice and pumas, Cotopaxi Park represents one of their few remaining sanctuaries. The population of majestic Andean condors has also declined considerably, but these magnificent birds, standing 5ft (1.5m) tall with a wingspan of 10ft (3m), can still occasionally be glimpsed among the rocks of Sincholagua. The National Park is also a breeding ground for the rare blue-billed duck and carunculated caracara, or orange-faced falcon. Much more common are humming birds, Andean plovers, red-backed sparrow hawks, owls and Andean gulls.

The snow-covered summit of Cotopaxi towers majestically above the high plateau of the Andes (above)

Extensive snowfields blanket the upper slopes of the volcano all year round (below)

Amid the high peaks of the Andes

Huascaran National Park in Peru protects the extraordinary flora of the Cordilleras

GETTING THERE:
Panamericana highway from Lima to Huaraz and then on to Callejon de Huaylas and Pativilca. Road up into the mountains to an altitude of 13,450ft (4,100m). Airport for charter flights

WHERE TO STAY:
Basic hotel accommodation; camping

CLIMATE:
Mountain climate with warm, moist winds from the Amazon basin. Rainy season from December to May; dry period from May to October. Temperatures up to 77º F (25º C)

MAIN ATTRACTIONS:
Hiking; mountain-climbing; mountain-biking; climb to the top of Mount Huascaran; prehistoric ruins

SPECIAL TIPS:
Risk of high altitude sickness

The high valleys of the National Park are flanked by 26 mountain peaks, each higher than 19,700ft (6,000m). Huascaran is the highest of these (above)

An unusual feature of this conservation area is the rare bromeliad, which blooms only rarely, but produces a flower that grows up to 33ft (10m) in height (below)

Some 170 million years ago, the Nazca Plate on the floor of the Pacific Ocean began to slide underneath the South American continent, pushing it upward. Over the course of millions of years, massive layers of rock were pushed into folds, rifts opened up and immense quantities of magma poured out from within the earth and overlaid the original rock. Just like the Himalayas, the Cordillera de los Andes is a chain of mountains that is still rising.

In Peru, the awe-inspiring mountains of the Andes Cordillera tower up into the tropical skies just 95 miles (150km) inland from the Pacific coast. The Cordillera Blanca, or 'white mountains,' situated beyond the wild, rushing torrents of the River Santa near Huaraz, is not only one of South America's foremost mountaineering regions, but its slopes and valleys are protected as part of the Huascaran National Park, one of the most breathtakingly beautiful high mountain ecosystems in the world.

Cotopaxi's outer, older crater rim, which stretches about 2,300ft (700m) from north to south and more than 1,640ft (500m) from west to east. Its external flanks are covered with a deep layer of snow.

For a very long time, this mountain refused to be conquered. The first person to attempt its ascent was Alexander von Humboldt in 1802. He failed, as did many others who followed him. It was not until 28 November 1872 that Wilhelm Reiss, a German scientist and explorer, finally succeeded in reaching the summit.

Nowadays, Cotopaxi, situated just 37 miles (60km) from Quito, is a popular destination for mountain climbing expeditions, accompanied by experienced local guides. The José

Over 600 glaciers

Twenty-six dazzlingly white mountain peaks rise to heights of more than 19,700ft (6,000m). Mighty walls of ice cover the steep rock faces surrounding the summits and some 660 glaciers descend towards the valleys, their melted ice water supplying at least 160 lakes. The region, which is a designated world heritage site, is also intersected by 41 rivers.

Situated in the Ancash province, Huascaran nature reserve extends across several provinces, including Recuay, Huaraz, Carhuaz, Yungay, Huaylas, Pomabamba and Mariscal Luzuriaga, Huari, Sihuas, and Bolognesi. It presents the visitor with a high-alpine landscape of indescribable beauty, full of cultural and natural treasures. The Park, which covers an area of 1,300 square miles (3,400km²), rises from an altitude of 8,200ft (2,500m) in the valley basins to the 22,200ft (6,768m) high summit of El Huascaran, the highest mountain in Peru.

Sheer walls consisting of thick bands of sediment, dating from the Calcareous and Jurassic periods, rise almost vertically. The rapid increase in height forces vegetation to adapt various ways and provides an explanation for the rich diversity of species found here – each of which has had to claim an individual niche for itself at various altitudes. Above the forests of gnarled quenual trees, which occur among the valleys and slopes, is a moist, sub-alpine habitat supporting Paramos vegetation, including a large number of grasses and shrubs in the higher areas, interspersed with an occasional low bush.

Around the summit is the barren alpine tundra zone. Scientists have so far managed to identify about 800 plants from 104 species and 340 subspecies.

Orchids and bromeliads are particularly prevalent here under the tropical, high-altitude sun and have evolved into a large number of different species. The area is home to a unique alpine bromeliad, the puya raimondii, which bears the largest flower in the world, growing to a staggering 33ft (10m) in height. It can live to be than 100 years old.

Rare bloom

The mountain Indians claim that this extremely large-flowering species of puya only blooms once every 8 to 12 years. Adult plants of the same species not only bloom together during the same year, but also develop at the same speed. This helps optimize pollination and seed production.

This varied mountain landscape, where it is comparatively easy to climb one of the awesome 16,400ft (5,000m) peaks, is home to ten species of mammal, the most spectacu-lar being the spectacled bear, puma, pampas cat, white-tailed deer, vicunas, and Andean huemol. These rugged mountains are home to about 115 different bird varieties, including magnificent birds of prey such as the booted eagle and Gurney's eagle, not to mention the superb Andes condor. Like the plant life, some species grow to enormous sizes in this part of the world; for instance, the giant coot or the giant humming-bird native to Peru.

This region has been populated by man for many centuries. Spectacular ruins, such as those found in Gekosh, Chuchumpunta, Willcahuain-Huyllap-Pumacayan, and Hechkap-Jonkapampa, some of them dating back to pre-Inca times, testify to past cultures and long vanished civilizations.

Paradise for sea lions

PARACAS National Park in Peru safeguards huge colonies of sea lions along its Pacific coast.

PERU
Lima
Paracas
National Park
PACIFIC
ATLANTIC

Paracas on the Peruvian coast is plagued by perpetual, strong, and searing winds. Scarcely anything thrives in this semi-arid region at the foot of the Cordilleras near the town of Pisco. The barrenness of the land stands in stark contrast to the astonishing diversity of life found in the ocean. This marine abundance was once a source of immense wealth to the region's early inhabitants and later settlers.

The constant trade winds and the Humboldt current swirling northward just off the coast stir up oxygen and nutrient-rich seawater from the depths of the Pacific, propelling it to the surface. Despite being 12-14° F (10-11° C) colder than the water in the surrounding open ocean, it nevertheless supports a huge population of algae and micro-organisms, providing plentiful supplies of food to nourish the prodigious shoals of fish that live off the Peruvian coast and making it one of the richest fishing grounds in the world.

For thousands of years, this superabundance of fish, particularly shoal varieties like anchovy and sardine, has inevitably attracted millions upon millions of sea birds to the area, first and foremost among them the cormorant. On the wind and wave-battered rocky islands lying off the coast, there are such vast colonies of these birds that their droppings accumulate as the recognized resource of guano, used all over the world as a natural fertilizer. Until the beginning of the twentieth century, these guano deposits were being blindly excavated without the slightest regard for the birds' breeding season. The population of guano producers has consequently declined, but so too has the demand for guano following the invention of artificial fertilizers. Nowadays, guano is harvested from the Chinchas Islands by a handful of individuals who appear to be inured to its reek. English sailing ships also used to anchor in the area to collect their cargo of guano for transport to Europe and North America.

Resting-place for migrant birds

A little to the south are the Paracas Peninsula and the Islas Ballestas, now comprising a national reserve which protects spectacular colonies of sea birds as well as considerable numbers of sea lions. Each year, the reserve also provides a refuge for dozens of species of migrating birds that choose the area to break their long, exhausting journey. Biologists have identified more than 200 varieties of birdlife, including pelicans, the rare blue-footed booby, Peruvian booby, and red-legged and Bigua cormorants. For some birds, such as the Humboldt penguin, flamingo, and Andean condor, the National Park represents a final refuge.

In 1804, Alexander von Humboldt, the German explorer, returned to Europe with samples of the remarkable guano, known as "Huanu" in the Inca tongue of Quechua. As a result, guano became highly sought after as a natural nitrogen and phosphorous-rich fertilizer, destined to revolutionize agriculture. A lively trade in this organic substance quickly developed. Peruvian guano from the Chinchas Islands became the world's first commercial fertilizer.

It was not, however, harvested with the same degree of concern for the environment displayed by the Incas in their day. Ruthless exploitation soon caused problems and it was not until 1909 that the "Compania Administradora del Guano" was founded in Lima, charged with the specific purpose of safeguarding the existing bird population and ensuring their protection. The organization simultaneously aimed at achieving a long-term increase in annual

guano production. By then, however, the bottom had already more or less dropped out of the guano market.

The nature reserve, two-thirds of which comprises the marine environment off the coast, covers an overall area of around 1,300 square miles (3,350km²) along the Pacific coast. The ocean and sea bed are home to toothed whales, seals, sea otters, turtles, and countless varieties of fish and invertebrates, not to mention the rare ratfish. Scientists have recorded a total of 19 species of mammal, 52 varieties of fish and six types of reptile in the National Park.

Barren coastal desert

The original varieties of Peruvian coastal flora have survived largely intact throughout the ages. Although most of the landscape consists of arid desert, dotted here and there with occasional grassy tussocks, the transition zone leading to the mountain tops supports some drought-resistant species of cacti, occasional bushy thickets of which occur on elevated areas and in a few places prone to moist mists.

The coast itself comprises a unique habitat supporting various types of grasses found in the brackish and salt marsh areas. These were once of great significance to the Nasca Indians, long before the advent of the Incas. Domestic items and clothes made from such grasses were unearthed from burial grounds discovered on Paracas in 1927 by the archeologist Julio C. Tello. The mummified remains found in these graves, along with tools, weapons, jewelry, and even food items, were wrapped in finely woven grave cloths – the fabric and enduring colors of which are still a source of wonder to scientists. Some of these items are on display in the Anthropological and Archeological Museum in Lima.

Water temperatures off the cliffs of Paracas are colder than in the open ocean. The resulting abundance of fish makes this inhospitable cliff landscape a paradise for migrating birds (above)

The area is home to huge colonies of sea lions - clearly at ease in these cold waters (below)

Floating islands of reeds

Lake **TITICACA** National Park is home to members of the Uro community who depend on the lake for their livelihood

PERU
Lima • Lake Titicaca
PACIFIC
ATLANTIC

GETTING THERE:
Regular flights from Lima to Juliaca, followed by a one-hour bus journey to Puno

WHERE TO STAY:
All categories of accommodation available in Puno and around Lake Titicaca, as well as on some of the islands

CLIMATE:
May to October sunny, with little rain; daytime temperatures up to

77º F (25º C), night temperatures around 32º F (0º C)

MAIN ATTRACTIONS:
Boat trip through the reserve; the floating Uro island dwellings; the islands of Taquile and Amantani

Lake Titicaca is the world's highest navigable freshwater lake (above)

Totora reeds provide all the Uro Indians' essential needs. They use reeds to build their floating island dwellings (below, center), their ships are built of reeds (below, left), and reeds harvested from the shore are transported into the hinterland to be used as building material (below, right)

Despite being regarded as an inferior race by the Incas, the Uros managed to survive invasions by would-be conquerors and even emerged intact from years of Spanish colonial rule. They are one of the oldest Indian peoples anywhere in America. Although their younger descendents have mixed with other Aymará tribes in the Lake Titicaca mountain region over the past 50 years, they have continued to uphold the traditions of their forefathers. Present-day Uros still live, as their ancestors did thousands of years ago, on floating islands in the middle of Lake Titicaca. There are more than 40 of these islands, artistically crafted from totora reeds, floating in the marshy wetlands of the Peruvian sector of Titicaca National Reserve at the northwestern end of the lake. The area is a mere 15-minute boat ride away from the bustling tourist city of Puno.

This national reserve was established in 1978 and covers an area more than 140 square miles (360km²). It is included on RAMSAR's list of the world's main wetland areas. The largest section, comprising an area of around 115 square miles (300km²), encompasses the Bay of Puno with its individual pockets of densely growing totora reeds. The Ramis sector, centering on the area around Huancané and extending about 7½ miles (12km) inland, was established to protect a large expanse of reed bed. The dominant emergent species here is totora, but 12 other sub-species of this flat, flexible-stemmed water plant are also present. This remote, inhospitable region, which nevertheless boasts a significant biodiversity, does not attract many visitors. Its indigenous plants and animals are consequently left largely undisturbed.

Floating houses

The Uro Indians' existence revolves entirely around the totora reed. Not only is it used as a building material for their dwellings, boats and islands, but it also provides a useful source of food. Each family occupies its own individual island which consists of a large quantity of individual woven mats which are tied together and anchored to the lake bed. Soil is collected from the shores of the lake and spread across the island in thin layers to create island gardens for growing root crops such as potatoes and yuccas.

Lake Titicaca, measuring around 3,200 square miles (8,300km²) and situated 12,500 ft (3,812m) above sea level, is the highest navigable lake on earth. It occupies the gap between two Andean mountain ranges. The lake is 460–590ft (140-180m) deep at its center, suddenly falling away to a depth of 920ft (280m) along the Peruvian-Bolivian border.

The fluctuating water table

Although 25 rivers discharge into Lake Titicaca, most of its water is derived directly from rainfall. Ninety-five percent of it evaporates as steam. The small Desagüadero River channels about 5 percent of Lake Titicaca's water into to Lake Poopó. During the Inca occupation, the lake was considerably larger than it is today. One thousand years ago, the Tihuanaco temple complex, now a distance of around 12½ miles (20km) inland from the lake, stood right on the lake shore. It is unlikely, however, that the lake will ever dry up.

It seems that the water levels undergo short-term fluctuations over the course of a year as well as regular, long-term changes over centuries.

Lake Titicaca is home to 14 different varieties of fish in the lake. Many of these have become endangered since the introduction of rainbow trout into the lake in 1939. These fish, which can reach lengths of 24in (60cm), have driven out virtually every other species and have become the most popular fish dish on the Indios menu. The only other species, which are still relatively common, are the Andean carp and a large species of catfish.

Another delicacy forming part of the Uros' diet is the giant, eyeless, Titicaca toad, which can also reach 24in (60cm) in length and lives on the lake bed. It is one of 18 species of amphibians residing in the lake. The majority of these are frogs, including a 12in (30cm) lake frog which is endemic to the region.

The protected areas of the reserve are a haven and breeding ground for many of the 60 different species of bird, including the flightless Titicaca diver, ibis, cormorants, ducks, rail, and three different species of flamingo, many of which are migratory and for whom the Park is an essential resting place.

The few mammals in the region are mainly rodents, such as the wild guinea pig, although Andean wolves and foxes are occasionally seen slinking their way through the grassy steppes that cover the slopes of the Andean mountains.

The forest of giant trees

JAU NATIONAL PARK on the shores of the Rio Negro protects a central area of tropical rainforest

The Amazonian rainforests are the green lungs of our planet. Around 30 percent of the earth's surface is covered with forest, half of which lies in the Tropics. The rainforest bordering the Amazon River covers an area of 3,250,000 square miles (8,500,000km²), and is the largest single forest in the world.

The Amazon River winds its way for 4,000 miles (6,400km) through tropical South America. It was so named in 1541 by Francisco de Orellana, the first European to set foot here. He hit upon this name after observing female Indian warriors on its banks who reminded him of the Amazon women of Greek mythology.

The river is known by several names, however. In the Peruvian Andes, it is called the Marañón River (or Maranhão in Portuguese). Until it merges with the Rio Negro, Brazilians refer to it as the Solmões River. Only then does it officially become the Amazon.

Unlike the whitish waters of the main river, the Rio Negro — literally "black river" — is very dark in color. For 1,550 miles (2,500km) between Columbia and Manau, it flows along a river bed channeled out of dense primeval forest and collects a great deal of plant detritus, such as leaves, roots, and fruit as well as sand or minerals, which explains its dark color.

The unique diversity of flora and fauna bordering both sides of this mighty river is protected by three huge national parks. One of these, the Jau National Park, lies some 145 miles (230km) upriver from Manaus. It spans the area between the Carabinani and Unini rivers, extending 155 miles (250km) into the rainforest itself.

Ideal habitat for epiphytes

The rainforest areas located on solid ground, or "terra firma," are home to giant trees that grow 100–200ft (30–60m) in height. The jungle is so dense and impenetrable here that most wildlife is restricted to the treetops. The rainforest does, however, support 180 different species of tree and plants per 2.5 acres (one hectare). In the Igapo region, which remains flooded for several months at a time, the river banks are lined with Mauritious palms and there is also a striking profusion of flora in the form of bromeliads and orchids. The region around the Rio Negro, where there is better water drainage, supports dense thickets of shrubs and trees in the Campinarana area.

There is still very little known about the 3,000 or so tree varieties found in the Amazon region. The consistent climate means that the trunks of these 200 to 250-year old trees do not produce growth rings. Some of them shed their leaves one by one during the year, while others lose them all in one go. These giant trees are frequently home to many epiphytes, particularly bromeliads, which are members of the orchid family. In order to get as close as possible to the light, they grow on branches, collecting droplets of the ever-present moisture in their funnel-shaped leaves. These leafy reservoirs constitute an ecosystem in themselves, supporting various varieties of fauna, especially frogs and insects, which in turn enrich the plants with their excreta.

Larger mammals, the most famous of which is the Amazon manatee, occasionally stray into this inhospitable region via the Rio Negro. These sizeable plant eaters differ from their marine cousins, the Dugongs, because they do not graze on plant life on the river bed, but feed on floating water plants. Consequently, the mouths of these slow-moving, extremely shy creatures are aimed upwards.

Adapted to an aquatic life

These former land animals have adapted well to an aquatic life. They

can close up their nostrils and ears, pick up ultra sound, their neck is foreshortened, their front limbs have evolved into fins, and their rear limbs have reverted to tail fins. The Amazon manatee has poor eyesight, but excellent hearing, and can remain submerged for up to 16 minutes before needing to surface for air.

Biologists have identified more than 120 mammals, 470 bird varieties, 15 reptiles and 320 species of fish in Jau National Park, Brazil's largest conservation area. Ten types of turtle inhabit the muddy shores of the river and three varieties of caimans, giant otters, and numerous species of monkey, jaguar and ocelot roam unchecked over the 1,040 square miles (2,700km²) of Jau National Park, which was established to protect this dense, evergreen jungle.

Marshland along one of the Amazon's largest tributaries, the Rio Negro. A unique diversity of flora thrives beneath the canopy of these jungle giants (above)

The abundant rainforest wildlife also includes squirrel monkeys (below, left)

View of the forested banks of the Rio Negro (below, right)

Paradise in the swamps

PANTANAL in northwestern Brazil protects a rich diversity of tropical landscapes and is a veritable Garden of Eden

GETTING THERE:
Flight from São Paulo to Cuiaba; by hire car to Poconé and Jofre, where boats and horses can be hired

WHERE TO STAY:
On ranches, or "fazendas," although several months' advance booking is required

CLIMATE:
Best time to visit is between April/May and September, when the climate is dry and hot. Rainy season from November to March

MAIN ATTRACTIONS:
A paradise for biologists and ornithologists. Piranha fishing; monkey watching

SPECIAL TIPS:
Substantial areas of the Pantanal can only be reached by boat or on horseback

The dark, leafy canopy of the dense riverine forest echoes with a cacophony of birdsong and the fluttering and flapping of wings. The swampy river is full of floating dead tree trunks, wading waterfowl, water birds, and jumping fish. These are the immediate, unforgettable first impressions of Brazil's Pantanal region, the world's most spectacular marsh area with its unparalleled biodiversity. It is hardly surprising that Brazilians call it the "Garden of Eden." Innumerable lakes and rivers, evergreen tropical rainforests, dry woodland, savannahs, and watery lagoons provide a range of habitats unequalled anywhere else in the world for many endangered species of animal and plant life. Not only do the Pantanal forests provide rich hunting grounds for jaguars, but the region is also a protected paradise for tapirs, giant monitor lizards, spectacled alligators, and countless species of waders.

Eighty percent of the Pantanal, a region comprising 54,000 square miles (140,000km²) of dense primeval jungle and dry steppe lands, lie in Brazil and extend into Bolivia and Paraguay beyond. The area is a marshy floodplain surrounded by moun-

tains, with a single runoff to the south. From October to March, when rainfall is heaviest, the mighty Paraguai River and its many tributaries, including the São Lourenso, Cuiaba, Taquari, Miranda, Negro, and Aquidaduana, burst their banks and form a vast marsh, ten times bigger than the Everglades in Florida.

The largest volume of water comes from the forests in the north, flowing down the Cuiaba tributary and emptying into this extensive wetland landscape. It discharges water into the Paraguai at the rate of 17,000 cubic feet (480m³) per second, so much that the river is obliged to create fresh channels for itself. Two-thirds of the Pantanal basin is submerged during the rainy period. In May, the floods recede, leaving behind a thick layer of sand, plant, and animal material. This silt makes a nutrient-rich, natural fertilizer.

Three ecological zones

The Pantanal can be divided into three ecological zones, depending on water quantity and water levels. In the Alto Pantanal area, the water remains up to 20in (0.5m) deep for two to three months, while the Medio Pantanal is inundated for three to four months at

a time. In the lower-lying Baixo Pantanal region, on the other hand, the water levels reach depths of 10–13ft (3–4m) during the rainy season.

The abrupt change from a dry to wet landscape is one of the reasons for the huge diversity of flora, which has only just begun to be explored. The terrain here comprises a gently undulating steppe landscape as well as paspalum grasslands. To the west, jojoba and jobo woodland stretch alongside permanently wet, green regions comprising riverine forest, with trees reaching 33–60ft (10–18m) in height and dense thickets of plant vegetation. The river tributaries contain floating islands of tangled reed roots known as "camalotes" and are dotted here and there with groups of assorted tropical palms.

The wildlife is equally abundant. Scientists have so far identified 80 different species of mammal, approximately 650 bird varieties, 50 types of reptile, and around 400 kinds of fish.

Above all, this tropical, watery refuge is paradise for a profusion of birds. One of the most famous of these is the Jabirú, or "Tuiuiú" as it is known locally. This is Latin-America's representative of the stork family. Standing up to 5ft (1.5m) tall, with a

wingspan of almost 8ft (2.5m), it is one of the largest birds in the world. It is the only stork in the world with entirely white plumage. The green forests are populated by 26 different species of parrot alone, including the world's largest parrot, the hyacinth macaw, measuring an incredible 39in (1m) in length. These extremely shy, blue-feathered parrots only live in one type of tree and an estimated 3,000 of magnificent them reside in the forests of Pantanal.

Refuge for waterfowl

The Pantanal also provides a perfect refuge for various species of heron, ibis and duck, while the wetlands provide a temporary home to huge flocks of waders and waterfowl from North America, which winter in the Pantanal.

Although large areas are inaccessible to man, the region is increasingly under threat. A significant proportion of the area, first developed during the early eighteenth century by Luso Brazilians in search of gold and slaves, is now cultivated for soybeans and sugar cane. Unfortunately, farming methods also include the use of fertilizers and pesticides, which are just as damaging to the wetlands as the few remaining pockets of gold and diamond mining.

Luckily, large expanses of the Pantanal have been acquired, however, by private purchasers and added to the 73 square miles (190km^2) of National Park conservation area that protects the unparalleled beauty of these wetlands.

During the rainy season, vast expanses of the Pantanal are inundated. The forests lining the rivers are left standing in water (above, left)

The marshlands provide a rich source of food for storks and herons, even during the dry season (above, right)

The abundant wildlife includes the stork-like Jabirú (center, right) and caiman alligators (below, right)

ATLANTIC
BRAZIL
Capivara •
• Brasilia
PACIFIC

Prehistoric treasure chamber

CAPIVARA National Park in Brazil contains some of South America's earliest cave paintings

GETTING THERE:
Flight connections to Petrolina in the Piauí, Bahia, and Pernambuco Triangle. By four-wheel-drive vehicle to São Raimundo Nonato

WHERE TO STAY:
Basic hotel accommodation in São Raimundo Nonato

CLIMATE:
Warm tropical climate

MAIN ATTRACTIONS:
Museu do Homem Americano in São Raimundo Nonato; caves: Boqueirao da Pedra Furada and Toca do Baixão da Vaca; more caves in Serra das Confusões National Park 60 miles (100km) away

SPECIAL TIPS:
Special permission required to visit the caves, and only with a guide

Until now, historians thought that man first crossed the Bering Straits to North America some 60,000 to 20,000 years ago, reaching South America a little more than 13,000 years ago. But the history of how South America was first settled will be re-written if the dating of prehistoric finds in Capivara National Park in northern Brazil proves to be conclusive. Some unique and extremely artistic cave paintings have been discovered in numerous caves in the province of Piauí. They have also found what may possibly be a place where early man used to make fire approximately 48,000 years ago.

Piauí is situated between the Amazon Basin and the Atlantic, where the climate is dry except for occasional torrential showers that descend upon the varied landscape. Most of the area is covered by bush and cactus landscape known as the Caatinga. To the east of the Bom Jesus da Guergeia Mountains lies the Cerrado, an increasingly rare landscape of tree savannah. This region is home to a wide diversity of wildlife, once a useful source of food to the region's early inhabitants.

Impressive canyons

This warm landscape with its relatively sparse forests and scenic beauty is a fascinating region. Spectacular canyons with sheer sandstone walls in a myriad of different hues, dotted with isolated, majestic rock pinnacles and arches, exhibit different colors of rock strata, testifying to the landscape's geological history.

The area is a significant sanctuary for some increasingly rare and special animals, such as America's largest bat, the "vampyrum spectrum," otherwise known as the large leaf-nosed or vampire bat. These nocturnal mammals have a wingspan of three feet. Despite their somewhat malignant appearance, they pose no threat to humans. The Park also boasts numerous types of parrot, snake, giant armadillo, giant anteater, jaguar, and puma, all of which are on the endangered species list.

The large number of natural caves in the white sandstone mountains of Capivara provided a haven for South America's earliest

inhabitants. Some of the caves have been gouged out and extended, their walls decorated with wonderfully intricate rock drawings depicting hunting scenes and people dancing or giving birth. There are more than 400 such sites providing considerable insight into these peoples' everyday lives.

Rock drawings in reds and browns

The most famous and grandest gallery of rock art is located in the rock shelter known as Toca do Boqueirão da Pedra Furada, literally the "rock of many holes." The reddish-brown paintings depict various animals as well as men wearing typical feather headdresses. Another important archeological site is located at Toca do Baixão da Vaca, an overhanging sandstone rock 375ft (114m) long. A total of 749 individual examples of rock art have survived here.

For the most part, these prehistoric artists used nature's own materials to lend color to their drawings, such as red hematite (iron oxide), yellow geothite, white plaster or kaolin, and their black was derived from burnt organic material such as bones or charcoal. They even used blue, a color seldom seen in cave paintings, to depict a deer.

The subject matter of these incredible rock paintings can be split into two different cultural strands or traditions. On the one hand, the Nordeste tradition, during the period from 12000 to 6000 BC, focused mainly on narrative rock illustrations, depicting scenes of animals and people presented singly or in groups. The later Agreste tradition dating from 8000 to 3000 BC was characterized, on the other hand, by peculiar lines and geometric patterns that some researchers have interpreted as an early form of script or code whose meaning has been lost in the mists of time.

Prehistoric animals

The animals depicted in these early paintings illustrate the fauna that once populated this magical landscape in the Maranhão Paraiba Basin of Brazil: emus, armadillos, panthers, alligators, fish, a variety of birds, and apes, which to this day still guard these caves and can often

Weather, wind,
and water have
sculpted remarkable
rock formations out
of the soft sandstone
of the National Park
(above)

This rocky karst
landscape is typical
of some parts of Piauí
Province (below, left)

Caves within the
National Park contain
prehistoric animal
paintings, some 14000
years old, illustrating
the wildlife of the time
(below, right)

be glimpsed during walks through this mountainous landscape.

The 500 square miles (1,300km²) of the Serra da Capivara National Park were originally intended to protect the Caatinga bush forest, but the 30,000 or so rock drawings that have come to light so far in this prehistoric treasure chamber have meanwhile been designated a world heritage site in themselves.

Meanwhile, similar caves in Serra das Confusões National Park 60 miles (100km) away have also been placed under protection, although these remain virtually unexplored.

In the shelter of the precordillera

LAUCA NATIONAL PARK in Chile lies at an altitude of 13,125ft (4,000m) in the northern altiplano

GETTING THERE:
By air via Santiago to Arica, then by bus to Parinacota

WHERE TO STAY:
Simple accommodation and camp sites within the National Park. Hotels in Arica

CLIMATE:
Summer temperatures are between 54-68° F (12-20° C), dropping at night to 14° F (-10° C)

MAIN ATTRACTIONS:
Parinacota; the hot springs of Jurasi; Salar de Surire; hiking; mountain climbing on Payachata

SPECIAL TIPS:
Risk of high-altitude sickness as most of the Park is situated at a height of around 14,800ft (4,500m)

Lauca National Park in northern Chile runs some 100 miles (160km) along the Bolivian border. Sheltered in the lee of the precordillera, whose volcanic heights rise to over 19,500ft (6,000m) in places, the Park extends across the northeastern altiplano, a high plateau situated some 13,000ft (4,000m) above sea level between the cordillera ranges. This nature reserve covers an area of almost 540 square miles (1,400km²) and is home to most of the great diversity of species found in the Andes. This high Andean consists of an endless expanse of grasslands with deep ravines cutting into the plains. The scores of shallow, shimmering lakes contrast sharply with dark lava fields, such as those in the Cotacotani region. The area is dotted with dazzling white salt pans glittering in the harsh, high-altitude sun. Freshwater, saltwater, and brackish lakes glisten on the plateau and raging rivers crash down into the valleys below. The most important of these rivers is the Lauca, which flows from the Parinacota. It meanders through the southern part of the Park before its waters flow into the Coipasa salt deposit in Bolivia, where they evaporate leaving nothing behind but the salt washed down from the mountains.

Dormant twin volcanoes

At the heart of the national park, the spectacular heights of the Payachatas, dormant twin volcanoes, soar skyward. The two snow-covered summits of Pomerape and Parinacota are around 20,700ft (6,300m) in height. Glittering at the foot of this magnificent picture is Lake Chungara, covering an area of over 8 square miles (21km²). This lake is one of the most elevated in the world. Located at an altitude of 14,810ft (4,514m), it is a full 2,300ft (700m) higher than Lake Titicaca.

Lake Chungara is home to the 130 or so bird varieties that occur in the Park: flamingoes, silvery grebes, night herons, and crested ducks as well as the ostrich-like rheas and giant coots. High above, condors circle majestically as they have done for thousands of years.

Huge flocks of flamingoes gather periodically at Salar de Surire salt lake, which is situated in a remote spot on the Park's southern periphery. This lake shore also provides a habitat for the vicuña, an elegant species of llama that grows to a height of 5¼ft (1.6m). Its wool is so greatly prized that it has been heavily hunted outside this conservation area and is consequently very scarce. Apart from these, alpacas are the only other mammals which have adapted to the lack of oxygen and extreme conditions of these altitudes of more than 13,000ft (4,000m).

The lower regions, however, are home to a further 30 species of mammal including wild guanacos and tarucas, which strut haughtily over the rocky landscape, while remaining on the alert for pumas. The Magellan fox hunts little vizcachas, Andean rabbits that are distantly related to chinchillas and guinea pigs.

Rare trees and shrubs

The vegetation, which grows between 12,500–13,800ft (3,800–4,200m), comprises a number of botanical rarities seldom found elsewhere. The hillsides support gnarled queñoa trees, whose trunks constantly shed their reddish bark, which peels off in flaps. Thickets of low, green bushes grow between these isolated groups of trees.

Up to an altitude of 13,800ft (4,200m), the cliffs are thickly covered with llareta, an unusual species of light green bush that grows in hard compact cushions. It grows very slowly, only three quarters of an inch a year, but was once very widespread. Nowadays, it is found only in Chile, and the best examples can be seen in Lauca Park. Llareta was used by the Indians for domestic fuel, but the mines and saltpeter refineries, which burnt vast quantities of this unique bush, brought it to the verge of extinction.

Lauca National Park has been designated an international biosphere reserve. The Park is inhabited by the Aymaran Indians who singlemindedly keep their ancient traditions alive. Archeological finds in the Las Cueva region are proof that they are the descendents of the hunters and gatherers that traveled across this plateau some 9,000 years ago.

While their owners are off shepherding their llama and alpaca herds over the high plateau, the Aymaran Indians' 50 or so dwellings remain unoccupied a good deal of the time. The Indians only return home at carnival time or for religious festivals, which are celebrated in Parinacota's distinctive church, built in the seventeenth century from volcanic material.

The snow-covered peaks of extinct volcanoes rear up from the altiplano (left)

Undemanding cacti populate the endless steppes of the altiplano (above, right)

The native Indians keep herds of llamas, much prized for their wool (below, right)

The end of the world

TORRES DEL PAINE NATIONAL PARK in southern Chile is still turning its back on civilization

GETTING THERE:
By road from Pintas Arena via Puerto Natales. Bus links available

WHERE TO STAY:
In lodges or at campsites within the Park. More expensive hotels along the boundary of the Park

CLIMATE:
December/January: 50°-64° F (10°-18° C), maximum 73°-77° F (23°-25° C). June/July: 32°-46° F (0°-8° C)

MAIN ATTRACTIONS:
Extensive network of hiking trails lead to the most interesting parts of the Park. The paths are safe and, for the most part, not particularly difficult

SPECIAL TIPS:
Vehicles prohibited in the Park

Aerial view of the Torres Park lake district (above)

Melted ice from the Grey Glacier flows into an inland lake (below, center)

Multi-colored grasses rippling across the flat steppes (below, right)

Traces of branches of low-growing trees on the rocks (below, left)

Torres del Paine epitomizes remote, faraway wilderness, the inaccessible end of the earth. Local people tell the story of Cai Cai, a wicked snake who caused a tidal wave to overwhelm Torres del Paine to eliminate an enemy tribe of warriors living there. After the flood waters had receded, Cai Cai seized the two biggest warriors and turned them into pillars of stone, the Cuernos del Paine, or 'horns of stone.' These pillars now dominate the Paine mountain massif, together with the Torres, three high, bare granite towers rising 7,385ft, 8,070ft, and 8,200ft (2,250m, 2,460m, and 2,500m) respectively.

Here in southern Chile just before the Andes plunge into the Pacific Ocean, a profusion of bizarre granite rock formations rear skywards, each of them over 6,600ft (2,000m) high. This must surely be one of the most beautiful and magnificent landscapes in all of Chile, supporting natural habitats that have remained untouched for thousands of years. These mountains were fortunately too inaccessible for European settlers and their vast herds of beef cattle.

Tongues of ice extend south from Campo del Hielo Sur, the Patagonian glacier and the world's largest single ice mass outside Antarctica.

The gradual demise of the glaciers

Despite their massive size and spectacular appearance, the Grey, Tyndall, and Balmaceda glaciers are mere remnants of what was once a vast system of ice-fields and glacial mountains. Like most other glaciers throughout the world, these too are gradually receding. Smoothly carved out, rounded valley bottoms and moraines below the lower edge of the glaciers testify how far these huge masses of ice extended only a few decades ago. Gigantic chunks can frequently be heard breaking off the Grey Glacier with a thunderous roar and plunging deep into the waters of the lake of the same name.

North of this glacier-filled, snowy mountain wilderness are the sparkling lakes known as Dickson, Paine, and Azule Lagune. To the south, are the finger lakes of Grey, Pohoe, and Nordenskjöld, while to the east is the Armarga Lagune.

The turquoise glacier water of the National Park's main river, the River Paine, springs in Lake Dickson from where it flows along the eastern flank of the massif before finally discharging into Lake Toro at the southern end of the Park. Along the way, it negotiates the various elevations in a series of three spectacular waterfalls: the Paine Waterfall, Salto Grande Waterfall, and Salto Chico Waterfall.

Sub-polar ecosystem

Torres del Paine National Park comprises more than 930 square miles (2,400km²) of extremely sensitive, but richly diverse, sub-polar habitat. Guanacos — smaller relatives of the camel that have become increasingly rare outside protected areas — are still fairly common here. The shy Patagonian red and gray foxes, on the other hand, remain hidden as they stalk the small Cuvier dormice or the European hares that were introduced into the country. As in all parts of the southern Andes, one must always beware of pumas.

The majority of the 106 species of birds, including numerous water birds and many endangered varieties, are generally found near the lakes and lagoons. Condors cruise above the mountain peaks, easily identified by their seven splayed primary feathers. Darwin rheas, a species related to the ostrich and equally under threat, inhabit the rocks and bushes alongside duck-sized Coscoroba swans with their spoon-shaped bills.

Striped woodpeckers, which can be spotted in the low-growing trees along Lake Nordenskjöld, have had to make a remarkable adjustment to the prevailing conditions: since there are no high trees available, they build their nests on the ground.

Waving grassland and vast planes, buffeted by incessant winds, stretch as far as the eye can see. The sloping mountain flanks are covered with coigue forest or Chilean cherry. Higher up, the coigue trees give way to Tierra del Fuego cherries, which get increasingly smaller the higher the altitude until they eventually form a natural bonsai garden, interspersed with the colorful yellow and red calafate bushes that are a species of berberis with berries resembling blueberries.

The plummeting torrents

The waterfalls in the Brazilian-Argentinean nature reserve of **IGUAZU** are among the most spectacular natural splendors in the world

The source of the Iguazu River rises at an altitude of 4,300ft (1,300m) in the Brazilian Serra do Mar mountain range not far from the Atlantic coast. No sooner has it emerged than it finds its direct route almost immediately blocked by the mountains themselves. Consequently, the Iguazu River, sections of which measure 1,650–4,950ft (500–1,500m) across, is obliged to wind its way more than 300 miles (500km) across the hinterland before discharging its waters into the Rio Paraná in the vicinity of Foz do Iguaçu in Brazil, Ciudad del Este in Paraguay, and Puerto Iguazu in Argentina. It begins by hurling itself more than 230ft (70m) over the precipice of a mighty lava plateau extending 400,000 square miles (1,000,000km^2) across Brazil, Paraguay, Argentina, and Uruguay, in what is one of the most magnificent waterfall spectacles on earth. This plateau of lava erupted 135 million years ago through cracks and fissures in the earth's surface, but no volcano ever formed here.

There is a stunning panoramic view from the Brazilian shore of the

crescent-shaped waterfall. During the rainy season, 230,000ft^3 (6,500m^3) of water thunder over its 8,900ft^3 (2.7km) lip, forming a roaring curtain of water, comprised of over 270 individual waterfalls. Great white clouds of mist rise up from this devil's cauldron of swirling water, producing numerous intersecting rainbows of spray in a unique spectacle of nature. During the dry season, the volume of water is a mere 10,600ft^3 (300m^2),

roaring its way down in around 150 separate cascades.

Just before the Iguazu reaches the precipice, it broadens out to more than a mile across, splitting into numerous tributaries that encircle the equally numerous islands and islets. Chunks of lava, which have broken away from the precipice over the course of time, have meanwhile become islands and islets, dissecting the wildly raging waters at the base of the falls.

Around 20,000 years ago, the waterfall was situated at the confluence of the Iguazu and the Paraná. Over thousands of years, however, it has carved itself a 17 mile (28km) long, 260ft (80m) deep channel out of the soft lava rock.

Below the Falls, a bridge leads across into Argentina. On this side, it is possible to approach within touching distance of the waterfall, either through winding hiking trails along the bank or by way of bridges or boat trips to the islands both above and below the actual waterfall.

These waterfalls are situated at the heart of a National Park area, which

straddles both Brazil and Argentina over an area of nearly 400 square miles (1,000km²) and is designed to protect this region's increasingly endangered primeval forest environment. Both Parks are part of mankind's natural heritage, preserving intact an area of almost pristine Paranaensic jungle, a type of primeval forest of which only 5 to 10 percent remains in Brazil and Paraguay.

Drenched by the cascades

The Park is a sub-tropical rainforest sporting an abundant diversity of species and several separate vegetation levels, starting with the high treetops 100ft (30m) above the ground, to the medium-sized trees and shrubs, and right down to the vegetation on the forest floor. One of the most beautiful trees is the jacaranda tree, which grows to a height of more than 130ft (40m) with a girth of around 5ft (1.6m). Dwarf palms are usually found growing in its shade. Altogether 2,000 different varieties of plant, including lianas, tree ferns, and numerous climbing plants, have been recorded here. More than 60 species of orchid and countless bromeliads are indigenous to this region.

The lion's share of the waterfall, encompassing one-and-a-quarter miles (two km) of this semi-circular spectacle, belongs to Argentina. The habitat that has evolved here reflects the constant humidity produced by the mists from the cascades. This relatively isolated biotope is also called kauri forest, after the Cupay tree, whose copper-colored buds unfurl into pendulous foliage. Lush Paspalum-Illoi grass flourishes between the boulders.

The fauna is equally diverse: biologists have recorded a total of 68 mammals, 422 birds, 38 reptiles, and 18 amphibians. Many of these are rare or even endangered species such as the giant otter, the La Plata otter, jaguar, ocelot, great anteater, lowland tapir, crab-eating raccoon, and South American coati.

The bird life is particularly eye-catching and colorful, with 44 percent of all bird species found in Argentina occurring here. These include brilliantly colored parrots, toucans with their enormous bills and helmet woodpeckers, not to mention the humming birds that dart in and out of the foliage. One of the most impressive birds, however, is undoubtedly the great dusky swift, which swoops gracefully over the cascades with the utmost precision, coming to rest among the rocks and even nesting on rocky outcrops, unperturbed by the surging torrents all around.

Specially constructed footbridges lead to an island at the foot of the waterfalls (above)

The water plunges down in a series of cascades from the high volcanic plateau above (below, right)

Aerial photograph of the precipitous rock walls of the falls, bordered by primeval forest (below, left)

The Patagonian ice field

Los **GLACIARES NATIONAL PARK** in Argentina incorporates several climatic zones

GETTING THERE:
Regular flights
from Buenos Aires to
Calafate. By car via
Santa Cruz on National
Route 3, or by bus via
Rio Gallegos. Don't
miss a drive along
National Route 40 from
Rio Gallegos or Esquel

WHERE TO STAY:
Hotels, guesthouses,
cabins, apartments,
camping sites

CLIMATE:
Moderate climate,
37º-54º F (3º-12º C).
Rainy season April
to May

MAIN ATTRACTIONS:
Glaciers: Moreno
(front edge of the
glacier) and Viedma.
Lakes: Argentino and
Viedma. Mountains:
Chaltén/Torre. Places
to visit: Calafate,
Chaltén. Glacier and
forest hikes. Boat trip
into the bays of Lake
Argentino

SPECIAL TIPS:
Puma territory! Camp
at least 165ft (50m)
from the lakeside
in case of swells caused
by collapsing sections
of glacier.

At 7.09 p.m. on 14 March 2004, watched by thousands of curious onlookers, an immense body of water burst through a 656ft (200m) high dam of pure, glittering ice, creating a mighty wave that traveled the 100 mile (160km) length of Lago Argentino in the west of the Argentina's Santa Cruz province.

During its advance, the Perito Moreno Glacier, one of the most imposing glaciers in the entire Andes, had pushed a tongue of ice across this narrow drainage arm of Lake Argentino, effectively blocking the channel and separating Rico Bay from the main part of the lake. Melted ice from the mighty glaciers in the Patagonian ice fields raised the water level in Rico Bay to 82ft (25m). The barrier of ice was eventually unable to withstand the growing pressure of water and a fracture appeared, creating a huge tunnel, which collapsed two days later with a thunderous roar, releasing the trapped volume of water.

The Moreno Glacier is just one of 47 icy giants within Los Glaciares National Park, an area covering around 1,740 square miles (4,500km²). It also encompasses two hundred or so smaller glaciers, each with areas of just over one square mile (3km²). Upsala and Viedma are the two largest glaciers in the park, each covering an area of approximately 230 square miles (600km²). Unlike most glaciers across the globe, Moreno Glacier is is actually increasing in volume.

The 3 mile (5km) expanse of its front edge is an unforgettable sight. The ice presents a magical scene: every conceivable shade of blue and white glitters and shimmers, depending on the angle of the tropical sun. It creaks and groans like a living creature when a section of the glacier is in the process of breaking loose and dropping away into the lake. When this happens, the collapsing chunk of ice plunges deep into the lake, creating a huge swell before resurfacing and finally coming to rest as a gently bobbing iceberg.

220 miles (350km) of white wasteland

Fifty percent of the National Park encompasses the southern section of the snow-covered Andes Cordillera, between whose summits and ridges this vast Patagonian ice field, a surreal and strange-looking landscape covering some 5,400 square miles (14,000km²), has evolved. Towering on the northern horizon are the highest peaks in Los Glaciares National Park: Chaltén and Torre, rising to heights of 11,073ft and 10,262ft (3,375m and 3,128m) respectively.

This white wilderness, measuring nearly 220 miles (350km) in length, is the largest single body of ice anywhere in the world outside the Antarctic. Its existence so far north is explained by the fact that the Andes Mountain chain forces moisture-laden westerly winds off the Atlantic upwards into much colder air. Any precipitation consequently falls as snow, which is compressed under its own accumulative weight into ice. To the east, the Park stretches across a relatively ice-free, pre-Andean zone into the middle of Lake Argentino Basin, where it merges into the steppes of Patagonia.

Vegetation within the Park reflects these two distinct geographical zones. The mountain slopes support the so-called Patagonian-Magellan rainforest, populated by southern beech and cypress, interspersed with the bright colors of red or golden-yellow catafate bushes. The steppe landscape is dominated by a waving sea of tussock grass stretching as far as the eye can see, kept in constant movement by the relentless, often stormy, west winds. Beneath the boundless sky lie the gentle hills of Patagonia, left over from previous Ice Ages and sculpted by giant glaciers.

Forbidding landscape

No matter how forbidding and harsh this singularly beautiful and captivating landscape might seem, it has nevertheless been occupied by man since prehistoric times. The hunter-gatherers, who appeared after the Ice Age, depended mainly on guanacos, small South American camels, for their survival. They were followed by the Tehuelchia Indians, vestiges of whose culture can still be visited in 14 different archaeological sites within the park. Their successors were driven out and killed by new arrivals from Europe.

The region's wildlife has not been thoroughly investigated, with the exception of the 100 or so species of birds, the most celebrated of which are the majestic Andean condor and the red-billed mountain duck. Although it was established in 1945, Los Glaciares National Park has only recently begun attracting world travelers to its frozen wastes, rugged mountains and infinite horizons. Meanwhile, Calafate, a small town with a population of about 4,000 inhabitants, has grown up between the mountain of the same name and Lake Argentino, becoming something akin to a tourist center. The settlement of Chaltén was established on the Park's northern boundary in 1985; its population now numbers 300. It is the starting-point for experienced hikers and mountain climbers wanting explore the Chaltén-Torre massif.

The advance of the ice
giants – shown here
near Santa Cruz – into
the colorful vegetation
zones (above)

Icebergs, broken
loose from glaciers,
floating off-shore
(below, right)

The impressive rock
faces found in the
Chaltén Torre range
represent an irresistible
challenge to mountain
climbers (below, left)

Tufa paradise

The bizarre lava landscape of **GÖREME NATIONAL PARK** in Cappadocia is a geological rarity

GETTING THERE:
Nearest airport: Kayseri
Good road access
from Nevsehir to Ürgüp

WHERE TO STAY:
All categories of hotel
available in Nevsehir,
Ürgüp, and Kayseri

CLIMATE:
Around 73° F (23° C)
May to September;
average around 32-34°
F (0-1° C) December
to January,
snow in January
and February

MAIN ATTRACTIONS:
Devrent and Catalkaya
valleys; Eustathios,
Kilise, and Elmali
churches; Ürgüp

The high valley landscape of Cappadocia between Nevsehír and Kayseri in Turkey is dominated by the silhouetted peaks of the mighty Hasan and Akdag volcanoes, not to mention Mount Erciyes, which towers to a height of over 13,000 ft (4,000m). Between two and five million years ago, these volcanoes paved the way for one of the most bizarre, yet beautiful, land formations on the planet. Past eruptions covered the area with soft tufa lava, which hardened into a mighty layer thousands of feet thick extending over an area of nearly 4,000 square miles (10,000km²) in the Kizilirmak basin. During subsequent eruptions one to two million years ago, this was in turn covered by a thin, solid layer of basaltic lava.

Central Turkey's harsh continental climate with its hot, dry summers and frosty, snowy winters has eroded this volcanic material to form spectacularly bizarre sculptures and fantastic rock formations.

Thousands of conical peaks, mushroom-shaped rock formations, chimney-like pillars, and towers strain skyward in an almost surreal kaleidoscope of colors, ranging from brilliant red to shades of yellowy-brown or greenish-gray. These tufa obelisks and pillars, some of which reach a height of 130ft (40m), are crowned with basalt caps that slow down the process of erosion. Each rocky outcrop promises a brand new vista of different shapes, with every valley holding a fresh set of surprises such as the fairy chimneys in Devrent valley, north of Ürgüp, or the original toadstool formations in Catalkaya valley.

Then man arrived on the scene. The first caves were excavated around 4,000 BC, but it was during the early days of Christianity that the first monks and nuns found their way to this beautiful landscape. Such surroundings were ideally suited to inward contemplation, an ascetic way of life, and prayer. Far removed from the Persian wars and incursions by other invaders, this rocky valley also provided a sanctuary for those seeking to escape persecution and destruction, with the result that primitive monks' chambers and hermitages soon sprang up alongside the simple peasant homes.

Cave dwellings and rock monasteries

These cave dwellings were soon followed by extensive monastery complexes. The region probably reached its cultural peak around AD 400, when a period of extremely intensive excavation work began on the orders of Bishop Basileio of Kayseri. The monks carved entire monasteries, including churches, sleeping quarters, and churches, out of the tufa rock walls high above the ground and tunneled entire underground cities out of the soft rock. All the hallmarks of Byzantine sacred architecture are in evidence here — even huge, cruciform, domed basilica churches. The walls are decorated with frescoes depicting the life of Jesus. Today, these sumptuously decorated cave walls are still potent reminders of the richness and overwhelming beauty of Byzantine fresco painting.

The Kara Kilise, or "dark church," is particularly well-preserved. This is due to its having been buried — probably during the eleventh century — throughout the Islamic iconoclastic period, thereby managing to escape the destruction of Christian symbols. Having had virtually no exposure to natural light, the brilliantly colored frescoes have retained their original vibrancy against a background of midnight blue.

Abandoned in the twentieth century

The Göreme cave settlement was abandoned around 1923–1924. In the mid 1980s, a National Park was established covering around 40 square miles (96km²) of this fantastic landscape. It was also designated a protected area in recognition of its status as one of the rare examples of a site combining outstanding natural beauty and interest with cultural heritage value. People form an important part of the scene as well, with around 20,000 farmers and artisans living within the Park. The local population is traditionally

dependent upon agriculture, including viniculture and fruit growing, and pottery, the weaving of rugs and carpets, and dyeing skills. Tourism also grew to become an important source of income during the eighties. Göreme Park now attracts around 600,000 visitors each year, captivating them with its surreal landscape. The flora and fauna are typical of a heritage site. Uncultivated areas are populated by sandalwood, leadwort and thrift. The ancient volcanoes encircle the valley to such an extent, however, that many species have evolved individually since the volcanic eruptions hundreds of thousands of years ago. Biologists have identified 110 species of plants unique to the rocky landscape of Göreme National Park.

Wolves and foxes, as well as otters, badgers and hares, may occasionally be glimpsed among these bizarre rock formations and in the fields. The birds that make their home here are mainly ground species, such as partridge and quail, which skulk among the shrubs and bushes.

ASIA

Many of the conical tufa hills have been carved into rock dwellings (above)

The National Park covers an area of nearly 4,000 square miles (10,000km²) (below, right)

The obelisks are crowned with rock "caps" that protect them from erosion (below, left)

King Kasyapa's rocky citadel

SIGIRIYA Mountain in Sri Lanka is one of the world's great cultural treasures

Bay of Bengal

Sigiriya
Colombo • SRI LANKA

INDIAN OCEAN

GETTING THERE:
By road or bus from Colombo to Sigiriya

WHERE TO STAY:
Hotels, guesthouses, lodges in Sigiriya, Habarana, or Kandalama

CLIMATE:
Humid, tropical climate

MAIN ATTRACTIONS:
Climb up Sigiriya mountain; tour of the palace gardens as well as boulder and water gardens; museum

Situated in the heart of Sri Lanka, a mighty, reddish-brown rock monolith rears 660ft (200m) out of the dark expanse of lush green jungle vegetation, interspersed with lighter patches of rice fields and glittering lakes. Long ago, the powerful ruler Kasyapa built the fortress for himself over a period of just seven years. It comprises an extraordinary system of steps, passageways, and walls within which he immured himself along with his followers, concubines, and treasures until his suicide in 495 AD.

The drama began over 1,500 years ago in Anuradhapura, the ancient capital of Sri Lanka. Kasyapa, the power-hungry son of King Dhatusena, overthrew his own father and had him chained naked to a rock face, leaving him to die. His half-brother, Moggallana, Dhatusena's legitimate heir, fled to India. From then on, Kasyapa lived in constant fear of his half-brother's return and transferred his residence in 477 AD to this huge rocky monolith surrounded by jungle. He converted it into a unique fortified palace with enchanting gardens and created a veritable work of art that has now been dignified with world heritage site status.

The entrance to this cliff-top citadel was originally guarded by the giant figure of a lion looking north carved partly out of rock and partly built of bricks and decorated with stucco work. The lion has not withstood the centuries well and only his paws remain today. The entrance to the palace once led up through the lion's gaping mouth to the main precinct, which covered 13,000 square feet (1,200m²) on this cliff-top plateau.

Erotic frescoes

Half way up the path to this hilltop palace, the staircase runs along the so-called Mirror Wall to a spiral staircase winding up to the dizzy heights above. The bricks of this wall used to be polished with egg-white and honey to such a high finish that they gleamed with a mirror-like shine. Well into the twelfth century and long after this rocky eyrie was abandoned, monks and visitors were still inspired to add hundreds of inscriptions and writings of their own to the Mirror Wall, some of which are acknowledged to be among the earliest examples of Singhalese poetry.

On reaching the top of this spiral staircase, the present-day visitor encounters around 20 captivating, erotic rock frescoes depicting bare-bosomed beauties of the fifth century. There were originally 500 such frescoes covering the rock face.

Having finally climbed the 1,860 steps leading up to the summit, the remains of the palace are visible scattered about the plateau. Kasyapa designed the palace so that its east wall would rise straight up from the vertical cliff wall. The remains of a carefully laid out kitchen garden can also still be seen on the western side, complete with a small pond and cisterns.

Breathtaking, panoramic views extend not only across the vast expanse of Sri Lanka's jungle plains, but also embrace the spacious and artistically designed layout of the palace, with its symmetrically planned gardens around the base of the cliff. The water gardens are a parti-

cularly impressive feature. They are based on a cleverly designed system, built over several levels and incorporating water courses, retaining basins, underground terracotta pipes, and cooling systems. The miniature water gardens, separated from the main water gardens by a wall, once contained numerous pavilions, shady courtyards, refreshing bathing pools, and cisterns. As a finishing touch, King Kasyapa also added pebbles to some of the waterways in order to recreate the sound of natural running water and other jungle noises.

Water from an artificial lake

The heart of the main water gardens is a central island surrounded by water, linked to the main precinct by a system of causeways radiating from the center. The garden was supplied with water from Lake Sigiri Maha Weva, an artificial reservoir created by a 7 mile (12km) dam situated immediately behind this rocky fortress to the south.

The asymmetrical boulder garden is situated higher up the rocky plateau. The area is full of narrow twisting paths, winding between giant natural boulders as well as the remains of the Audience Hall with its 16ft (5m) long throne hewn out of rock. Almost every boulder once sheltered a brick or timber building.

In 495 AD, Kasyapa's worst fears became reality when his half-brother Moggallana returned from India with his own army. Deserted by his own followers, Kasyapa committed suicide and his luxurious citadel gradually disintegrated until British game hunters happened across it in 1828.

Sigiriya Mountain is a huge monolith of reddish-brown rock rearing up out of the surrounding jungle. Its plateau once housed a fortified palace, surrounded by ornamental water gardens and a natural boulder garden (above)

Erotic frescoes are reminders of those bygone days (below, right)

This memorable scenery is further enhanced by traditionally robed monks (below, left)

On the roof of the world

SAGARMATHA NATIONAL PARK around Mount Everest in Nepal protects the flora and fauna of the Himalayas

GETTING THERE:
Flight to Syangboche;
flight to Lukia, followed
by two days' trek,
or flight to Phaplu
followed by 5 days' trek,
or flight to Tumlingtar
and 10 days' trek

WHERE TO STAY:
All kinds of accommo-
dation available from
luxury hotels to simple
lodges, Sherpa hotels,
and private accommo-
dation

CLIMATE:
Best time to visit
is between October
and November

MAIN ATTRACTIONS:
Mendalphu in the
center of the Park;
Tengboche monastery;
hiking trails

SPECIAL TIPS:
Collecting wood for
fires is forbidden. Beer
bottles, mountain
bikes, and motor-bikes
are also banned.

*Giant ice fields moving
down Mount Everest
toward the valleys (above)*

*Gokyo River is one of the
most spectacular sights in
the Himalayas (below, right)*

*Local people use sticks to
mark prayer sites on the
mountain (below, left)*

In the shadow of Mount Everest, which at 29,028ft (8,848m) is the world's highest mountain, lies the highest national park on earth. Even its deepest gorges are situated 9,335ft (2,845m) above sea level. Sagarmatha National Park is located on the Nepalese side of Nepalese-Tibetan border. Its 443 square miles (1,148km²) comprise the Khumbu region and the upper reaches of Dudh Kosi River, which eventually becomes the Ganges. Its fan-shaped basin is surrounded on all sides by high, rugged mountain scenery. Glaciers at the head of the four main valleys of Chukhung, Khumbu, Gokyo, and Nangpa feed the river with large quantities of cold, crystal-clear water, the quantity of which increases each year as global warming accelerates the rate at which these ice masses melt.

Not only does the park contain the highest spot on the planet, but it also encompasses eight other mountain giants whose peaks exceed 26,250ft (8,000m) above sea level: Lhotse Shar, Cho Oyu, Ama Dablam, Pumori, Kangtega, Gyachung Kang, Thamserku, and Kwangde.

The National Park was established in 1976, mainly because mountaineering tourism had assumed such destructive proportions that wildlife habitats were seriously shrinking and many animals had disappeared altogether. Having settled here 500 years ago, it was the Sherpas themselves who had begun forest clearance, but the situation became much worse around 1960 when a wave of refugees poured in from Tibet. Reforestation is now hampered by the fact that the layer of humus in the cleared areas has largely been washed away.

The Park was designated a world heritage site in 1979. This made little impact on the mountain climbers flocking to the region. A clean-up operation by 150 Sherpas in 2001 harvested a staggering four tons of discarded refuse over a period of five days. It is estimated that a further thousand tons of garbage still lie in the valleys.

Sagarmatha National Park was founded not only to preserve the habitats of different plants and animals, but also to safeguard the culture and lifestyle of the inhabitants of Khumbu, the Sherpas. Around 3,500 of these people now live within the Park's boundaries in 63 different settlements. They left their homeland in Salmo Gang, eastern Tibet, around 1500. One group of them settled in Khumbu, while the other continued on to Solu.

The blessing of the potato

Before the mid-nineteenth century, daily existence must have been a struggle for the Sherpas since only a very robust variety of barley could be cultivated in such harsh conditions. Everything changed, however, when the potato was introduced into this remote mountain area in 1850. The population grew and a large number of ornate monasteries were built. The second major change in the lives of these mountain people came when teams of western mountaineering expeditions climbing up to their valleys realized that Sherpas make outstanding and skilled mountain guides. Since those days, Sherpas have become almost totally economically dependant on mountain tourism.

The dramatic Himalayan mountain range was formed when the Indian plate collided with the continent of Asia around 70 million years ago, pushing up the first ridges. These two tectonic plates have continued colliding intermittently for many millions of years, forcing the Himalayan Mountains ever higher. The last major height increase is thought to have occurred 500,000 to 800,000 years ago: in other words, after the dawn of mankind. The Himalayas are still rising at the rate of one-fifth of an inch (five millimeters a year); most of this is lost, however, as a consequence of natural erosion.

Where only lichen grows

While the majority of the nature reserve is desolate wilderness, it is not entirely without vegetation. Almost 30 percent is pasture land and nearly 3 percent is forest. The vegetation on the mountainsides alters according to altitude, as do the wildlife habitats. Above 9,900ft (3,000m), the landscape is dominated by sparse forests of silver fir, Himalayan white pine, juniper and birch. The forest gives way to a dense covering of alpine rhododendron bushes at altitudes of around 12,500ft (3,800m). These burst into bloom in spring, providing a stunning spectacle of color during the monsoon season. At an altitude of 14,800ft (4,500m), dwarf shrubs and grasses gain the upper hand, and between 18,100–19,800ft (5,500–6,000m), the vegetation is limited to a few varieties of low-growing rhododendron. Altitudes higher than this can only support various species of lichen, which

somehow manage to survive by clinging to the exposed, often snow or ice-covered rocks.

Animal life has dwindled dramatically as a result of the influx of more than 35,000 mountain climbers and trekkers who visit this delicately balanced, high mountain ecosystem each year, keen to experience its majestic, snowy peaks first-hand. You would be very lucky indeed to get a glimpse of even one of the 28 indigenous mammals, which include snow leopards, red pandas, yellow-throated martens, common langurs and musk deer. Far more likely is an encounter with a Goral or Serau chamois, or the Himalayan tahr, a breed of sheep.

The region is home to 152 species of birds, 36 of which are rare. It is astonishing how many of them actually manage to breed at such high altitudes. Many of the small glacier lakes are important resting places for migrating birds obliged to cross this huge range of mountains. At least 19 water birds occur here, even in the midst of all the mountains.

Regards from the rhinoceros

KAZIRANGA NATIONAL PARK in India is a last refuge for the one-horned rhinoceros

GETTING THERE:
Entrance to the Park along the NH 37 highway in Kohora. Bus connections from Guwahati, Furkating, and Tezpur. Railway station in Furkating; airport at Jorhat

WHERE TO STAY:
Hotels in Kaziranga. Bungalows and two lodges within the Park

CLIMATE:
Best time to visit: between November and April

MAIN ATTRACTIONS:
Elephant safari; jeep safari; observation towers in the Park

SPECIAL TIPS:
Park open November to April only

A herd of Indian elephants with the Mikir Hills in Assam in the background (above)

Placed under the protection of the National Park, the rhinoceros population, once on the brink of extinction, now numbers several hundred (below, right)

During the summer monsoon period, the Brahmaputra River floods a major portion of the conservation area (below, left)

Kaziranga National Park represents a spectacular success story for the Indian rhinoceros, which at the turn of the nineteenth century was verging on extinction. In the space of only one hundred years, the species increased from just 12 to 1,500 animals. These prehistoric-looking creatures, unlike others of their species, have just one horn. In 1908, a protected area was specifically created for these incredible animals on the southern banks of the Brahmaputra River in India's northeastern province of Assam. In 1974, this was incorporated into a 165 square mile (430km²) national park and since 1985, the area has been designated a world heritage site.

The flood plains between the mighty, fast-flowing Brahmaputra River to the north and the Mikir Hills rise steeply some 4,000ft (1,200m) or more in the south and have meanwhile become home to 80 percent of all Indian rhinoceroses as well as 15 other species of Indian mammals that are running out of living space on the sub-continent. These include more than 1,000 Indian elephants, as well as capped langurs, sloth bears and a small population of gibbon.

Shaking your quarry to death

Tigers and leopards have a rich choice of prey among the numerous wild boar, wild cattle and swamp deer. The lakes and shores of the Brahmaputra are frequented by water buffalo, while otters dart about, at home both on land and in water. The Brahmaputra River is teeming with fish and Ganges dolphins can occasionally be seen leaping out of the water, killing their prey by shaking it to death above the waves. Unlike other dolphins, this species has no back fin, just a thick protuberance.

The gentle hills of the Brahmaputra's floodplains are largely covered by waving grasslands interspersed with open, tropical forests and numerous interconnecting streams, rivers, and small lakes. Once a year, when the Brahmaputra bursts its banks during the monsoon period between June and July, some three quarters of the Park is inundated by murky floodwater, depositing nutrient-rich, alluvial soils from its upper reaches.

The animals seek refuge on the Park's higher ground or else abandon the area entirely, migrating across the fields and bringing road traffic to a standstill. Once animals leave the confines of the Park, they automatically become prey to poachers and cause problems for farmers whose crops they trample. During the past few years, floodwaters have been getting increasingly higher and heavier as a result of the tree-felling along the upper reaches of the Brahmaputra and because the river keeps having to force its way between dikes.

The higher ground is generally populated by tall "elephant grass," while shorter grasses flourish on the lower ground around the small lakes and ponds that are often barely visible beneath the dense thickets of reeds. Thousands of years of annual flooding have shaped and preserved this unique habitat. Amid the grasses are scattered groups of kapok trees, elephant apple, and Indian gooseberry.

Marabou storks and gray pelicans

Tropical, wet, evergreen forests dominated by mahogany and magnolia species are found near Kanchanjhuri, Panbari, and Tamulipathar, while drier tropical forests occur near Baguri, Bimali and Haldibari, populated by species such as albizia procera, banaba and karaya trees.

These wetlands are bursting with life and provide rich reservoirs of food for thousands of birds of

passage, some of which visit the Park from Siberia during their annual migration. Near the village of Kaziranga is a gray pelican colony, while rare giant storks and Sunda marabou storks patrol the shallow lakes, their bills underwater, filtering the lake for food. Around 25 to 30 Bengal floricans still nest in the Park while high above, birds of prey including buz-

zards and eagles, not to mention the rare Pallas's fish eagle and headed-headed fish eagle, ride on the thermal updrafts of the nearby mountains. The air is filled with the raucous twittering of innumerable red-breasted parakeets. The avifauna in Kaziranga National Park comprises over 300 species and is a veritable paradise for bird-watchers.

The vast, open terrain of the National Park enables visitors to get close to the rich diversity of wildlife. The region is dotted with small observation towers, providing a panoramic view of the landscape and different herds of animals. Although the Park has three different routes suitable for off-road vehicles, visitors usually opt for the traditional method of transport, i.e., specially trained elephants. Led by experienced guides, this is the only way to ensure a really close encounter with the herds of rhinoceros and elephants.

Kingdom of the royal Bengal tiger

The **SUNDARBANS** mangrove forest surrounding the vast Ganges and Brahmaputra river delta is a haven for wildlife

BANGLADESH Dacca
Sundarbans
Bay of Bengal

*INDIAN
OCEAN*

GETTING THERE:
By car, bus, or boat
from Dhaka. Airport
near Jessore

WHERE TO STAY:
Accommodation avail-
able at Hiron Point in
Mongla Port

CLIMATE:
June/July: 99°-108° F
(37°-42° C);
December/January:
48°-84° F (9°-29° C).
Monsoon season from
June to October

MAIN ATTRACTIONS:
Wildlife watching at
Hiron Point, Katka, and
Tin Kona Island. Fish-
ing village at Dubjar
Char

SPECIAL TIPS:
Guided package tours
available from Dhaka
between October to
March

In southern Bangladesh, three main rivers, the Ganges, Brahmaputra, and Meghna, along with their thousands of tributaries, canals, and creeks, converge over an area of 31,000 square miles (80,000km²) to form the world's largest river delta. The western section of the delta emptying into the Bay of Bengal is called "the Sundarbans," an inhospitable landscape of mangrove swamps, islands and a few dunes thrown up by the wind and tides. The Sundarbans extend over an area of 3,900 square miles (10,000km²) and extend across the border into India. On the Bangladeshi side, 2,300 square miles (6,000km²) of this area are preserved as a wildlife sanctuary and natural heritage site, while 500 square miles (1,300km²) are situated over the border in India.

Twice a day, the tides in the Bay of Bengal inundate the countless, shallow waterways, some of which are a mile wide, while others are just narrow tidal creeks. They wash the sand from the rivers and deposit it in sandbanks wherever tributaries flow into the sea. Once these sandbanks have reached the high-water level, the strong, south-westerly monsoon winds begin whipping them into dunes. This creates fresh mudflats that eventually become islands supporting salt grass vegetation. Wind and water are constantly altering the blurred lines between land and sea, a pattern representative of the eternal cycle of growth and decay in nature.

A dense jungle of mangroves covers this landscape of land and water. The almost impenetrable maze of root systems holds the soil together on hundreds of islands. The mangroves form a mosaic of shore and tidal forests, some of which are no taller than bush height, while others consist of high trees with light leaf canopies. In other places, some emergent species live with their roots in saltwater or freshwater. Palm trees grow on some of the younger mud flats. So far, biologists have identified 334 plant species from 245 different families — a most unusual diversity of fundamentally different species.

Rescue cabins in the trees

The Sundarbans are a last refuge for numerous animals. Even so, no less than five out of a total of some fifty species of mammal have completely vanished from certain areas: for example the Java rhinoceros, water buffalo, certain types of deer, and gaur wild cattle.

The Sundarbans are, however, home to the largest population of magnificent royal Bengal tigers now

left in the wild. Around 300 of these majestic, nearly 10ft (3m) long, big cats still roam the dense forests. They are regarded here as man-eaters and the local inhabitants, who live mainly on houseboats, live in fear of them. Wood gatherers and honey collectors, who empty the beehives in the mangrove swamps in April and May, build emergency cabins for themselves high up in the trees so they can take refuge if a tiger gets too close. Even so, people get attacked and killed by tigers every year, although how these big cats in the Sundarbans ever acquired a taste for human flesh is a mystery. The fact that over the years these waterways carried many human corpses out to sea in the wake of a flood disaster may well have played a role.

Between land and water

Three other, smaller members of the cat family also roam the jungle here: leopards, fishing cats, and jungle cats are at home in the region. The Axis deer with its wonderful markings and wild boar are the Bengal tigers' favorite prey. Ganges River dolphins are also found in some of the larger waterways. While lacking the charac-

teristic back fin, they just have a hump or protuberance with a small point instead. They frequently swim and hunt in a line. They hold larger prey above water and shake it to death.

The profusion of bird life here is spectacular. The air is filled with fluttering wings and twittering while some species just quietly search for food in the still waters beneath the comparatively light canopy of trees. So far, 315 different species have been identified, including 95 types of moor hen, 38 birds of prey, and 9 different varieties of kingfisher. Magnificent sea eagles are particularly easy to spot with their brilliant white underbellies. Each one of these birds occupies a territory covering some 30 miles (50km) of waterway, circling above the wet woodland area.

The peaceful lakes and swamps are home to herons and storks, while numerous water birds search the shallows for food and terns swoop and soar along the waterways. The Sundarbans are also home to some true woodland birds. Numerous woodpeckers, barbets, shrikes, and drongos — a species of starling — are present here, twittering and calling in the tree canopy. There are also occasional

glimpses of crocodiles' eyes and snouts, the only features visible as they lie in wait for prey just beneath the surface of the shallow waterways. Once hunted ruthlessly for their skins, crocodiles are no longer present in their former quantities and swamp crocodiles have completely vanished. However, estuarine crocodiles are still fairly common.

Because their root systems grow upward, mangrove trees in the swamp retain a foothold in the water-logged mud (above)

The Sundarbans' villages are under constant threat from flooding (below)

The sacred mountain

TAI SHAN NATIONAL PARK combines sacred sites with unspoiled nature

GETTING THERE:
Good road, bus, and rail links to Tai'an. Airport at Jinan

WHERE TO STAY:
All categories of hotel available in Tai'an and Jinan

CLIMATE:
Moderately warm climate. Occasional frost on the Tai summit

MAIN ATTRACTIONS:
Eastern route good for cultural sites (up 6,000 plus steps); western route better for natural scenery. Trip on one of the three cable cars; helicopter round trip

The most important of China's five sacred mountains rises dramatically and steeply out of the plains in China's eastern province of Shandong. Wu Tai Shan mountain rises to a height of 5,070ft (1,545m), making it the highest summit in the Tai Shan massif. This mountain region is situated to the north of the city of Tai'an, and is regarded as one of the cradles of Chinese culture. It would seem that this mountain was already drawing prehistoric man under its spell 400,000 years ago. During the Neolithic period, it became the focus of two cultures, namely the Dawenkou on its northern flank and the Longshan on its southern side. Thousands of years later, these evolved into the rival states of Qi in the north and Lu in the south. Between 475 and 221 BC, Qi went so far as to erect a 310 mile (500km) wall to protect this sacred mountain from hostile forces. Ruins of this early precursor of the Great Wall of China can still be seen to this day.

Tai Shan Mountain forms the focus for a number of different faiths that have been associated with Taoism and Buddhism for the past 2,000 years. It is regarded as the center of Yang, the positive masculine principle, and the well-spring of life. Indeed, the mountain has become a deity in itself.

From the Qin dynasty (221–206 BC) to the Qing dynasty (1644–1911), every Emperor of China has climbed this holy mountain to offer a sacrifice to the gods. More than 20 groups of buildings and over 2,200 memorials and stone carvings still exist, a powerful testimony to the spiritual significance of Wu Tai Shan.

Granite and gneiss

The most important edifice is the Dai Temple at the foot of the mountain. This was built between 221 BC and AD 220 during the Qin and Han dynasties. During the Tang and Sang dynasties (AD 618–1279) the buildings were substantially extended. Tiangung Hall, the main building, rivals both Taihe Hall in Beijing's Imperial Palace and Dacheng Hall in the Confucian Temple of Qufu, ranking as one of China's largest palace-style buildings.

These cultural sites are in perfect harmony with the impressive diversity of nature. The sacred stature of the mountain has made it virtually inviolable and its original ecosystems have therefore survived intact. Extending to nearly 100 square miles (250km^2), the Park now protects Tai Shan's treasures as an area of natural and cultural heritage.

Geologically speaking, the Tai Shan massif is the oldest and most significant geological fold in eastern China. The spectacular, towering rock formations of granite and gneiss were formed 170–200 million years ago. Rich fossil layers on its northern flanks contain clear evidence of petrified remains of long extinct plants and animals.

Thousand-year-old trees

Around 80 percent of the nature reserve and cultural park is covered with a remarkable diversity of dense vegetation. There has so far been very little research carried out on the different habitats in this region. So far, 1,000 plant species have been identified, including 433 tree varieties. Some individual trees are extremely ancient and steeped in legend: the Han dynasty cypress trees were planted by Emperor Wu Di 2,100 years ago, and the Tang, or scholars' tree, has been growing here for the past 1,300 years.

The forests are home to around 200 species of animal, not counting the 122 different types of birds fluttering around in the treetops and from rock to the rock, although biologists as yet know very little about these populations. Rivers situated at altitudes of around 1,000–2,600ft (300–800m) support a species of fish known as the Common Chramuija, a carp that grows to more than 15in (40cm) in length and was regarded as a culinary delicacy during the Qing dynasty.

Two main routes lead up to the summit of Tai Shan. The western trail passes through virtually untamed and unspoilt natural scenery. The route is lined with magnificent fir trees and numerous waterfalls. From Tianwaicun, it leads up to Zhontianmen Gate, passing through a number of scenic sights, with picturesque names such as "Black Dragon Pool," the "Bridge of Longevity," and "Fan Crags."

The eastern trail is better known for the cultural sights en route. A series of 6,293 steps climbs from Hongmen to Nantianmen Gate, passing the Hongmen Palace, the Wanxian building, Doumu Palace, Jingshi Gorge and the Zhongtian Gate en route. The last stretch of the Shibapan path winds up to the summit of Yuhuangding in a series of 18 hair-pin bends.

The 1000-year old trees are one of the National Park's most spectacular sights (above)

This holy mountain accommodates more than 20 temples on its slopes (below, left)

A bordered pathway consisting of 6,293 stone steps climbs up to the Nantianmen Gate

The pandas have all the bamboo they need

WOLONG NATIONAL PARK on the eastern flanks of the Himalayas is China's foremost protected area for pandas

GETTING THERE:
By road or regular bus service from Chengdu (airport) to Sawan. Tours arranged by specialist travel organizations

WHERE TO STAY:
Hotels in Sawan; private accommodation also available

CLIMATE:
Mild mountain climate; frequent mists and rain

MAIN ATTRACTIONS:
Panda breeding station at Wuyipeng (former research station); panda museum; mountain hiking (Wuyipeng is the starting-point for several trails); bird watching

SPECIAL TIPS:
Hiking trails often impassable after heavy rainfall

On the eastern flanks of the Himalayas, surrounded by giant mountains towering to heights in excess of 16,500ft (5,000m), is the last main sanctuary of the Giant Panda, a species of bear currently teetering on the brink of extinction. Wolong National Park, which extends across an area of 770 square miles (2,000km²), lies 145 miles (230km) northwest of Chengdu in the Chinese province of Sichuan. It is here that the Quinhai mountain plateau, itself part of the Qionglai mountain range, drops abruptly down to the broad, flat Sichuan basin, situated at an altitude of around 4,100ft (1,250m).

Wolong National Park borders the banks of the Pitiao River as carves its way between steep mountain slopes and deeply incised valleys. The surrounding mountain giants tower to heights of 16,500ft (5,000m) and more. Even the Balang Shan Pass is 15,100ft (4,600m) above sea level, a twisting road of hair-pin bends winding its way up the river valley from Dujiangyan via Sawan.

Surrounding the reserve is a landscape of gnarled larch trees, dense rhododendron bushes, impenetrable bamboo thickets, and swirling rain clouds – scenery that could be straight out of a delicate Chinese silk painting. The Park represents an ecological oasis amid a desert of deforested and denuded mountain slopes. Yet this conservation area boasts one of the richest biodiversities in the world, combining both high alpine vegetation and tropical plant life. The higher altitudes are naturally subject to a variability of factors governed by weather, sun radiation and air pressure, which in turn have produced a variety of vegetation zones supporting several different habitats.

Biologists have so far identified more than 1,500 different plant species, including 16 varieties of rhododendron, 59 species of mammal and 155 different bird types, which attract large numbers of bird watchers from all over the world each year.

Around 100 species of flora have additional significance as medicinal plants, a valuable resource of which it is hoped better use can be made in future. The root of the fritillary can be used as a remedy for heart and circulatory problems. Extracts of Gastrodia, a type of orchid, are beneficial in improving brain function in stroke victims and one special type of fungus is said to be effective in increasing energy and boosting the immune system.

Persecuted by poachers

Needless to say, Wolong National Park, which is also a significant international biosphere reserve, revolves almost entirely around the Giant Panda. Nearly ten percent of all wild pandas live in these mountains. Protecting the pandas means preserving their habitat as well as the dense thickets of the bamboo which are the staple of the panda's diet.

It is somewhat ironic that, after this protection zone was established in 1987, far more panda habitats were destroyed within the Park than outside it. More and more forested areas are being cleared by the valley dwellers for farmland and poachers continue to hunt the panda for its fur. For this reason, the intricate network of trails, often extremely steep in places, is regularly patrolled by heavily armed members of the People's Police.

Solitary creatures of the forest

Scientists disagreed for a long time as to whether pandas were in fact bears at all. For although they look like bears, with the exception of their black-and-white fur and distinctive black eye-patches, many aspects of their behavior are quite different. For instance, these mammals, which stand 5ft (1.5m) tall and can weigh over 350lb (160kg), do not hibernate. Nor do they need to, since bamboo is evergreen and plentiful all year round — provided it does not suddenly bloom, as it does once every 30 to 80 years, causing it to die off across large areas. In the past, the pandas could migrate to other areas if this eventuality arose, but increased human settlement of the region, road building and deforestation have cut them off from other feeding areas further away and, as a consequence, many of them have starved to death.

Pandas are solitary creatures; they mate only every two years. The female remains fertile for a very brief period of just a few hours in spring, rearing only one of her offspring, and even this is likely to fall prey to snow leopards or eagles. Pandas consequently have a very low reproductive rate, which is the main reason why they require such stringent protective measures.

The task of saving the panda population has fallen to the "Chinese Research and Preservation Center for the Giant Panda," located at the heart of the Pitiao river valley, where baby pandas are reared and gradually prepared for return to the wild in the Wolong Reserve.

Affection in the panda forest: two pandas exchanging a kiss while climbing a tree (right)

Pandas are vegetarians, with their primary diet consisting of evergreen bamboo. A bear seated on a rock making himself comfortable at meal time (below, left)

Fantastical rock formations

SHILIN STONE FOREST in the Chinese province of Yunnan is famous for its fairytale scenery

GETTING THERE:
Bus service from Kunming

WHERE TO STAY:
Wide choice of hotels in Kunming; an hotel within the Park

CLIMATE:
Mean annual temperature around 59° F (15° C) with high humidity. Very little seasonal fluctuation

MAIN ATTRACTIONS:
Liziqing; Naigu; Zhiyundon (underground); Lake Changhu; Dadieshui waterfall

Around 55 miles (90km) southeast of Kunming, the capital of Yunnan province in China, nature has created a truly fantastical limestone landscape, known as the Shilin Stone Forest. An amazing landscape of extraordinary limestone rock formations covers an area of 135 square miles (350km²) and stretches as far as the eye can see is. Wind and rain have eroded the rock to form three-feet-high mushroom shapes, petrified waves, teeth, and even animal figures out of the soft limestone. Spectacular cave systems have been carved out by subterranean rivers that appear above ground in the form of thundering waterfalls or tranquil lakes.

This whole region was still at the bottom of the sea 270 million years ago. Organisms with calcareous shells, including corals, built their intricate homes on a thick layer of sandstone that gradually became overlain with a layer of limestone three feet thick. As the sea retreated from the area over the course of millions of years, the undulating limestone plateau that had previously formed the seabed now rose 5,600–6,600ft (1,700–2,000m) above sea level. Weather and climate immediately set to work eroding the soft stone and sculpting these 100ft (30m) high pillars of rock into bizarre pinnacles, often resembling the shapes of plants or animals. They have been given a variety of imaginative names, such as "Phoenix smoothing its wings," "Rhinoceros looking at the moon," and the "ten-thousand-year-old mushroom." These rocky columns stand so close to one another that the effect is like walking through a maze of trees.

Smaller pinnacles, barely higher than 30ft (9m), populate the higher areas, while giant columns, obelisks, and ridges up to 100ft (30m) in height rise up out of the valleys. In the

heart of this fairyland setting is the Liziqing Stone Forest, covering an area of 6 square miles (16km²) and encompassing more than 100 smaller rock formations. Stone Age and Bronze Age settlers have left large numbers of rock drawings in the area, depicting scenes from their everyday existence.

Gateway to the underworld

Naigu Stone Forest, 5 miles (8km) further north, covers an area of some 3 square miles (8 km²) and incorporates several cave openings leading into an underground world, where erosion has fashioned an amazing collection of strange rock formations.

There is even a subterranean stone forest, known as the Zhiyundon forest, covering an area of one square mile (three square kilometers) and extending nearly 330ft (100m) into the earth through a series of vast caves. The Qifeng cave system, through which a

river has carved out a channel, is subject to such substantial differences in air pressure between August and November that a strong wind sweeps through its underground passages every thirty minutes.

There are more than 80 lakes in this stone forest region, created when the cave ceilings weakened and collapsed. The largest of these is Lake Changhu. It lies at an altitude of 6,257ft (1,907m), is 3 miles (5km) in length and nearly 1,000ft (300m) across. Stalactites and stalagmites can be seen beneath its crystal-clear waters, which descend to depths of 100ft (30m). The remains of columns that once supported this former cave now poke above the water in the form of four small, densely forested islands.

Nine subterranean river systems have so far been explored, including the Baijang River, which plunges 300ft (90m) down into the Nanpanjiang River, just southwest of Liziqing Stone Forest

near the 100ft (30m) wide Dadieshui waterfall. This is one of the highest waterfalls in China. The surrounding landscape forms some of the most spectacular scenery in the entire stone forest. The Xiaodishui waterfall is also situated nearby. Crystal-clear water gushes out of this captivating cascade, bordered with lush green vegetation, forming a gateway to the Xianren cave.

Myths and legends

Large expanses of the stone forest have been landscaped in the manner of a garden with pathways and lawns to make it more accessible to the streams of visitors. In some parts, however, the original vegetation has been left to its own devices. This consists mainly of subtropical trees such as the cluster-leaved oak, Chinese and Mason pine and Nepal alder, interspersed with lime-loving species such as pepper, pistachio, berberis and various species of African boxwood.

Many myths and legends have been woven to explain how this stone forest originated. One such relates how the dreaded Asi Abo was carting rocks to the area in order to dam up the Nanpan River. His devious plan was that the ensuing floods would destroy the fertile fields belonging to the Sani and Yi people, the original inhabitants of the region. By daybreak, however, he had only got as far as the site of the present-day stone forest. Fearing that his hideous features might be recognized in daylight, he dropped everything and the rocks he abandoned now form the stone forest.

Myths and legends surround the stone figures in Liziqing Stone Forest (above)

Some limestone pillars can reach up to 100ft (30m) in height (below, left)

Some of the scenery in this natural garden is strongly reminiscent of a Chinese ink drawing (below, right)

A paradise for wildlife

KUSHIRO NATIONAL PARK on Hokkaido Island is home
to the legendary red-crested cranes

**Low hills surround
the moors and marshes
of Takkobu area.
Unusual grasses
produce a colorful
landscape (right and
above, left)**

Just 3 miles (5km) away from Kushiro, the island's capital, in the southeastern corner of Hokkaido in northern Japan, is an area of marshland that is home to the world's most significant population of red-crested cranes. These majestic white birds with black and gray trim on their faces and throats and their scarlet caps are on the list of internationally endangered species. Fortunately, however, their numbers are slowly recovering and 1,000 of them now live and breed in Kushiro National Park, an area of some 104 square miles (270km²). This represents one third of the world population of these birds. For centuries, red-crested cranes have been a national symbol of long life and prosperity, yet very few Japanese are actually likely ever to have seen one.

Eighty years ago, the "tancho," or "red crest," as the cranes were known in the Land of the Rising Sun, teetered on the verge of extinction. Towards the end of the nineteenth century, Hokkaido began developing rapidly into a heavily populated, industrial island. The cranes were thought to have vanished from the region, but in 1924 a hunter discovered one of these symbolic birds in the marshes. A thorough search ensued, resulting in a dozen of these spectacular birds being found in other remote parts of the marshes. This marked the start of an unprecedent-

ed rescue program to save these birds from extinction. Following some particularly severe snow storms in 1952, which left many of them on the brink of starvation, local residents undertook to feed the cranes with grain until they had recovered their strength. Each winter, 200 birds still visit the feeding grounds at the Tsurui crane observatory, where visitors are rewarded with a close-up view of these magnificent creatures.

The swamps of Kushiro Park also provide a refuge for many other species of bird. European sea eagles come here to breed and, in winter, the marshes provide a home for the Steller's sea eagle from Kamchatka and Sachalin. The rare Japanese fish owl also breeds in this protected area.

Lakes and swamps

Kushiro National Park, measuring some 70 square miles (180km²), protects Japan's largest marsh, the sweeping bends of the Kushiro River and its tributaries as it meanders across the plains at the foot of the Oakan and Meakan mountains. The Park encompasses Lake Toro, the Shirarutoro Marsh, Takkobu Swamp, and the surrounding low hills as well. Almost 30 square miles (80km²) of Japan's last remnant of surviving swampland have been placed under special protection as a significant wetland area.

In the center of this vast wetland environment are a few scattered areas

of ancient high moorland and, to the east, three large, freshwater lakes. This seemingly endless expanse of wetland, populated by turf and mosses, reeds, and sedge, began forming 4,000 years ago while it was still a bay on the shores of the Pacific Ocean. Sea currents and waves created shallows and the constant winds continued the process by forming sand dunes, which eventually blocked off the bay from the sea altogether.

There are even alder woods growing around the hills. The rainwater runoff deposits considerable amounts of nutrients in these areas so that alders can grow to heights of around 32ft (10m) in some cases. By contrast, trees growing in the much poorer soils of the open moor reach 16ft (5m) in height at most. Usually, alders sprout several trees from a single root system. Once they have reached their optimum height they die, by which time some of the new shoots will have developed into trees themselves.

Unspoiled nature

For thousands of years, nature remained completely undisturbed on Hokkaido Island. It was not until 1870, when 537 Japanese immigrants came to settle in what is now the city of Kushiro, that the island began its rapid development. More than 2,000 different varieties of plant and animal life still exist in the region's marshes and waters, many of which are rare species.

The Siberian salamander, for example, which is fairly common in other parts of Asia, only occurs in Japan's Kushiro Marsh. It has only recently been discovered that this reptile's main distribution area actually lies just outside the Park's boundaries so that it is still at risk from agriculture and industry. Similarly, the region contains Japan's last remaining population of the mosaic damselfly, a wonderful species of dragonfly whose limited habitat is restricted to high moorland.

The importance of this vast moorland area lies not just in providing a habitat where nature may develop without interruption. Equally important is the fact that these moors store up rainwater, thereby ensuring that in the lower reaches of the Kushiro River, the water levels remain constant. The marsh serves as a giant filter and drinking water reservoir for the city and surrounding villages.

On the floor of the Aso volcano

The collapse of the Aso crater on the Japanese island of **KYUSHU** created the largest caldera on earth

GETTING THERE:
Take the Minami-Aso train from Tateno station to Takamori. By car or bus from Tateno and Beppu. Airport at Kumamoto

WHERE TO STAY:
Minami-Aso Vacationland Hotel and campsites. Further hotels in the vicinity

CLIMATE:
Cool, but sunny, in summer; snow on higher ground in winter

MAIN ATTRACTIONS:
Naka summit (by cable car); Taka; Neko; Miyamakirishima and Senui-kyou gorges; Koga-no-taki waterfall Cultural attractions: the Avenue of 100 Cherry Trees near Takamori-Toge; Kuju flower gardens; mountain climbing

Steam still billows up from the Aso crater, the world's largest active caldera, situated at the heart of Kyushu Island in southern Japan. A caldera is the saucer-shaped depression formed when a volcano collapses and the outer walls of the volcanic cone are left standing. Aso extends over some 70 miles (110km), stretching 17 miles (27km) from north to south and 10 miles (16km) from east to west.

The lava that the volcano has spit out over the past 30 million years has created the island of Kyushu. Four gigantic explosions have occurred over the past 300,000 years, the last of which occurred around 90,000 years ago. This was one of the most powerful eruptions in geological history and signaled the end of Aso. Forty cubic miles (160 km^2) of lava poured out over central Kyushu, a volume so vast that the magma chamber beneath the volcano collapsed under the sheer weight of it. The ash cloud from Aso deposited a 6in (15cm) thick shroud over the island of Hokkaido, 1,050 miles (1,700km) away in northern Japan. The collapsed crater gradually filled with water, forming a giant lake. In time, however, five new volcanic cones have gradually emerged from the caldera basin. These are strung out in a line along an east-west axis across the center of the caldera. The volcanic peaks of Kishima, Eboshi,

Naka, Taka, and Neko form the incredibly spectacular, lunar-like landscape of Aso Gogaku. The bizarre shapes left by the once molten rock as it solidified around the crater rims have a unique and eerie beauty.

Countless picturesque waterfalls cascade over the rocks to the valley below, many of which consist of hot, steaming water. Sensui-kyou, one of Aso's most enchanting gorges, is a refuge for a rare alpine plant, the Kyushu alpine rose, a small, pink species of rhododendron.

Taka, now extinct, is the highest of the five volcanoes, rising to a height of 5,226ft (1,593m). Naka, on the other hand, is still active. This 4,340ft (1,323m) high volcanic cone frequently emits black clouds of pungent and sulfurous gasses, sometimes to the accompaniment of rumblings from deep within the earth. A cable car ascends to a viewpoint from which

visitors can peer over the rim of the crater and look down into the swirling chasm below. To protect visitors from sudden ash emissions, thick-walled concrete bunkers have been built in which they can take cover in the event of an eruption.

Traditional pasture farming

An overhead view sweeps across an unexpectedly charming landscape within the caldera. Lush green fields and meadows extend right up to the edge of the crater on the horizon. The gently undulating terrain is dotted with peacefully grazing cattle and horses. The cars on the roads look tiny, as do the three villages and three small towns, which now accommodate around 100,000 people. Near the village of Tateno, rain and wind have eroded the caldera's crater wall to such an extent that it collapsed between 30,000 and 50,000 years ago, releasing the volume of

water that once formed the crater lake and allowing it to drain away to the sea.

The Aso caldera has been populated since time immemorial. In early March, the farming community burns the dry winter grass to eliminate pests. They have followed this practice for centuries and nature has learned to adapt itself to this annual burning procedure by evolving a unique variety of meadow vegetation.

Nowadays, the entire Aso region forms part of the Aso-Kuju National Park, which extends over an area of 280 square miles (727km²) and was established not only to protect the magnificent natural scenery, but also to preserve traditional farming methods.

The park also comprises the mighty Kuju volcanic group, all with summits in excess of 4,950ft (1,500m). The highest of these is Mount Kuju

itself, at 5,876ft (1,791m), the highest elevation on Kyushu. Plumes of white smoke occasionally billow out of Iwo, one of the craters. Kuyu lies along the same volcanic belt as Aso. The area is dotted with numerous hot springs, bubbling up from beneath the earth's surface. Beppu, Chojabaru, Yuno-Tani, and Uchino-Maki are spa resorts popular with visitors seeking health cures or simply relaxation in the natural, hot spring baths.

The Kuju uplands are regarded as one of the last natural paradises left in Japan. From the base of these mountains, the slopes rise gently and gracefully upward to a high plateau. Here, too, the luxuriant meadows are grazed by cattle and horses. Higher up, the volcanic slopes support a rich diversity of flora and fauna. These mountains are particularly famed for their displays of wild azaleas, which bloom here during the summer in a dazzling riot of color.

Individual volcanic peaks, such as the extinct Taka, rear up from the flat plain within the Aso crater (above)

This large expanse of land at the bottom of the crater has been populated since prehistoric times. Farmers have cultivated the land in terraces in some areas (below, left)

Land of rocks and water

A coastal bay National Park:
HA LONG CLIFFS in Vietnam
are a stunning natural spectacle

GETTING THERE:
Good roads from Hanoi
to Halong. Bus and
helicopter connections

WHERE TO STAY:
The town of Ha Long
offers a wide choice
of all types
of accommodation

CLIMATE:
Hot and humid tropical
climate

MAIN ATTRACTIONS:
Boat trips on Halong
Bay, including stops
at some of the grottoes
and floating villages

Possibly no other bay on earth presents as magnificent a sight as Halong Bay near Hong Gai, southeast of Hanoi on the Gulf of Tonkin. Halong Bay's tranquil waters are dotted with hundreds of islands and islets, jutting dramatically out of the sea to heights of 330–660ft (100–200m). The entire area is strewn with bizarre, jagged limestone rock formations, which have been sculpted into fantastic shapes by thousands of years of wind and weather erosion. These strange shapes are individually named: for example, the Pencil, the Saddle, the Junk Sail, the Bat, Fighting Cocks, the Turtle, the Buffalo, and many others are named after spirits. The majority of the 1,600 or possibly even 3,000 islands are uninhabitable, since their steep cliffs are impossible to climb. Along the water line, where the tides eat away at the limestone, deep grottoes have been hollowed out. The clefts, overhangs, and summits of these stone giants and rocky pillars are populated by green jungle plants. The larger islands, such as Ba Mun and Cat Ba, support undisturbed, pristine tropical rainforests. The area's inaccessibility has safeguarded a unique and rare ecosystem that remains largely untouched.

Bamboo-covered boats

The approximately 300 families in Ha Long National Park have lived here for generations, living on the water in bamboo-covered boats or, more recently, in floating houses. The largest of these floating villages is To Bo Nau, located right in the middle of the bay. These people are fishing folk, but some of them have learnt how to breed all kinds of exotic marine life in cages beneath their houses: rock lobsters, for example, which they sell directly to the many passing tourist boats full of visitors from all over the world.

Although the bay has never been heavily populated, traces of the Hoa Binh culture were found in archeological remains discovered on Giap Khau Island (Hon Gai). During the Stone Age, this region was home to the Ha Long, a unique culture that had no equivalent on the mainland. Archeological evidence testifying to this was found on the islands of Tuan Chau, Ngoc Vung, Cai Dam, Dong Naim, and Cat Ba. Cave findings testify to an earlier culture, known as the Soi

Nhu, which evolved in this area perhaps 25,000 years ago. These people were followed 7,000 to 5,000 years ago by the Cai Beo culture, which mastered the technique of pottery making and paved the way for the Ha Long. Evidence of their presence can sometimes be found on the beaches of isolated bays and in the limestone mountains. The early Ha Long people were still predominantly land dwellers, occupying the dry, flat land between the bizarre peaks of the limestone mountains until the sea rose and covered the region. Nowadays, Ha Long Bay is home to altogether 21 different ethnic groups.

Whenever a tropical cyclone threatens to blow in off the South China Sea, the boat folk seek refuge in the large grottoes and tunnels that the rain has gouged out of the soft rock. Many grottoes lead through to

circular lakes nestled in the center of karst islands, snugly sheltered thanks to their steep vertical rock walls. These are saltwater lakes, which are connected to the sea by underwater tunnels.

Colliding tectonic plates

The most spectacular grotto of all is Hang Dau Go, which consists of three giant caverns in whose deeply fissured walls nature has carved a variety of bizarre shapes. Sung Sot is as big as a cathedral. Stalactites, several feet in length, hang from its ceiling, shimmering in a rainbow of colors thanks to the atmospheric lighting and throwing mysterious shadows onto the craggy walls.

This stunningly breathtaking scenery of rock and water owes its existence to one of the most spectacular geological events in the earth's history, which took place around 50

million years ago approximately 1,250 miles (2,000km) northwest of Vietnam. It was then that the Indian subcontinent, which had split away from the supercontinent of Gondwana some 100 million years previously, collided with the Asian continental plate. Not only did this thrust the seabed between India and Asia upward to form the 29,500ft (9,000m) high Himalayas, but it also ripped apart the earth's crust all over southeast Asia, including the 3,300ft (1km) thick limestone plate of Halong Bay.

For millions of years, the tropical monsoons, with the help of wind and heat, then set to work on the exposed rock. As sea levels rose following the last Ice Age 7,000 to 8,000 years ago, the ocean slowly began laying claim to this remarkable and distinctive landscape of limestone pillars.

Ha Long region has been inhabited by people living on houseboats since time immemorial (above)

The traditional-style, bamboo-covered boats are gradually being replaced by more comfortable, wooden boats (below)

Home to troops of frolicking monkeys

ANG THONG NATIONAL PARK is a unique island
reserve with its own coral reef

THAILAND
Bangkok
South China Sea
PACIFIC
Ang Thong
(Ko Samui)

Endless palm forests and dense jungle cling to the steep slopes and ravines at the heart of the island of Ko Samui, which covers an area of 95 square miles (250km²) in the Gulf of Thailand, 20 miles (30km) off the mainland. The highest elevation is Khao Phlu. Its summit, rising to 2,100ft (640m), is hidden by a thick canopy of tropical rain forest in which primeval ferns and banana trees are interspersed with splashes of bright red hibiscus blossoms. The innumerable streams that spring from Khao Phlu teem with colorful tropical freshwater fish, while the shady valleys below are populated by coffee bushes and rubber trees.

The bays, surrounded by bizarre rock formations sculpted out of the steep, limestone cliffs, are edged with miles and miles of idyllic, white, sandy beaches.

Beneath the palm trees

Like its neighboring islands, Ko Phangan and Ko Tao, Ko Samui Island was formed during the cold, rainy Pleiocene period around 10 million years ago. It was during this period that a limestone plateau was pushed up from the seabed and finally emerged above the surface of the ocean. Wind and rain gradually eroded this plateau, leaving behind strange, steep, rocky columns and islands.

Ko Samui is Thailand's third largest island and exactly represents the stereotypical island paradise. Eighty percent of the 40,000 Thailanders that live here earn their living from western tourists, who come here in search of peace, recreation, and relaxation. However, the view across the green hills and blue sea is not marred by any hotel buildings because none of the buildings are higher than the tops of the palm trees.

The most spectacular beaches are found along the north and east coasts, the most popular of which are Chaweng and Lamai. Families tend to seek out the quieter beaches of Bophut and Mae Nam. Chaweng beach, which stretches for 4 miles (6km) along the coast, is considered the island's most beautiful beach.

Intrepid snorkelers are rewarded with a breathtaking glimpse of the colorful underwater world that surrounds a coral reef. The flora and fauna here are similar to that found on all Thailand's other reefs, although the colorful coral fish are not quite so common here.

South of Lamai Beach, nature has sculpted two extremely erotic male and female forms into the cliffs between the villages of Ban Hua Thanon and Ban Lamai, known as Hin Ta and Hin Yai, the phallus-like "Grandfather" and "Grandmother" rock formations. This area is a popular holiday

destination, particularly for native holidaymakers.

Above the beach, a concrete road leads to two unusual waterfalls, the 60ft (18m) high Na Muang 1 and Na Muang 2, which plummet with a deafening roar through a series of cascades 260ft (80m) down into a lake which can only be reached from Na Muang 1 by way of a steep natural staircase of rock and tree roots. These spectacular cascades were formed as the result of calcium encrustations left by mosses that form a thick carpet over the damp cliffs and deposit calcium sediments in the water, thereby accumulating layer upon layer of porous, calcareous tufa, which creates an ever-increasing number of barriers and small terraces. These tufa formations grow about three-quarters of an inch to an inch (two to three centimeters) each year.

Emerald-green saltwater lake

One of the most scenic waterfalls, only 13ft (4m) in height, lies very close to the island's capital of Na Thon. It can be reached only via a steep path, winding through an enchanting, dense forest of giant trees, fern fronds, and intertwined lianas. This landscape offers a glimpse of how Ko Samui looked before coconut palms were planted here.

A two-hour boat ride away is a miniature, fairytale world, consisting of 40 uninhabited islands strung out to the west of Ko Samui and known as the Ang Thong Marine National Park. Weirdly shaped cliffs overgrown with dense jungle vegetation and umbrella trees tower up out of the calm, azure-blue sea to heights of 1,300ft (400m).

These islands provide a largely undisturbed habitat for macaques, sea otters and countless numbers of brilliantly colored, tropical birds. The dramatically sheer coastal cliffs are peppered with mysterious limestone caves, such as Tham Bua Bok with its spectacular stalactites. The picturesque bays are lined with dazzling white, sandy beaches. Glittering right in the center of Ko Mae Kok Island and surrounded by sheer cliffs is the emerald-green saltwater lake of Tale Nai, which can be reached by a steep cliff path.

Not far from the island of Ko Sam Sao, where a giant rocky arch spans the sea, lies an extensive, colorful coral reef, a popular destination for snorkelers.

GETTING THERE:
Wide choice of package tours. Independent travelers: bus and rail links from Bangkok to Chumpon. Airport in the northwest of Ko Samui. Daily boat trips to the Marine National Park or by kayak

WHERE TO STAY:
Included in package tours. Independent travelers: wide range of hotel accommodation available out of season. Cabins and tents bookable via the park authorities in the Marine National Park.

CLIMATE:
December to February around 86º F (30º C); March to June around 104º F (40º C) and high humidity levels. Monsoon season with daily downpours from July to November

MAIN ATTRACTIONS:
Beaches; Samui Everest viewpoint; Na Muang, Hin Lat, and Big Buddha waterfalls; butterfly garden; snake farm; aquarium; tiger zoo. Secret Buddha garden; mummified monk. Marine National Park with Tham Bua Bok cave, Tale Nai saltwater lake, coral reef near Ko Sam Sao, Had Chan Charat Beach, and viewing platform

SPECIAL TIPS:
Four-wheel-drive vehicles recommended for trips into the island's interior. Many routes impassable during the monsoon season

Ko Surin Island off the coast of Thailand is a holiday paradise for tourists (left)

The Ang Thong islands remain uninhabited (above, right)

Waterfalls beneath a canopy of palm fronds are a common sight (below, right)

Walkways over the jungle

TAMAN NEGARA NATIONAL PARK
in Malaysia provides access into the jungle

GETTING THERE:
By car, taxi, or bus from Kuala Lumpur (daily or park shuttle service) to Kuala Tembling. From there, by jungle boat to the Kuala Tahan visitors' center

WHERE TO STAY:
Park guesthouse with dormitories and several well-equipped chalets with bathrooms and air-conditioning. Simple fishermen's huts on the opposite side of the river and outside the park boundary. Wide choice of hotels also available outside the Park. Adventure camping sites and tree-houses in idyllic locations, but with no facilities. Camping equipment hire available

CLIMATE:
Tropical heat and humidity throughout the year

MAIN ATTRACTIONS:
Jungle treks; boat trip; "Canopy walk;" a night in an observation hide; guided night safaris

SPECIAL TIPS:
Getting around the Park is only possible by boat or on foot. Catering facilities available in the Kuala Tahan visitors' center

Centrally situated on the Malayan Peninsula is one of the most untouched tropical jungles in the world, which has been carefully developed to accommodate visitors. Covering an area of 1,677 square miles (4,343km²), Taman Negara National Park is situated between the Banjaran Timur mountains in the east and the Banjaran Titiwangsa chain in the west. These warm, humid forests consist of high plateaus and green valleys interspersed with clear, unpolluted streams. Here and there, the peaks of majestic mountains emerge above the lush, green canopy. This virgin jungle has remained undisturbed for over 130 million years — despite the Ice Age and other geological calamities. At the northwestern end of the Park, Gunung Tahan, Malaysia's highest mountain rises 7,175ft (2,187m) above the jungle greenery. It can only be reached after a four to five-day trek through unmarked lowland rainforest, which becomes shrouded in mist at higher altitudes. Good mountaineering skills are essential for anyone intending to ascend its precipitous rock faces.

Up the Tahan River
Although it is quick and easy to reach its boundaries, the Park is not accessible by road or path. The Taman Negara Resort visitor center, the starting-point for all the treks and boat trips, can only be reached after a several-hour boat trip from Kuala Tembling up the Tahan River. After just a few miles, the last of the huts on the river bank disappears from sight and the mighty green jungle starts pressing in toward the river. Tree branches reach across the water, thick lianas hanging from their limbs. Dead tree trunks, sometimes barely above water level, have to be circumnavigated.

After approximately 40 miles (60km) the jungle clears, revealing boats and rafts along the shore and, perched above the bank, the buildings of the Taman Negara Resort, a unique hotel complex in the heart of the jungle.

Near the visitor center, a nature trail comprising a 1,640ft (500m) long "canopy walk" leads through the forest. It consists of a system of rope bridges, suspended 100ft (30m) above ground, which wind through the jungle canopy. The trunks and branches of these giant old trees form the basis for a natural habitat that supports the rich diversity of life found in every tropical rainforest. Here you will find plants growing on other plants. These have achieved a sensitive balance within a complicated system of interdependence. Butterflies and other insects pollinate the flowers and utilize the remains of plants. Birds build their nests here and monkeys use the flat branches as nurseries for their young. The aerial walkway is not just a tourist attraction, but is also used by scientists investigating the various factors that interact with one another within the complicated jungle ecosystem.

The cacophony of sound within the rainforest is incredible. From dawn to dusk, 250 different varieties of birds try to outdo each other with their songs, all to the underlying accompaniment of the shrill chirping of innumerable cicadas and the croaking of rare species of frogs. This is frequently interspersed with the shrieks of gibbon monkeys.

Tree houses in the branches
Several marked trails lead into the jungle from the visitors' center. Some of these can be followed for several days. The further they get from the resort, the lonelier they become, not to mention the more difficult to follow. Tree houses or hides have been built up in the branches in many places along the routes. These can provide basic shelter for the night, as well as being an ideal observation hide for watching the animals. The larger mammals, such as elephants, tigers, leopards, bears, rhinoceros, and tapirs are rarely spotted. They are very shy

and remain perfectly camouflaged by the jungle.

A 5 mile (8km) trail follows the Sungai Tahan River and leads up to the magnificent Lata Berkoh Cascades, whose cool, crystal-clear waters plunge via a roaring, foaming waterfall into the valley below. The water has carved out pools in the rock, a tempting spot for a refreshing bath.

In the north of the National Park are some karst caves, lying deep within the limestone cliffs. Some of these contain impressive, if somewhat faded, cave paintings – reminders that this area has been inhabited since prehistoric times. Small bats populate many of the caves. Hundreds of thousands of them hang from the ceilings of these hidden habitations which reek with the overpowering odor of bat guano.

The walls of the jungle crowd in along the river's edge. The National Park is only accessible by water (above)

Floral splendor in the rainforest (below)

The land of dragons

Giant lizards find their last refuge on **KOMODO ISLAND** in Indonesia's National Park

PACIFIC

INDONESIA

Jakarta   Komodo
           Islands

GETTING THERE:
Flights from Bali and overland buses to Bima (East Sumbawa) and Labuan Bajo (West Flores). Ferries to Komodo from Sape on Sumbawa and Labuan Bajo on Flores

WHERE TO STAY:
Simple bungalows, rooms, and a restaurant at the Loh Liang ranger station, otherwise very basic accommodation in rangers' cabins

CLIMATE:
Best time to travel is during the dry season from May to October, when temperatures are around 90° F (32° C)

MAIN ATTRACTIONS:
Scuba diving; guided walks

SPECIAL TIPS:
Do heed any travel warnings

The barren, grass-covered hills of Komodo rise gently above the choppy, blue-white waters of the Sape Straits between the Indonesian islands of Sumbawa and Flores. Here and there, a slender lontar palm tree reaches skyward and mist-shrouded forests are visible higher up the mountain slopes. The coastline alternates between sheer rock faces dropping abruptly away to the sea and tranquil bays featuring small, sandy beaches or dense mangrove vegetation.

Komodo is the largest island within the National Park bearing the same name. The reserve also includes Komodo's smaller sister islands, Rinca and Padar, as well as numerous tiny islands and the entire marine world off Flores in the eastern Sape Straits. Most visitors come here to see the legendary giant monitor lizards or to dive in one of the world's most fascinating underwater reserves.

Unpredictable predators

Komodo's main attraction is without doubt the giant monitor lizards, known as Komodo dragons. They can grow to almost 10ft (3m) in length and are the biggest, if not the longest, of their kind. Despite their fearsome reputation, they no longer eat human beings. Yet Komodo dragons are still unpredictable, like all wild animals. However, knowledgeable and experienced park guides can lead the visitor within an arm's length

of these prehistoric-looking creatures, which spend most of the day sunbathing or wandering through the savannah, their long tongues darting in and out in search of prey.

The oras, as they are known locally, are primarily carrion-eaters. Their sense of smell is so acute that they can detect decomposing flesh from a distance of 6 miles (10km). Thanks to their Jacobson's organ, a sensory detector in the roof of their mouth, they are able to smell by sticking out their forked tongue. Thus they are constantly "scenting" the air with this sensitive organ, which flickers in and out continually.

If they cannot find any carrion, as is often the case, they will resort to goats, wild boar, horses, or even water buffalo. An untreated bite from a giant monitor lizard can lead to death within days, if not hours. The saliva contains bacteria which infects its victim with a deadly septicemia. This creature with its ancient origins developed over 4 million years ago from the "varinides" family that was indigenous to Asia 25-40 million years ago. Today, there are only around 2,900 of these giant lizards left on Komodo, 900 on Rinca, and fewer than 100 on Gili Motong, as well as a few in the western corner of Flores Island, which is also part of the National Park. Their numbers have remained quite stable since the Sultan of Bima designated them a protected species in 1915. The huge

migration of people from other Indonesian islands to this conservation area has meant, however, that an increasing number of the animals on which the giant lizard preys are being poached.

Wildlife from two continents

Meanwhile, the National Park is more than just a habitat for Komodo dragons. Komodo, like the rest of Indonesia, is a transition zone between the Australian and Eurasian animal kingdoms. Consequently, the resulting wildlife population is a mixture of mammals, such as sambars, wild boar, macaques and civet cats of Asiatic origin, and various reptiles and birds, such as scrub fowl and sulfur-crested cockatoos, from Australia.

The number of different species is small because the islands are situated in one of the driest regions of Indonesia. For eight months of the year there is little or no rain at all. Only during the monsoon period between November and March do the small, mist-covered, tropical forests

on the mountain heights receive occasional, hefty downpours unleashed by low-lying clouds.

The underwater world, however, constitutes two-thirds of the National Park area. Divers in these waters will encounter a myriad of colors and a breathtaking variety of life in and around the coral reefs, the mangrove swamps and seaweed forests, as well as in the smooth, calm bays. Naturalists have identified 1,000 species of fish, 260 reef-forming corals and 70 varieties of sponge. Furthermore, at least 14 species of whale, dolphin, and turtle have also made their home here.

Underwater, a similar collision of two different worlds is taking place. Coming from the Indian Ocean, cold, nutrient-rich, deep water from Antarctica rises up, encountering a warm, tropical stream from the Flores Sea. Strong tidal currents and whirlpools also help oxygenate the water making the seas between Sumbawa and Flores some of the richest marine environments in the world.

A Komodo dragon can grow up to 10ft (3m) in length. The giant lizard is predatory, but does not deserve its reputation as a man-eater (above)

View over the Komodo Sound to Rinca (below, left)

Australian birds have become resident here along the shores of the National Park (below, right)

Volcanic paradise in Java

The **BROMO-TENGGER-SEMERU NATIONAL PARK** protects the unique natural landscape around the extinct Tengger volcano

PACIFIC

INDONESIA

Jakarta Bromo-Tengger-Semeru

GETTING THERE:
By car from Malang via Tumpang through approximately 12¹/₂ miles (20km) of picturesque mountain scenery from Probolinggo to Ngadisari. Steep road from Ngadisari to Cemoro Lawang on the edge of the Tengger crater

WHERE TO STAY:
Simple guesthouse in Ngadisari at the park entrance. Thirty-bed hotel on the slopes of the Tengger Caldera ring near Cemaralawang. Numerous campsites available

CLIMATE:
Monsoon climate with warm rainy season between December and March. Daily temperatures around 64° F (18° C), falling to 37-39° F (3-4° C) at night

MAIN ATTRACTIONS:
Bromo; the sand sea; viewpoint from Penanjakan; the crater lakes of Pani, Regulo, and Kumbolo; tropical rain forest around Lake Darungan

SPECIAL TIPS:
Special permission required to climb Mahameru issued by the National Park office in Malang. If visiting the Semeru volcano, be wary of toxic gasses and hot lava

Millions of years ago, the gigantic Tengger volcano in the volcanic region of East Java collapsed upon itself when the magma chamber in the earth's crust emptied beneath it. Java's largest and most impressive caldera measuring around 6 miles (10km) across remained. The high plateau has still not settled down, however, and five new volcanic cones have erupted here at heights of 6,500ft (2,000m), each one more picturesque than the other.

Towering in the south, outside the 165–1,650ft (50–500m) high caldera, is the massive cone of the Semeru crater. Rising to a height of 12,000ft (3,676m), it is Java's highest mountain. It is also the most active, as evidenced by the thick plume of steam that rises every eight minutes from its interior and floats away across the tropical blue sky as a light white cloud. Lush, green, and dense tropical vegetation covers the lower half of the slopes, while above 8,000ft (2,400m) this gives way to sparsely covered, sub-alpine pine forest. Nothing grows at the highest elevation: the top of the cone is covered with ash and stones.

Sacred mountain of the Hindus

Bromo-Tengger-Semuru National Park comprises almost 225 square miles (580km²) of this volcanic region, which extends some 25 miles (40km) from north to south and over 12¹/₂ miles (20km) from east to west.

In the center of the circular Tengger Caldera, surrounded by sheer precipices ranging from 165–1,650ft (50–500m) in height, are the symmetrical cones of the two volcanoes Bromo and Batok. Batok is dormant whereas Bromo continues to spew clouds of steam into the atmosphere. Bromo is also a sacred mountain to the Hindus, who retreated to this area when Indonesia was being converted to Islam. Each October, thousands of the faithful make the pilgrimage to take part in the Yadnya-Kasada ceremony, a type of thanksgiving festival. They celebrate the event in a small temple complex on the barren plateau.

A series of 140 steps leads up to the rim of the crater, where the pungent smell of sulfur makes breathing difficult. Thick steam rises from the vents in the 2,000–2,600ft (600–800m) wide crater. But the view into the fiery depths below and across the Tengger Caldera to Semeru in the background is breathtaking. The part of the caldera south of the Bromo cra-

ter is a green savannah filled with undulating grasslands. To the north is a sea of sand, a featureless moon landscape of lava and ash, poured onto the Tengger crater ring by the Bromo volcano.

Although sparse and unvarying within the Tengger crater itself, the plant life along its outer periphery, and indeed throughout the entire mountain massif, is amazingly varied due to the dramatic differences in elevation within this volcanic landscape. Biologists have identified 1,025 different species of plants, including 226 orchids and 260 used locally for medicinal purposes.

Depending on their elevation, the extensive forested areas provide three different habitats. The lower zone up to 5,000ft (1,500m) is colonized by primeval tropical rainforest with a large diversity of species. The dense leaf canopy of ancient trees protects the lower reaches of this jungle environment. Its branches are festooned with various species of lianas, forming an impenetrable thicket.

Above this, at a height of 5,000–8,000ft (1,500–2,400m), is a band of secondary forest consisting of pioneer plants, which cannot flourish in the half-light beneath the tropical rainforest canopy. These are mainly kangaroo trees, a species of birch and acacias.

Edelweiss blooms here occasionally

The sub-alpine zone above 8,000ft (2,400m) consists of pine trees, which diminish in size as the elevation increases. Meanwhile, the forest floor is home to a type of blueberry and even occasional edelweiss.

There is little wildlife in the park. The 22 species found here include red deer, wild boar, porcupines and also cheetahs. But the animals were apparently hunted so zealously before the National Park was established in 1982 that their numbers have never recovered. Nevertheless, the bird world is well represented with 130 different species, including doves, parrots, orioles, jungle hens and the unusual mountain duck with its soft, flexible bill.

Arguably the most spectacular view across this unique volcanic landscape is from the summit of Penanjakan. From this viewpoint, the backdrop of the volcano's symmetrical flanks contrasts dramatically with the lush, green slopes and the desolate sand sea. At sunrise or sunset, the beauty of this volcanic massif is virtually unparalleled.

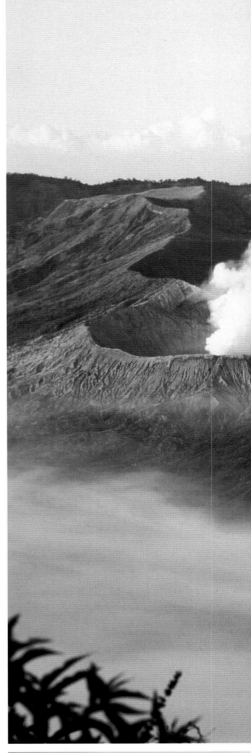

The blunt volcanic cones in the Bromo region were created by violent eruptions within the earth (above)

Toxic sulfurous fumes bubble up from inside the volcano (below, left)

Away from the crater, the mountain slopes are covered with deciduous forest (below, right)

Sunbathing on the "Cold Coast"

SPITZBERGEN is home to almost as many polar bears as people

GETTING THERE:
Summer flights from Oslo via Tromsø, ships from Tromsø and Honningsvåg/Nordkap. Longyearbyen is a popular destination for cruise ships

WHERE TO STAY:
Several hotels and bed and breakfast establishments; accommodation available in former workers' quarters. Indoor heating is excessively warm.

EXCURSIONS AND MAIN ATTRACTIONS:
Svalbard museum in Longyearbyen; Spitzbergen cruise (1 week); easy one-day hike through the Advent valley (fossils, reindeer, flora). Tourists not admitted to Ny Ålesund

CLOTHING:
Warm clothing, waterproofs, sunglasses, stout shoes

SPECIAL TIPS:
Do not stray from inhabited settlements without a weapon or armed guide. No roads or tracks away from inhabited settlements. No formal emergency services

The first people who accidentally found their way here were Vikings, who stumbled upon Svalbard, the "cold coast," in 1194. They very quickly forgot about it again and it was not until 400 years later, in June 1594, that another ship approached the precipitously steep mountain peaks of the main island. On board were two Dutch explorers, Willem Barents and Jacob van Heemskerck, who named the island Spitzbergen.

It is the largest of Svalbard's nine major islands and comprises over half the archipelago's overall landmass of around 24,300 square miles (63,000km²). To the northeast, the region's highest mountain, Newtontoppen, rises to a height of 5,634ft (1,717m), standing out in dramatic relief between the other peaks.

Svalbard is home to three national parks, two nature reserves, two areas of plant conservation and 16 protected bird sites. Almost 50 percent of its entire area is consequently under protection and entry is either forbidden altogether or restricted to authorized trails.

A surprisingly mild climate

Despite their position on the Arctic Circle, the islands enjoy a mild climate. The west coasts remain ice-free from June to December, thanks to warm currents from the North Atlantic Drift, a northern extension of the Gulf Stream. In July, when the sun is shining and there is no breeze, temperatures can easily rise to 68º F (20º C), high enough to shed the weatherproof clothing and sunbathe. However, despite the midnight sun, which never sets here between 21 April and 24 August, the mountaintops are often shrouded in cloud and the val-leys frequently veiled in mist.

The ground remains frozen for most of the year, only thawing a little along the coast during the summer. During this period, the tundra becomes a carpet of mosses, lichen, ferns, grasses, and even 40 varieties of flowers bearing tiny, vividly colored blooms in spring and summer. Incredible though it may seem, biologists have even identified two unprepossessing tree species among the 170 different varieties of plant: a robust, weather-resistant arctic willow and a bushy miniature birch, which grows to a height of just 6in (15cm).

Spring witnesses the arrival of millions of birds, which migrate here from the south to breed. Svalbard boasts around 150 varieties of bird, including eider ducks, puffins, ptarmigans, barnacle geese and numerous species of gull. However, it is a little warm at this time for the estimated 3,000 polar bears, which prefer the feel of ice under their paws and consequently retreat to the polar ice floes in the north, thereby affording a brief respite to the numerous seals and sea dogs that are the polar bears' staple diet. This is also the season when herds of walrus begin to gather on the beaches to fish for eels and indulge in their courtship rituals beneath the midnight sun.

For the small, tough reindeer that live on Spitzbergen, summer is just one long picnic. No more strenuous scraping and digging to uncover tasty morsels of lichen beneath the snow. They become popular photo models for the brightly-clad tourists clutching shiny cameras in their gloved hands. They are obliging animals and often allow people to get within a few yards of them.

This is not so in the case of the blue or white arctic foxes, which slink away to seek cover among the rocks. Another animal that prefers to keep its distance is the almost prehistoric-looking musk ox, introduced from Greenland in 1929.

Port of call for cruise ships

These islands, whose majestic mountains provide a landscape of jagged outcrops and bizarre rock formations, constitute the highest eleva-

For the small Spitzbergen reindeer, summer is just one long feast when lichen, their favorite diet, is easy to find (right)

tions on a splinter of continent that has, for the past 600 million years, been drifting across all the climatic zones on earth at the rate of 1¼ in (4.5cm) a year – and is still doing so.

Nowadays, around 3000 Norwegians and Russians, as well as an equivalent number of polar bears, inhabit the three settlements of Longyearbyen, Barentsburg, and Nyålesund. During the summer months, cruise ships disgorge around 60,000 tourists at Longyearbyen on the Advent fjord. The eastern shore of this fjord is a popular destination for day excursions into an unspoiled natural environment, where visitors frequently encounter unlikely reminders of earlier human activity in the region that have survived for centuries in this unpolluted and cold atmosphere: abandoned trappers' cabins, ghost towns once populated by whale hunters, the remnants of polar expeditions.

Only about 2000 people, who are eager to know this magnificent landscape more intimately, remain on Spitzbergen for any length of time. Nor is this an easy matter. The Sysselsman, the Norwegian governor, and his colleagues are very strict in ensuring that the natural environment remains in pristine condition. It is essential to carry a rifle and know how to use it if you are venturing beyond the boundaries of human habitation. However, experienced tour operators know their business and take every precaution when organizing and leading excursions.

The edge of a glacier where a section has broken away. Spitzbergen glaciers are constantly collapsing into the sea. These massive chunks of ice break away with a thunderous roar (above)

Magdalena fjord is accessible in summer from Trinity harbor (below center)

The seals are quite at home on drifting ice floes (bottom right)

89

The Vidda uplands

HARDANGERVIDDA in Norway is home to Europe's largest reindeer herd

GETTING THERE:
Several highways lead along the National Park boundaries. The Oslo-Bergen line has several stops at the northern end of Hardangervidda. No trucks are permitted within the Park.

WHERE TO STAY:
Comfortable hotels in the towns and villages bordering Hardangervidda. Numerous overnight cabins located along the hiking trails (750 miles/1,200km of marked trails). Camping permitted

CLIMATE:
Arctic; rarely exceeds 50° F (10° C) even in summer

MAIN ATTRACTIONS:
Nature center in Øvre Eidfjord; wildlife watching; hiking; fishing and hunting by special permit; Oddatal with its numerous waterfalls; Utne Hotel dating from 1722 and Kjeåsen mountain inn from around 1300; Stone Age settlements

SPECIAL TIPS:
Open fires, including camping stoves, prohibited within the Park from 15 May to 15 September

In contrast to the mountain regions of Central Europe, Ice Age glaciers in Norway eroded the mountain peaks into broad, high plateaus and rounded domes. Extending across an area of almost 3,500 square miles (9,000km²), Hardangervidda in southern Norway is Europe's largest peneplain, an eroded, almost level plateau, roughly the same size as Cyprus. Approximately one third of this plateau, which lies at an altitude of between 3,950–4,600ft (1,200–1,400m), has been awarded National Park status and placed under protection. Since the tree line in the central part of southern Norway stops at 3,300ft (1,000m), this wide expanse of high plateau, a gently undulating landscape of moor and marsh criss-crossed with streams, is typical Arctic tundra, known locally as "fjell."

Apart from occasional dwarf shrubs, which provide a habitat for blue-throats, winchats, meadow pipits, and reed buntings, the terrain is mainly covered with a dense carpet of lush grasses and lichens.

In the west, just before dropping abruptly away into the Sørf and Hardangerfjords, a few steep mountain ridges up to 5,600ft (1,700m) in height rise up from the plateau. During the tourist season, from 1 June to 15 September, the magnificent Vøringsfoss waterfall plunges down into the fjord at the far end of the Måbødalen valley. Outside the tourist season, it supplies Norway's largest power station, the dynamo of which is housed 2,300ft (700m) deep within the mountain.

Hard, primeval rock

An unusual, dome-shaped mountain, Mount Hårteigen, rises from the flat center of the Vidda plateau to a height of 5,550ft (1,690m). It is a significant landmark in the region and its snow patches are visible for miles. Its rock is so hard that glaciers have been unable to erode it.

The hard bedrock in the southeast of Hardangervidda is the last vestige of a mountain landscape before it was eroded, eventually sinking into the sea a thousand million years ago. Limestone rocks in the northwest testify to the fact that they originally formed from deposits accumulating on the sea bed. Millions of years later, a large tectonic plate pushed the submerged mountains back up to the surface again. Mount Hårteigen and

Mount Hardangerjøkulen are relics of this mountain chain.

When the ice shield retreated after the last Ice Age 9,000 years ago, the Hardangervidda plateau was left free of ice, as were the summits of the surrounding mountains. The bare rocks were quickly covered with a dense carpet of lichen and during the next 2,000 years forests reclaimed the high plateau. Consequently, there was adequate food for reindeer, who were hunted by early settlers. Around 250 Stone Age dwellings dating from around 6300 BC have been discovered on the Vidda plateau, as well as numerous pits for trapping wild animals.

Glaciers on the high plateau

When the climate cooled again 2,000 to 3,000 years ago, a giant glacier formed on the 6,250ft (1,900m) high Hardangerjøkulen. By 1750, the mountain reached its peak. The forest vanished and the high plateau was abandoned by human settlers. Between 1930 and 1970, the Hardangerjøkulen glacier, like the rest of Norway's glaciers, retreated and a few

rocky peaks, still buried under the ice at the dawn of the twentieth century, gradually became visible again. Although the surrounding mountains are ice-free, a 28 square mile (72km²) glacier still survives on Mount Hardangerjøkulen due to the high amount of precipitation from the southwest, nearly of all of which falls in this very spot.

In search of snowflakes

Higher levels of precipitation also mean much lusher vegetation during the summer months in the western part of Hardangervidda. This is the season that sees the arrival of Europe's largest reindeer herds in time for the females to calve in May. During this time, between 10,000 and 15,000 animals move across this high tundra region seeking even higher terrain in order to escape from the midges and mosquitoes. Herds of several thousand reindeer may be seen congregating near the few remaining areas of snow. They remain here until the autumn, when they return to the windy valleys of Ostvidda.

These huge herds of reindeer are accompanied by Arctic foxes, skulking among the rocks and crags. This National Park marks their southernmost distribution area in Europe. The Vidda plateau likewise provides an ideal habitat, undisturbed by humans, for the rare snowy owl, golden eagles and ospreys, gyrfalcons as well as Tengmalm's owls, which prey on lemmings, fjell rats and snow grouse chicks.

During the short summer months, a colorful carpet of flowers springs up between the rocks, across the high moors, alongside streams and around the shores of lakes. Cotton grass bursts into balls of fluffy white blooms, while purple gentian, campanulas and reddish-yellow moorland berries provide a splash of color amid the barren lichen vegetation.

Along Hardangervidda's western edge, the fjord's fingers penetrate deep into the surrounding terrain. Even during the summer months, the wide expanse of the Vidda plateau is never entirely free of snow and is often veiled in mists (above)

Patches of snow and barren, lichen-covered rocks are typical of the type of scenery found in parts of the Vidda (below)

The Saami herdsmen

Four major national parks protect the tundra in the Swedish sector of **LAPLAND**

Sarek/
Padjelanta/
Lapland

ZWEDEN

North Sea

Stockholm

Baltic Sea

North Sea

GETTING THERE:
The region is easy
to reach by train, road,
plane, or helicopter

WHERE TO STAY:
Hotels and cabins
in Abisko. Padjelanta:
overnight cabins along
the trails. Camping
permitted everywhere,
but all litter must be
removed

CLIMATE:
Cool and damp
in summer. In winter,
-4° to -22° F
(-20° C to -30° C)

MAIN ATTRACTIONS:
Abisko: Njulla summit,
Torneträsk Sea;
Padjelanta: flora
and fauna, Lakes
Vastenjaure and
Virihaure; Stora
Sjöfallet: Akka Massif,
pine forest near Vietas,
Teusadel Valley, Kierkau
cliffs; Sarek: scenery
and fauna

SPECIAL TIPS:
Some areas are
off-limits during
the early summer
breeding season
and have virtually
no tourist infrastructure.
The Saami have special
rights with regard
to use of motor
vehicles in the tundra

A rugged, ice and snow-covered mountainous region in the west and large expanses of swampland, dense forest, sparkling lakes, and numerous rivers in the east comprise the largest single area of continuous primeval landscape in Europe. Extending into Sweden from beyond the Arctic Circle are four large national parks, two equally sizeable reserves, and three other conservation areas, all part of an area encompassing 3,630 square miles (9,400km²) that has been designated a natural world heritage site.

Above the tree line, the bleak, blustery heights of the steep mountains on the Norwegian border are mainly barren and strewn with bare boulders and rocks. Wherever the rocks are not covered by glaciers, the summit areas are populated with a few alpine heathers, mixed with various types of scrubby vegetation, grassy tussocks and sedges.

Between the treeless heights and vast pine forests that cover most of central Lapland is a belt of heath land with dense thickets of diminutive, windswept birch. This is an unusual type of vegetation to find along the tree line as, in other parts of the world, it is mainly pine trees that grow at this altitude. The only other area in the world where this type of birch forest occurs is on the Kamchatka peninsula in Siberia.

Padjelanta National Park comprises 766 square miles (1,984km²) of an elevated plain surrounding the large lakes of Vastenjaure and Virhaure. The park has an extremely rich diversity of flora and fauna. Despite its Nordic alpine character, its rolling plains, softly rounded mountain ridges and vast areas of water are unusually open and accessible.

Arctic foxes and wolverines

The limy soil of the National Park supports over 400 different plant species, quite impressive for this type of remote mountain landscape. The lush alpine meadows are home to scarce species such as potentilla hypartica, a type of cinquefoil, and creeping sandwort. Arctic foxes and wolverine stalk the undergrowth and snowy owls breed here undisturbed. Padjelanta also provides valuable grazing pastures for the semi-wild reindeer, driven here each summer by the Saami, Lapland's native inhabitants.

The two National Parks of Sarek and Stor Sjöfallet, on the other hand, are dominated by the towering peaks of the Scandinavian mountains and separated by deep, trough-shaped valleys and mighty rivers. The wild,

alpine Arctic mountains and flat high plains of Stora Sjöfallet support very little vegetation. Bare boulders, snowfields, and glaciers dominate the landscape and it is only the depths of the valleys that are populated by primeval forests and birch woods.

Sarek National Park, with more than 200 peaks rising to over 5,900ft (1,800m), is extremely inaccessible. Six of Sweden's highest mountains are located here, along with some 100 glaciers. Sarek National Park's main artery is the Rapaätno River, one of Europe's most breathtaking water landscapes, which sweeps along the broad, majestic, U-shaped Rapadalen valley.

Ultimate, inaccessible wilderness

The green water from around 30 melted glaciers roars down into the valley in the raging torrents of the Rapaätno River. The river valley is carpeted with an almost impenetrable thicket of mountain birch, osier, and other vegetation. Nevertheless, only a few plant species actually manage to survive here. However, an unusual variety of wildlife compensates for the paucity of plant species. Bears, wolverine, lynx, and moose remain virtually undisturbed by man. Sarek is indeed one of the world's most remote wild places, with no trails or accommodation facilities for visitors.

Abisko National Park, on the other hand, provides much easier access to Lapland's bleak beauty. Situated in a broad valley in one of Sweden's sunniest regions, it is sheltered by high mountains to the south and west, while the large expanse of Lake Torneträsk sparkles to the north. Just before the mighty Abiskojokka River empties into the lake, it forces its way through a canyon 65ft (20m) deep, whose steep cliff walls document Lapland's geological history. From the summit of Mount Njulla, accessible by cable car, there are simply breathtaking views across the tundra and the lake.

Lapland is the land of the Saami who settled here 7,000 years ago as hunters and fishermen and began domesticating and breeding reindeer during the eighteenth century. However, the nomadic Polar Saami has left almost no visible traces of their presence. The lack of arrowheads, walled enclosures, or pits for trapping animals gives this unique and original tundra region the appearance of being virtually untouched. Today, between 200 and 250 Saami still inhabit the region with their 30,000 to 35,000 reindeer.

The shores of Lake Torneträsk are covered with dense coniferous forest. In the background, low hills form part of the tundra landscape (above)

Reindeer are an integral part of traditional Saami culture (below, left) Every autumn, the tundra bursts into a blaze of color (below, center)

A tiny, round church is one of the more unusual features of Padjelanta National Park (below, right)

Finland's island kingdom

Between the **ÅLAND ISLANDS** and the mainland is the largest archipelago in the world

Despite their slender legs, elks are excellent swimmers and are found on several of the islands (above, left)

The Bengtskär lighthouse is a beacon to ships navigating their way between the islands (above, right)

Water and rocks, water and woodland: colorful flora decorating the shores of the Dragsfjord in the Turku Archipelago

The southern and southwestern coast of Finland is fringed with clusters of tiny islands and islets, the remnants of an ancient, slowly disintegrating section of the Baltic Shield. Between 2,300,000 and 10,000 years ago, Ice Age glaciers smoothed away the last traces of erosion and any veins of soft rock between the hard masses of granite, scouring the land surface bare and leaving behind a landscape of softly rounded humps.

When the ice melted, the land was initially inundated by a sea of freshwater, which built up between terminal moraines and the glacier. When the Baltic Shield rose, these numerous small hills were pushed up above the surface of the water.

Southwest of Turku, a group of islands stretching over a distance of 50 miles (80km) emerged from the Baltic, forming part of the world's largest archipelago, situated between the Åland Islands and the Finnish mainland. The rocky coastal cliffs on the mainland and the belt of tightly clustered, mainly forested islands lying just offshore form the inner archipelago. The islands and islets of the outer archipelago are often no more than bare rock, buffeted by the wind and sea.

Even so, the clefts in the rock bloom throughout the summer with chives, coastal chamomile, and common scurvy grass, while the sandy islands in the center of the Park are also populated by stonecrop and wild strawberries. Since the Baltic's saline content here is no more than five parts per thousand, the shores are also home to wild angelica and longwort, Dyer's woad, yellow toadflax, and fescue grass.

A thousand islands

Many of the people who once occupied these isolated islands and eked out a living from fishing and agriculture have departed. Nowadays, only about 1,200 remain — apart from the rash of holiday homes. This has meant changes to a traditional culture that supported a unique biodiversity. This natural and cultural landscape is now protected by a National Park and also forms part of an international biosphere reserve encompassing 1,620 square miles (4,200km^2) and approximately 1,000 islands and islets.

The soil on some of the larger land masses is relatively fertile, thanks mainly to the veins of limestone that surface amidst the granite rocks. Farmers used to graze cattle in mixed woodland consisting of fir, spruce, and birch interspersed with oak,

alder, ash, and aspen. This practice produced wooded meadows filled with colorful flowers such as buttercups, goldilocks buttercups, and heath pinks. Some of the flat and relatively stone-free meadows were mown. Even the lower tree branches could be used as winter fodder. This created areas of open terrain and a few of these lightly wooded meadows still survive even now.

Since the islands were abandoned, this traditional landscape is increasingly in danger of disappearing altogether as nature reclaims its own and the region becomes overgrown. There are a few dominant species, which tend to squeeze out all the others. The main culprits in this respect are the dark fir forests, which deprive flowering plants of adequate light. In an effort to preserve the individuality and diversity of this heritage landscape, some of the island inhabitants, supported by the park authorities, have begun reintroducing traditional farming methods.

Gray and ringed seals

Animal life is surprisingly abundant. Twenty-five different species of mammal have settled in this island kingdom. The majority of these are small rodents, although elks too have swum across the water to occupy the islands' woodland. Despite their thin legs, they are actually very good swimmers. Sometimes, gray seals and even Baltic ringed seals are sighted, a species that is teetering on the brink of extinction.

The islands are home to 132 different bird species and, during the breeding season, many of the islands are closed to visitors. Gulls, terns, eider ducks, and razorbills inhabit the bare rocks, not to mention the black guillemots with their white wing tips and bright red legs. Some endangered species, like the Caspian tern and scaup duck, also nest here undisturbed. The sea eagle is a success story in itself. These birds had almost disappeared from the region, but can now be seen circling majestically high in the sky.

Only a small number of organisms have managed to adapt to the aquatic world of the skerries, such as bladder wrack, green and red algae, and a few types of crab. The Baltic Sea is, after all, too salty for freshwater creatures, yet not salty enough for marine ones. With no competition to speak of, the few organisms that do live here often multiply in vast numbers – for example, the green algae in summer and the balanids, brought in by ships from the North Sea.

Black organ pipes

The lava pillars of the **GIANT'S CAUSEWAY** rise up from the Northern Irish coastline

GETTING THERE:
Flights to Dublin airport. By road from Antrim and Ballymena to Ballycastle or Portrush

WHERE TO STAY:
At the historic Causeway Hotel in Giant's Causeway Park; all other categories of hotel in the surrounding towns. Bed-and-breakfast establishments available. Camping site

CLIMATE:
Temperate Atlantic climate. Stormy weather in spring and autumn

MAIN ATTRACTIONS:
Port Reostan viewpoint; Organ, Giant's Eyes, Harp, Camel's Hump, and Chimney Tops (site of the Girona wreck); walk along the former hydro-electric tram tracks or to Dunseverick Castle

Even though Finn MacCumhail (also known as MacCool) was 50ft (15m) in height, he is one of the smaller giants in Irish mythology. According to legend, it was he who built this spectacular formation of basalt pillars that project out into the sea off the coast of Northern Ireland as a causeway designed to connect Ireland with the Scottish isle of Staffa. There are differing versions of the legend of the construction of the pillars. According to one, MacCumhail built it to save the woman he loved from getting her feet wet when he brought her over to Ireland. Another says he constructed them to enable him to do battle with a rival giant in Scotland, thus explaining the existence of similar pillars on Staffa.

These strange, five and seven-sided basalt pillars, have diameters of 12–20in (30–50cm) across and range up to 82ft (25m) in height. They form a tightly packed arrangement of black columns rising from the shoreline on the edge of the Antrim Plateau between Causeway Head and Benbane Head. They look as if they are reaching up from the seabed toward the 330ft (100m) high cliff tops. From above, they look like a piece of honeycomb, while viewed from the side they resemble steps leading down into the sea.

The Antrim Plateau extends over an area of 1,500 square miles (3,800km^2) and is Europe's largest surviving lava plateau. It was formed 50 to 60 million years ago during the early Tertiary period when hot, molten lava erupted through fissures in the limestone landscape. The remains of some of these larger clefts in the limestone rock near the shore can still be seen today. There were three main periods of volcanic activity during which the lower, middle, and upper basalt layers were deposited. The Giant's Causeway columns originate from the middle lava emission, when five or six outpourings of molten rock flowed into the sea where it instantly solidified. The subsequent pressure between the lava flows compressed them into the angular columns we see today. There are around 40,000 such columns rising up from the sea around Giant's Causeway.

Giants' Eyes

Sixty thicker columns, all of equal height and size, soar upward in the formation known as Giants Organ. At Chimney Tops, erosion has separated the pillars into impressive, single chimney stacks.

The coast to the north of Port Ballantrae is peppered with fantastic structures of this kind, created by lava, water, and weathering.

Names like "The Harp," "Camel's Hump," "Amphitheater," or "Wishing Chair" encourage the imagination to run riot.

Erosion of the lower basalt layer, on which the columns stand, runs for approximately $3^{1}/_{4}$ miles (6km) along the coast in the form of a reddish band. The black cliffs, comprising innumerable bays and rocky promontories, end abruptly in a steep, luminous-white ridge of limestone. The round shapes, which have resulted in several places from erosion of the lower basalt layer, are known in Ireland as the Giants' Eyes.

During the seventeenth century, the Giant's Causeway became so popular that people came in droves to see it, often incurring the displeasure of local farmers and fishermen. It was not until 1897, following a lengthy legal battle, that local inhabitants were obliged to accept a road being built enabling people to visit this natural phenomenon on payment of a hefty admission fee. In 1961, however, Northern Ireland's National Trust association purchased the entire area and made it a protected area, at the same time abolishing all entry charges. Around 160 acres (0.7km²) of this breathtaking natural coastal spectacle now enjoys official protection. Thousands of visitors come here not only to marvel at the mighty pillars and steps, but also to enjoy the plant life and observe the animals. Its flora and fauna is one of the reasons this section of coastline was designated a world heritage site.

Scree, grassland and heath

Over 200 species of plants make this strip of coastline a fascinating area for botanists. This biodiversity represents a whole range of different habitats, comprising seashore, cliffs, scree, grassland, scrub, and heath as well as marshland. Some of the rarer varieties found here include maidenhair spleenwort, hare's foot clover, wild garlic, and fescue grass.

Such a varied coastline is a paradise for birds and birdwatchers alike. In addition to a large number of songbirds in the hinterland, fulmars, petrels, cormorants, shags, redshanks, guillemots, and razorbills can all be seen along the coast.

Giant's Causeway is a breathtaking landscape. Apart from the unforgettable coastal scenery and basalt formations, not to mention the rich diversity of flora and fauna, walkers can stumble upon tiny fishermen's huts around little harbors tucked away in sheltered bays. The rocks of Giant's Causeway, however, have also been the undoing of several ships, most notably the "Girona," which ran aground here in October 1588 during a strong northwesterly gale with the loss of around 1,200 men. Only five souls survived and their descendants still live in the area. The "Girona" was a Spanish Armada galleon, which had rescued the crews of two other wrecked ships and was consequently heavily overloaded. Its fate was sealed when its rudder snapped.

View of the valley featuring the black pillars of Giant's Causeway (above)

The rocky coastline around Port Ballantrae consists of cooled lava (below, left)

The eroded remains of once tall lava pillars (below, right)

Land of moors and peat bogs

NORTHUMBERLAND NATIONAL PARK IN NORTHEAST ENGLAND
is a unique nature reserve

North Sea
North-umberland
GREAT BRITAIN
London
ATLANTIC
English Channel

GETTING THERE:
By motorway from Newcastle, Carlisle, and Edinburgh. Train stations in Newcastle and Carlisle have connecting bus links to most places in the National Park. Regular shuttle bus service along Hadrian's Wall

WHERE TO STAY:
Large choice of all categories of accommodation in and around the National Park

CLIMATE:
Damp, temperate, northern climate. Cool in the Cheviot Hills

MAIN ATTRACTIONS:
Hadrian's Wall; Simonside; Yeavering Bell; Thirlwall Castle; Harbottle Castle. Hiking in the northern sector

The far northeastern corner of England is a landscape of uninterrupted horizons, tranquility, and spectacular natural scenery. This landscape has known the influence of man for thousands of years and so far his efforts to preserve it have proved successful. Northumberland National Park extends over an area of some 400 square miles (1,000km²) from the Scottish border in the north to Hadrian's Wall in the south. It is intersected by the idyllic Rede and Coquet Rivers, whose waters teem with vast quantities of salmon while otters play along their banks.

Stretching along the border with Scotland are the majestic, gently-sloping Cheviot Hills, a mountainous massif consisting of ancient volcanoes. Over many thousands of years, wind, rain, snow, and ice have combined to erode them into soft, smoothly rounded hills, the highest of which is Cheviot itself, rising to a height of 2,675ft (815m). Despite its remoteness, this hilly region is inhabited and farmed mainly by sheep farmers who maintain the heath moorlands and watch over the wild flora and fauna, thus helping to preserve this unique landscape.

Toward the south, the Cheviots give way to the gentler slopes of Coquetdale and the Rede and North Tyne river valleys, their grassy slopes rolling away into the distance. Beyond the Park's boundaries, Kielder Forest, the largest man-made European forest, forms the backdrop to a scenic landscape of fields interspersed with small pockets of mixed woodland and intersected by numerous small tributaries and streams, flowing through the side valleys toward the major rivers.

During the fifteenth and sixteenth centuries, this border country next to Scotland formed a buffer between two warring nations. The region is full of medieval fortresses and strongholds that were once the heavily fortified domains of pugnacious landowners.

Today, an idyllic and peaceful landscape, harmoniously shared between man and nature, greets the visitor. A healthy balance between conservation and tree-felling has been struck in the small forests. This approach is working so well that the rare red squirrel, driven from its traditional habitats elsewhere in England by the larger gray squirrel, has successfully found a home here.

The northern outpost of the Roman Empire

Hadrian's Wall is the most important Roman structure in England. This famous Wall, built by Roman Emperor Hadrian in AD 122, is more than just the route leading hikers through the magnificent and dramatic landscape in the southern part of the National Park. It has been placed under international protection because of its Roman origins and its watch towers, roads and settlements provide excellent examples of how the ancient Romans organized their occupied territory. The 75 mile (120km) long military fortification, running from east to west, has bisected this barren countryside for the past 2,000 years, at one

time defining the northernmost frontier of the Roman Empire.

The legionaries built this defense barrier on a hard ridge of volcanic outflow known as Whin Sill, which drops away steeply on its northern side, making the fortification unassailable. Following the Romans' departure from Britain around AD 400, much of the Wall was carted off and used in the construction of other buildings, such as Thirlwall Castle near Greenhead. Even today, the area is not without its military connections. A large army training area separates the northern part of this nature reserve from the southern sector.

A protective blanket of turf

Northumberland National Park is a protected sanctuary for many species of flora and fauna, most of which have adapted to the specific types of environment found here. Although fairly common within the Park itself, some species are very rare elsewhere in Britain and Europe.

Ancient forests, for example, have become extremely scarce in the United Kingdom, even though they once covered the entire country. Nowadays, only a few small pockets of such forest are left, even in Northumberland National Park. The presence of the wood anemone indicates that forest has covered a particular area for hundreds of years. This plant is not

found in younger woodlands, but is present in many parts of the National Park.

Northumberland nature reserve also contains some of the most significant peat bogs in Europe. These are among the most unspoilt areas in the National Park, thanks to their extreme inaccessibility. Over the past 10,000 years, they have become covered with

a blanket of turf overlaid with a thick cushion of moss. In spring, the landscape is dotted with the luminous, fluffy, white heads of cotton grass, followed during the summer months by yellow bog asphodel. In the cooler, even wetter Cheviot Hills, where crowberries and cloudberries can be found, this layer of turf grows at a much slower rate.

Castles and fortified strongholds are frequent sights in this border country (above, left)

Large flocks of sheep are still helping to keep this idyllic moor and heath landscape intact (above, right)

Hadrian's Wall was built in AD 122 by the Roman army. Substantial sections of this ancient defense barrier are still standing (below)

High fells, brooding lakes

The LAKE DISTRICT in northwest England: a varied landscapes in the British Isles

GETTING THERE:
Direct train link from
Manchester airport. M6
motorway. Coach link
from Hull ferry terminal

WHERE TO STAY:
Hotels, guesthouses,
self-catering cottages,
bed and breakfast
establishments,
and camping sites

CLIMATE:
January around 43° F
(6° C), August around
73° F (23° C). October
to March frequent
rainfall. August is
a relatively dry month

MAIN ATTRACTIONS:
Hiking; Ullswater
and Langdale (rock
carvings); Cunsey Beck
(smithy); houses where
famous English artists
and poets lived

SPECIAL TIPS:
No fossil-collecting
permitted

**View of Scafell from
Wasdale near Nether
Beck (left)**

**Pine trees along the
shores of Buttermere
on an autumn day
(above)**

**Bucolic landscape near
Mill Brow, on the
Brathay river
(below, right)**

**Twilight descending
on Derwentwater
(below, center)**

The Lake District in the northwest of England is one of the country-'s most popular tourist destinations and Lake Windermere is the largest of its many lakes. Its 865 square miles (2,240km²) were designated a national conservation area in 1951. It was established in order to testify to thousands of years of human habitation in the area and to safeguard various ancient habitats, which have dwindled dramatically throughout England.

This grandiose landscape of fells and mountains is so named because of the 60 or more lakes in the region. Many of the mighty mountains with their soft contours and bare summits rise to 2,300ft (700m) or more in height. Foremost among these are England's three highest peaks: Scafell Pike (3,210ft/978m), Sca Fell, (3,195ft/974m), and Helvellyn (3,115ft/950m).

The lakes at the southern end of the National Park are surrounded by low, elongated fells, carved into softly rounded shapes by the glaciers of the last Ice Age. These glaciers cut ever deeper through the U-shaped trough of the major valleys, sheering off many of the side valleys. These so-called "hanging valleys" now end abruptly part way up the mountainside, their river tributaries plunging in spectacular waterfalls over the precipice into the main valleys below.

Recent discovery of prehistoric rock art

For centuries, its endless expanses of moorland and fells, unfathomable black lakes, and sinister forests have set the Lake District apart from the scenery found in southern and eastern England. Stone Age settlers began cutting down the forests on the coasts 5,000 years ago.

A few years ago, rock carvings were discovered in the Ullswater and Langdale valleys, bearing witness to prehistoric settlement during the Late Stone Age. The Ullswater finds show that these early settlers hollowed out different-sized depressions in the rock, connecting them with carved lines. The carvings found in the Langdale Valley consist of sets of concentric circles and spiral designs. These are the first such finds in England to be completely unconnected to any prehistoric stone circle, several of which also exist within the Lake District National Park. Similar carvings have also been found in southern Scotland and Ireland, a sure indication of the links between the two cultures either side of the Irish Sea. It is thought that the stone axe factories, frequent evidence of which can be found throughout the Lake District, date from this same period.

From AD 200-500, England was occupied by the Romans. It was they who built the first two roads through this inhospitable landscape. The Romans were followed by the Norman invaders, who began widespread tree-felling throughout the region in order to procure timber for their ships. The monks of the Cistercian monasteries at Furness and Byland continued with this policy, to provide grazing pastures for their flocks of sheep. Wool from these sheep was, after all, a lucrative form of trade. The last of the region's great forests disappeared when iron smelting got underway along the shores of various lakes and lead and copper mining began in the area. By 1870, it was clear that not all these industrial experiments were proving profitable and focus eventually shifted primarily to quarrying stone for slate and building requirements.

The forest authorities and many private landowners have gradually begun reforesting this mountain landscape, albeit with economically lucrative conifer plantations, a type of tree not indigenous to the region.

Despite this, many areas of deciduous woodland have been preserved in the Lake District. The mixed woodland is dominated by oak and ash and provides essential habitats for various species of plants and wildlife, such as the rare red squirrel that depends on these trees for its survival.

Grasses and weeds

Another important Lake District habitat is the grassy terrain carpeting the broad, flat valleys. Soil quality, nutrients, and climate all determine the type of grassland. Every bit of ground in each meadow nurtures a unique combination of grass and weed vegetation which, in turn, attracts certain specific varieties of butterflies and beetles. Despite needing regular mowing, these meadows are a breathtaking sight in spring and summer, with brilliantly colored butterflies flitting back and forth amidst a profusion of bright flowers.

Heather-clad slopes and vast expanses of moorland carpeted with dense, green moss lead up to the bare mountain summits. The views across the fells in late summer when the heather is in full bloom are spectacular. A little later in the year, the rust-red autumn foliage of the ubiquitous bracken is equally stunning.

The Lake District National Park, bordered on the west by the Irish Sea, also incorporates a marine habitat. The sand dunes around the Ravenglass estuary are an important breeding ground for the increasingly rare natterjack toad and the sand dunes of Drigg Nature Reserve support the breeding colonies of black-headed gulls.

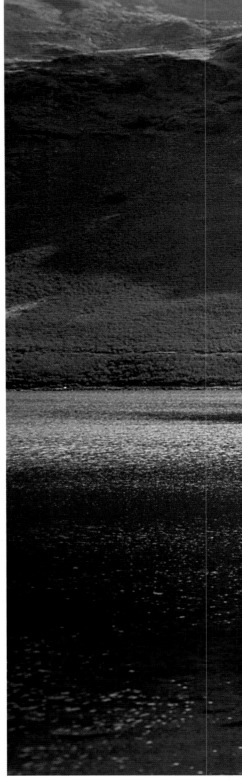

The mists could swallow the world

DARTMOOR NATIONAL PARK in the southwest corner of England is one of the largest in Europe and the site of many Stone and Bronze Age finds

A granite plateau, rising 1,650–2,000ft (500–600m) above sea-level, extends some 465 square miles (1,200km²) across the county of Devon in southern England. Much of it is covered by wide expanses of bleak and desolate moorland dotted with great, gray, granite rock formations, known as tors, rising out of the landscape like sculptures from some past age. The largest of these is Yes Tor, its summit rising to 2,065ft (629m) above sea-level.

Dartmoor's landscape can suddenly disappear behind an abruptly descending curtain of swirling mists, making the plateau resemble the ill-defined shadow of a large, slinking beast. Its moors have always fuelled the imagination of novelists, serving as an effective setting for innumerable tales of mystery and suspense. Dartmoor's forbidding atmosphere lent additional menace by the presence of Dartmoor Prison, built in the heart of the moor to house Napoleonic prisoners in 1806. The settlement of Princetown was built specifically to provide accommodation for the personnel of the prisou and is still the main town in these inhospitable moorlands. The real core of Dartmoor, which was designated a National Park in 1951, is the high moorland known as Dartmoor Forest, covering 365 square miles (945km²). It is situated to the northeast of Plymouth and stretches from Tavistock and Oke-hampton in the west to Exeter in the east.

High, moorland forest

Despite its inhospitable landscape and air of mystery, Dartmoor has, in fact, been inhabited by man for over 10,000 years. In its early days, this moorland plateau was thickly forested. During the Stone Age, between 8,000–4,000 BC, groups of hunter-gatherers began felling areas of forest to make it easier to hunt the wild animals that came to graze in the clearings. The first farm dwellings probably began to appear in the valleys sometime during the late Stone Age between 4,000–2,500 BC. By the middle of the Bronze Age, all the moorland forests had disappeared.

The National Park contains numerous prehistoric Bronze Age remnants dating from 1600–800 BC which testify to Dartmoor's ancient past. These include settlements,

dwellings, burial mounds, and standing stones, as well as stone circles and solitary obelisks of religious significance.

Around 1700 BC, people began to cultivate fields and enclose pastureland with stone walls, some of which have survived until this day. Very little evidence of any other kind has survived to provide insight into life in prehistoric times, since any ceramics, bones, or metal artifacts have been destroyed by the acid soil that is typical of moorland areas.

The National Park protects a number of increasingly rare habitats. The two main areas comprise a substantial expanse of peat bog on the northern plateau and a similar, smaller area to the south. Both are ringed by a mixture of grass and heather moors, while the more sheltered valleys are populated with oak woodland. The craggy, exposed tors and roaring rivers surging through deep ravines also provide uniquely individual habitats, as do the cave systems and former stone quarries found in the limestone rock of southeast Dartmoor.

Prehistoric animal remains

Britain's largest selection of prehistoric animal remains, some of which are over 150,000 years old, were discovered in Dartmoor's limestone caves. Joint Mitnor Cave,

for example, contains the prehistoric bones of hippopotamuses and straight-tusked elephants, as well as the fossilized remains of early wild boar, hyenas, and lions.

Most of Dartmoor is consists of what is known as blanket bog, one of the earth's increasingly rare landscapes, seldom found nowadays anywhere south of Dartmoor. The bogs themselves lie under a layer of turf at least 20in (50cm) deep and measuring 23ft (7m) thick in some places.

There is one other spectacular and even rarer area of peat bog within the National Park, namely the Tor Royal Bog, measuring 3 square miles (8km²), where the peaty ground bulges up like a dome arching above the surrounding moorland.

Dartmoor is one of the few remaining havens for moorland birds, many of which are found here. Another unique feature of Dartmoor is the large mammal population that it supports. Dartmoor ponies have roamed the plateau for centuries, along with sheep and cattle. They run wild on the moor and the harsh climate has made them very hardy. These tough breeds even rated a mention in the writings of Awlfwold of Crediton, who died in 1012. Nowadays, the ponies are regarded as excellent mounts for children and good breeding-stock for producing larger ponies.

GETTING THERE:
By rail from London to Southwest Eng, then bus. By car from Exeter to Easton, Chagford, More-tonhampstead, or North Bovey, from where narrow roads lead up into the heart of Dartmoor

WHERE TO STAY:
All categories of hotel available in Exeter, otherwise mainly bed-and-breakfast establishments and camping facilities within the Park itself

CLIMATE:
Frequent rain and wind

MAIN ATTRACTIONS:
Hiking; Castle Drogo; Sir Francis Drake's house; Widecombe-in-the-Moor with the Cathedral of the Moor

SPECIAL TIPS:
Compass and up-to-date maps are essential

Dartmoor's deciduous woodlands provide a feast of color against the first frost (right)

A September day on Dartmoor. Numerous streams help soften the wild and lonely landscape (left)

The past and the present: stone bridges within the nature conservation area (above, center)

View of Widecombe-in-the-Moor (below, center)

Salt marshes and mud flats

The "VORPOMMERN BODDENLANDSCHAFT" NATIONAL PARK lies off the coast of Mecklenburg

Vorpommern-
Boddenland-
schaft
National Park
GERMANY

GETTING THERE:
By car from Rostock via
Barth to the Zingst-Darß
peninsula.
To Hiddensee
(vehicles prohibited)
by boat from
Schaprode on Rügen

WHERE TO STAY:
The National Park
is a popular holiday
area with a large choice
of accommodation
available

CLIMATE:
Temperate central
European climate with
continental influences.
Daily summertime
temperatures around
68° F (20° C); often
below 32° F (0° C)
in winter; occasional
drift ice

MAIN ATTRACTIONS:
"Bodden" landscape
along the Darß-Zingst
shores; dune landscape
on Hiddensee Island.
Autumn is the best time
for watching the crane
migrations

In spring and autumn, some 60,000 cranes en route to or from Scandinavia glide gracefully down to the strange and rugged coastal area between Rostock and the island of Rügen on Germany's Baltic coast. During this time, more than a third of Europe's entire population of these large, elegant birds with their long, slender necks feast on the rich pickings yielded by the salt marshes and sand banks, mud flats and shallow lagoons located in the transition zone between land and sea, before resuming their journey across the wide expanse of Baltic Sea or continental Europe.

The "Vorpommern Boddenlandschaft" National Park covers an area of 310 square miles (800km²) and comprises one of the last surviving natural landscapes in Europe. Not only is it a breeding ground for numerous species of rare water birds, but it is also a spawning ground for fish and a sanctuary for amphibians. The Park encompasses two extensive lagoon areas. To the west, the Darß-Zingst peninsula protects a chain of shallow inlets, or "Bodden," from the pounding Baltic seas. To the east, the island of Hiddensee forms an effective breakwater for Rügen Island. Fifty percent of the National Park lies underwater, forming part of the largest inland sea in the world. Over the course of thousands of years, numerous species of flora and fauna have managed to adapt to its low saline levels. Although the fish found in the Baltic are derived from species that also live in the open oceans, they have evolved as an individual sub-species, fundamentally different from their cousins in ordinary seawater habitats. The "Bodden" lagoons are home to creatures from two different environments. Mud snails, for example, which normally only occur in the

open sea, co-exist with melon shells, which are traditionally freshwater creatures.

Steep cliffs, flat shorelines, coastal lakes, land spits, dunes, forest, marshland, salt marsh, and sand bars are all part of this diverse landscape, which provides plants and wildlife with a variety of habitats. Geologically speaking, this is a very young landscape, formed after the last Ice Age around 10,000 years ago. Once the weight of the glaciers lifted, the Scandinavian shield rose in the north and east, while the southern Baltic coast sank accordingly. Six thousand years ago, the North Sea gradually broke through into this giant inland sea left behind by the retreating glaciers. Water inundated the land, transforming the higher elevations into islands from which the sea continued to wrest substantial chunks, depositing them elsewhere as sand spits, sand bars, or peninsulas.

First shallows, then sand banks

The present "Bodden" lagoon landscape looks much as it did 4,000 years ago, yet it is still undergoing changes. Wave action and currents are still transporting sand from one place to another. The once individual islands of Darß and Zingst have gradually merged together, forming a peninsula. The island of Hiddensee is likewise linking up with Rügen. Currents are gradually removing the sand from the southern tip of Hiddensee, carrying it northward along the shoreline and depositing it at the northern tip of the island. Areas with shallow water eventually become sandbanks and ultimately small islands. Meanwhile, the wind whips the dry sand into dunes where salt-tolerant plants can establish themselves, stabilizing this new land with their roots. Final-

ly, dwarf shrubs, juniper, and the first conifers appear, forming the sparse beginnings of a heath. Meager though this plant life may be, it nevertheless paves the way for the birch, beech, and oak that will eventually populate the area with dense, mixed woodland.

Non-tidal mudflats

The flat coastal areas, which are subject to periodic high-water flooding, sustain the salt marsh vegetation found along all Central European coasts. For some plants, such as sea lavender and sea wormwood, the water is not saline enough, making them something of a rarity. Other plant species, such as wild celery, salt marsh flat sedge and sea purslane, which once grew abundantly throughout the Baltic region, have dwindled dramatically. They have at last found refuge in the sheltered waters of the lagoons.

Although the Baltic Sea is not tidal, an extensive area of mud flats, known as the "Windwatt," still spre-

The reed beds along the shore and flat coastline are typical of the "Bodden" landscape (above)

One of the most popular harbors is Ahrenshoop on the western edge of the National Park (below, right)

Visitors can enjoy boat trips through the flat "Bodden" landscape in traditional fishing boats

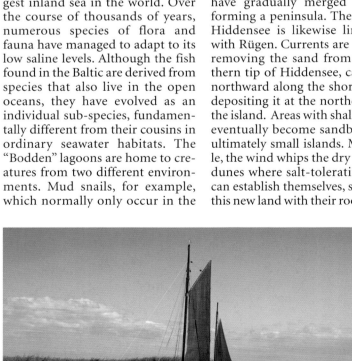

ads across the wetlands. If the wind blows for several days from the same direction, the Baltic Sea builds up a large swell. Once the wind drops, this build-up of water falls back as a wave, flooding the low-lying sandy areas. The vagaries of the weather mean that it can also remain dry for weeks on end. As the sun dries up the residual water, salinity increases. If it rains, on the other hand, the salt is washed out. Only a few creatures, such as rag worms, can withstand such conditions. These species reproduce so successfully, however, that birds such as saw bills and sanderlings are able to eat their fill.

Below the steep cliffs, known as "Dornbusch," is a totally different type of mudflat. The cliffs that abound here overlook rocky mud flats. The large boulders found in this area are encrusted with bladder wrack and other large types of algae. This ecological niche provides an ideal feeding ground for birds such as the turnstone and sandpiper.

A kaleidoscope of colors

The **LÜNEBERG HEATH** and **SÜDHEIDE** Nature Park in northern Germany are ancient cultural landscapes

North Sea
Baltic Sea
Lüneberg Heath
Berlin
GERMANY

GETTING THERE:
Via the Hamburg-Hanover Autobahn.
Train and bus links to Schneverdinge, Soltau, Celle, Bergen

WHERE TO STAY:
Hotels, rural inns, and holiday parks

CLIMATE:
Moderate climate with continental influences

MAIN ATTRACTIONS:
Wilsede with its museum and 16th century farmhouses; Undeloh and its Magdalena Chapel; Totengrund

SPECIAL TIPS:
Vehicles prohibited in the nature parks

The Lüneberg Heath, measuring 2,780 square miles (7,200km²), is a unique area of man-made heath land situated in the lowlands of northern Germany between the two major cities of Hamburg and Hanover. It is the last remnant of the landscape that once stretched all the way from Denmark to Belgium, encompassing the entire Geest region of northern Germany. When the last Ice Age glaciers retreated northwards 10,000 years ago, this predominantly flat landscape was covered with dense forest.

The first settlers arrived around 5,000 years ago during the Bronze Age and began farming the land. Their livestock grazed on the young saplings and the forest receded in many places for lack of fresh growth.

Large tracts of forest were also felled for firewood. The settlers hit upon a new method of enriching the poor-quality, sandy soil. It became known as "heather farming." They cleared away the thin surface layer of humus along with its sparse covering of vegetation and scattered it in the cattle sheds. They then fertilized their fields with the resulting mixture of soil and livestock dung. This method of soil enrichment, known as "Plaggen," was an early method of manuring to improve soil quality and was common practice on the Lüneberg Heath until the nineteenth century. In order to maintain sufficient supplies of humus for their fields, farmers needed to retain a reservoir of heath land that was ten times larger than their arable acreage. The exposed sand was often blown by the wind into sand dunes. During the nineteenth century, this method of farming became uneconomical and many farmers lost their farms. Forest began to regain a foothold in unused areas.

Thousands of years of human intervention in the natural environment have played a key role in shaping this unique landscape. Many plants and animals have successfully adapted to life in this habitat and found a niche here. The region includes wide expanses of savannah-style plains, with broad grassy areas, crystal-clear streams, silent moorland, forests, and heaths.

Common heather and bell heather

The heath vegetation consists predominantly of common heather and cranberries, with bell heather replacing common heather wherever the soil conditions are wetter. Other varieties of vegetation thriving here include various grasses, lichen, and moss, dotted with occasional juniper bushes and common broom. The rare bog asphodel, marsh gentian, and heath pinks can also be found here.

It is also a good place for observing rare birds, such as great gray shrikes, black storks, woodlarks, nightjars, whinchats, and stonechats. Adders and smooth snakes, which have disappeared elsewhere, can be seen slithering over the sandy ground among the heather. The most significant mammals found on the Lüneberg Heath, however, are the horned moorland sheep. Without moorland sheep, there would no longer be any heath left. This small, modest sheep is believed to have been introduced during the Bronze Age and is descended from the Mouflon, a tough breed of mountain sheep found in Corsica and Sardinia. It is also related to the Gotland sheep, which was introduced to that Baltic island around 3,000 BC. The majority of today's moorland sheep were crossed with another breed during the 1970s. These cross-breeds differ from their pure-bred ancestors because the females no longer have horns.

The advent of modern farming methods and commercial conifer plantations around the turn of the twentieth century threatened to destroy a thousand-year-old natural ecosystem. Around 1904, nature conservationists decided to try and preserve the landscape, using tradi-tional, if not cost-effective, methods of farming. Thanks to them there are still flocks of moorland sheep grazing peacefully among the juniper and broom. The process of "Plaggen," i.e. the heavy task of removing the top layer of humus, is now accomplished by machines.

Famous Mount Wilseder

The Lüneberg Heath is rich in reminders of earlier human settlement, ranging from Bronze Age barrows, ancient tracks, and boundary markings to thatched farmhouses, originating in the sixteenth and seventeenth centuries.

Two nature reserves have been established to protect what is left of this once vast landscape: the Lüneberg Heath Nature Park, covering around 90 square miles (230km²) between Lüneberg and Hamburg, and the Südheide Nature Park, extending nearly 200 square miles (500km²), between Munster and Celle. This unspoiled natural oasis so close to civilization also boasts northern Germany's highest elevation, the 555ft (169m) high Mount Wilseder, and comprises almost 30 percent of original heath land and associated habitats. It has become a major attraction for many city dwellers who flock here from Ham-burg, Bremen, and Hanover to seek rest and recreation at the weekends.

The more southerly Park is almost completely covered in woodland and forms part of one of the largest, continuous forests in northern Germany. Because of its situation a fair distance from any roads or towns, very few visitors make their way here. As a result, it has become a sanctuary for shy animals, such as European otters and cranes.

In late summer, when the heather is in full bloom, the landscape is a mass of brilliant purple. The stunning colors are as unusual as the rest of the heath vegetation: Juniper bushes (above, left) thrive well on sandy soil and the silver birch is also a typical feature of heath vegetation (above, right)

Shepherds move their flocks of moorland sheep around whatever the season (below)

Eerie forest wilderness

The **BAVARIAN FOREST** and **BOHEMIAN FOREST** National Parks, situated on both sides of the German-Czech frontier, form a conservation area for some rare sphagnum bogs and for the remnants of the great Central European primeval forests.

For centuries, smugglers, quartz seekers, and treasure hunters have found this hilly region, extending along the border between Bavaria and Bohemia, a wild and frightening place. This great expanse of primeval forest in the heart of Europe stretches over an endless landscape of rolling hills and ridges. It is singularly lacking in properly defined tracks — an eerie environment, inhabited by wolves and wildcats, where it is all too easy to lose one's way and perish. Even the 19th century novelist, Adalbert Stifter (1805-1868), who grew up in the region, still regarded this forest wilderness as a dangerously alien and hostile landscape.

Even now, as we enter the third millennium, the Bavarian and Bohemian Forests, which straddle the German-Czech frontier, still constitute the largest continuous forest region in central Europe. This once menacing ancient forest, however, has long since been forced to make room for cultivated plantations of fast-growing spruce. Only a few pockets of ancient woodlands have managed to survive, tucked away in parts of the German and Czech reserves. These primeval forest areas are one of the main attractions of the Bavarian Forest National Park, established in 1969 and the first of its kind in Germany. Many of the hikers, visiting the National Park, head for the 90 acres (36 hectares) of ancient forest around the Mittelsteig lodge, south of Bayerisch Eisenstein, where spruce, fir, and beech trees as high as church towers surround the isolated village of Zwieslerwaldhaus. After receiving special protected forest status in 1763, this woodland no longer had to sacrifice its trees to the axe. If its trees succumbed at all, it was to old age, parasites, damage caused by wild animals, or lightning storms. Some dead trees manage to remain upright for many decades, providing a home for woodpeckers, pygmy owls, and dormice, before they finally rot and break down completely.

A forest of old-timers

High up on the Grosser Falkenstein (4,315ft/1,315m) and in Sumava National Park in the Bohemian Forest across the border, tall mountain spruce, beeches, mountain maples, fir, and ash trees can be found growing on steep precipices, jutting out from beneath rocky outcrops, or leaning out over rushing mountain streams. These trees, some of which are 300 to 400 years old, were not planted by any human hand, but are survivors of the original primeval forest. Some of these old-timers have reached 130ft (40m) in height, their

massive root systems resembling pythons, gripping rocky promontories in a stranglehold. One such wild spot has been known since time immemorial as the "Höllenbachgespreng" because it is here that the stream rises. According to superstition, its source is the gateway to Hell. The surrounding rocks are covered with brimstone-yellow sulfur lichen, while the stream itself plunges into the Höllbach gorge below.

This German-Czech frontier area abounds in legend, and Lake Rachel is no exception. It lies at an altitude of around 3,300ft (1,000m) and was left behind by the retreating Ice Age glaciers. It is now surrounded by ancient forest, comprising trees over 500 years old whose mighty crowns tower over the younger competition. This primeval lake is consequently so well sheltered that scarcely a breath of wind ruffles its surface. The water appears either blue or black in color, depending on atmospheric conditions, making the lake appear strangely devoid of life. For this reason, it too is reputed to be a gateway to the netherworld.

Steinberg hiking area

While less eerie, the Steinberg hiking territory between Weidhütte and Glashütte is nevertheless a perfect setting for games of trappers and Indians. Situated in the heart of an tranquil forest is a 650ft (200m) high knoll, furrowed with

narrow ravines, dotted with strange-looking gneiss boulders, and populated with spruce, fir, and beech trees, all several hundred years old. An arduous climb winds through dead trees, between sheer rock walls, and up through clefts in the rock to pulpit-like projections along the ridge of gneiss rock. From these splendid natural viewpoints, one can look out over a sea of treetops to Mount Lusen (4,500ft/1,373m) on the German-Czech frontier, where the Bavarian Forest merges imperceptibly into the Bohemian Forest.

The Bavarian Forest National Park comprises altogether 50 square miles (130km²), of which an astonishing 98 per cent is covered in forest.

A similar situation exists on the Czech side. Apart from examples of primeval forest, both National Parks comprise areas of sphagnum bog, ancient stands of narrow-crowned mountain spruce, and mixed mountain forests, as well as riverside forests supporting marsh birch in the valley depressions. Around 40 square miles (100km²) of forest, including former spruce forests, enjoy full protection: no tree-felling, no planting, no cattle-grazing, and no hunting. The forest is to be allowed to develop as nature intended and trees that were originally artificially introduced as part of a forest management scheme now have the opportunity to revert to natural forest.

GETTING THERE:
Rail links to Zwiesel, Spiegelau, and Grafenau in the vicinity of the National Park. By car via the A3 Autobahn, Hengersberg junction, then along the B 85 to Grafena. The National Park area can be reached via the B 11 from Deggendorf and the B 12 from Passau

WHERE TO STAY:
Varied and plentiful accommodations available in private houses, bed and breakfast establishments, and smaller hotels. More expensive accommodation available in the "Hotel Sonnenhof" near Grafenau

CLIMATE:
Frequent rainfall. Cold winters, moderately warm summers

MAIN ATTRACTIONS:
Ancient forest areas near the Czech frontier. Well-marked hiking trails, to the Lake Rachel and Arbers region among others

SPECIAL TIPS:
Trips into Sumava National Park (Bohemian Forest) in the Czech Republic can be arranged from Bayerisch Eisenstein

Lake Rachel with its dark, brooding waters is surrounded by legend. Superstition has it that the lake is the gateway to the netherworld (above, left)

The delightful scenery within these two National Parks includes an abundance of streams whose brownish waters indicate the close proximity of bogs (below, left)

Over the past few years, lynx have re-established themselves in these protected forest areas. These beautiful animals have been successfully bred and returned to the wild (below, right)

Primeval forest setting

BERCHTESGADEN National Park
is Germany's oldest nature
conservation area

Towards the end of the nineteenth century, Berchtesgaden decided to follow the example of Yellowstone National Park in the United States and place the flora and fauna within this alpine region under protection. The decision came almost too late for many species, however, as by then entire areas of ancient mountain forest had already been felled. Giant larches had been used to build wooden walkways around Lake Starnberger, magnificent firs were used as firewood to heat ovens, and aromatic arolla pines had been fashioned into wood paneling to decorate expensive villas. Approximately one third of the alpine forest had already vanished in the Berchtesgaden region as a direct result of felling, forest clearance, karstification, and a drop in the altitude of the tree line due to climatic influences.

By the dawn of the twentieth century, the damage to wildlife was also irreversible. While inordinately large populations of chamois, red deer, and roe-deer populations had been deliberately bred on the traditional hunting grounds of Bavarian kings, any other wild animals regarded as dangerous or useless to the hunting fraternity were mercilessly slaughtered. The last bear was killed in 1835 near Ruhpolding; the last wolf in 1836 on the Steinernes Meer Mountain. The last bearded vulture was blasted out of the sky in 1855 by a smug marksman in the Wimbachtal Valley, although a harmless carrion eater would have been completely uneatable. The last surviving lynx was also killed around the same time.

Alpine flowers for festival decorations

Following lengthy discussion, conservationists succeeded in 1910 in getting 20,500 acres (8,300 hectares) of land around the Königsee Lake and part of the Watzmann Mountain designated as the "Berchtesgaden Plant Protection Area." A vast number of rare alpine flowers had already been "harvested" from this same area to decorate the tables of elegant hotels for various festivals. These flower displays consisted of edelweiss, for example, alpine roses, Christmas roses, lady's slipper, and other types of orchid.

This protection area later paved the way for other conservation areas and in 1978, the Berchtesgaden National Park was established, covering an area of 80 square miles (210km²). Since then, there have been systematic attempts to preserve these last pockets of alpine wilderness and encourage the remaining woodland, mostly state-owned forests, to return to

a natural development process. The forests have been left mainly to their own devices and tree-felling, removal of dead wood, clearance work are not allowed. Only occasional attempts to encourage mono cultures of natural species, in order to give the forest a helping hand with its recovery and return to mixed alpine woodland, are permitted. At the same time, the amount of game in the forest is being reduced to a manageable level, thereby considerably limiting the amount of damage caused by wild game.

The last remnants of the ancient forest that once covered the entire Alps right up to the tree line are mostly located off the main tourist track. On Mount Rotofen (4,490ft/1,369m) in the Latten Mountains and in the Gamskendl region near Reichenhall, there are still ancient stands of firs, spruce, and beech. The Untersberg Mountain and Reiteralm on

the lower slopes of the Mühlsturzhörner mountains are also home to larch and beech trees, which are several hundred years old. In Wimbachgrieß, an ancient forest of dwarf pine has survived intact, and on the Hochkalter (8,555ft/2,607m) are remnants of an ancient spruce and larch forest.

Wilderness around St. Bartholomä

Natural areas of forest, which have gradually regained the character of ancient woodland now that commercial forest management has ceased, can be reached either via the main hiking trails traversing the National Park or by boat. The Königsee peninsula with its pilgrimage church of St. Bartholomä is situated right on the fringes of this wilderness area of mixed alpine forest. The shores of the Obersee Lake are populated by ancient

mountain maple and spruce completely covered with moss and ferns. A few dead trees, which are now bare of needles, have tipped into the lake and from a distance resemble gigantic fish skeletons. Species of plants growing beneath these trees include alpine honeysuckle, red-berried elder, spindle, and dog rose. Yellow globe-flowers and blue alpine clematis bloom long into the autumn.

Nature is slowly regaining the upper hand in the National Park, as the ancient forest re-establishes itself. Previously managed forest is reverting to its natural state, but bears, lynx, and wolves are unlikely ever to return to their old haunts. Only the bearded vulture has returned to circle above these mountains after an absence of over 150 years. These birds are visitors from the Rauriser Valley in neighboring Austria, where conservationists are hoping they will settle again.

Looking down on the Königsee nestling at the foot of the Watzman massif (above)

The stunning beauty of the lake glimpsed through the breaks in the trees (below)

Sometimes sea, sometimes land

The **WADDENZEE** between the West Friesian Islands and the Dutch coast is a unique type of sea landscape

Waddenzee

North Sea

● Amsterdam

NETHERLANDS

HOW TO GET THERE:
By road or train to
Den Helder and
Leeuwarden. Onward
journey by ferry

WHERE TO STAY:
Wide choice
of accommodation
all along the coast
and on the holiday
islands of Texel,
Vlieland, Terschelling,
and Ameland

CLIMATE:
Temperate, marine
climate. Average
January temperature:
35º F (1.7º C), average
July temperature 63º F
(17.2º C)

MAIN ATTRACTIONS:
Visits to the islands
of Texel, Vlieland,
Terschelling, and
Ameland; Den Helder
Ijsselmeer Dam; guided
walk across the mudflats

SPECIAL TIPS:
Ferry traffic ceases
during gales

Extending from Den Helder to the mouth of the River Ems on the coast of Holland is a landscape which alternates twice a day between sea and marshland. This sweeping, muddy coastal plain, known as the Waddenzee, is criss-crossed by islands, shallows, sand banks and creeks and is a designated biosphere reserve extending over some 965 square miles (2,500km²).

A chain of islands including Texel, Vlieland, Terschelling, Ameland, and Schiermonnikoog, curve gently around the Waddenzee. These West Friesian islands form a protective barrier, sheltering the wetlands against the onslaught of the North Sea. Over the past 10,000 years, an unparalleled landscape has evolved, supporting an ecosystem that could scarcely be more diverse or more delicately balanced. Every 12 hours and 25 minutes, the channels between these islands fill up or empty as the saline North Sea waters ebb and flow. These tides originate far out in the Atlantic. As the moon orbits the earth, its gravitational pull builds up a swell of water, drawing a giant wave along in its wake. Fingers of this massive wave thrust their way across the English Channel, pouring into the North Sea between Scotland and Norway. The two waves converge off the coasts of Holland, Germany, and Denmark. If the crests of these waves collide, the mudflats are flooded, but if the troughs collide, the ebb tide draws the water away.

Ever-changing dunes

The islands off the Dutch coast are relatively young. Wave action created the first sandbanks around 10,000 years ago after the end of the Ice Age. As soon as they were exposed above sea level, the wind was able to blow the sand into dunes. Sheltered from the sea on the side facing mainland, salt marsh has managed to gain a foothold.

This landscape is in a constant state of flux, however, due to the action of the wind and the North Sea. Most of the dunes visible today are at most 600 to 900 years old. Sand is removed from the western ends of the islands and re-deposited at the eastern ends. Shallow areas are washed away, only to reappear elsewhere. Since the Middle Ages, man has also played a key role in shaping this environment, not least by constructing dikes, originally as a protection against unexpectedly high tides, and later as a means of creating new agricultural land.

These island dunes have, in the meantime, been stabilized by a dense cover of vegetation. The seaward side of the dunes has, in some cases, been sheltered by additional protective measures and man-made sea walls. These sea defenses have, however, thwarted the natural process of sand dune renewal. Nor can any windborne sand be added to the mud flats, a process that would once have helped firm up the mainland side of the dunes. The mature dunes, therefore, are being gradually depleted of their nutrients and the vegetation cover is becoming sparser and more fragile. Tourists trampling their way through this unique dune landscape after the end of World War Two caused so much damage to local vegetation that the wind was able to blow away entire stretches of dunes. In consequen-

ce, the area where great dunes once dominated the landscape has been transformed into an irregular, undulating landscape.

This amphibious landscape between the islands and the mainland is so highly productive from a biological point of view that it would be difficult to find its equal elsewhere. Not only are the mud flats well supplied with oxygen, but they are also well fed with large amounts of nutrients from freshwater from the Ijssel and Llauwers seas and Ems and Westerwoldse Aa Rivers, which produce huge quantities of tiny, microscopic plankton organisms. These, in turn, provide the necessary nutrients for innumerable creatures that are at home in the mud, such as soft-shelled clams, cockles, Baltic tellins, mussels, mud snails, lugworms, mud shrimps, and starfish. Many young fish can feast at low tide, undisturbed by larger predatory fish, in the shallow pools and channels left by the receding sea.

Stopover for migrating birds

Any creatures or fish that live in these mudflats are, in turn, prey to others, such as the common seal, the only mammal that lives here. Above all, however, they are a vital food supply for the two to three million migratory birds that stop here each spring and autumn to recharge their batteries in preparation for the next stage of their long flight. When the mudflats dry up, hikers can enjoy a much more intense encounter with

this unique natural landscape. Trails through this muddy terrain, sometimes soft and oily, sometimes firm and sandy, open up a whole new world. Ameland and Schiermonnikoog can be reached at low tide after a three-hour hike. The other islands are separated from the mainland by fast flowing creeks. It is not advisable for the uninitiated, who may be unaware of these hidden and unpredictable hazards, to venture out alone onto these mudflats, nor should they stray far from the mainland or attempt to wade across creeks. Special guides are available to lead tourists safely across the muddy landscape, and acquaint them with the unparalleled flora and fauna that lies hidden just a few inches beneath the surface.

An area of lush, green salt marsh extends between the mudflats and the mainland and the landward side of the islands, providing a unique habitat for some highly individual plants, including glasswort, false spike grass, common salt marsh grass, and sea asters which have successfully adapted to saline soil. They remain equally unperturbed by their periodic submersion in salty North Sea water.

Currents carry the water, which collects in creeks and channels at low tide, back out to sea, draining the mud flats (above, left)

Plants that are adapted to tidal conditions, such as glasswort, have established themselves along the fringes of the mudflats (above, right)

A walk across the mudflats is an unforgettable experience for any tourist (below, right)

Europe's biggest shifting dune

The **PYLA DUNE**, sculpted by wind and waves, is a unique natural monument

GETTING THERE:
Good roads, bus, and rail links from Bordeaux to Arcachon. Bordeaux airport

WHERE TO STAY:
The beaches of Aquitania are popular tourist destinations. Wide choice of holiday accommodation

CLIMATE:
Around 45° F (7° C) in January; 77° F (25° C) in July

MAIN ATTRACTIONS:
Climbing to the top of Pyla Dune; paragliding; water sports

The power struggle between water, sand, and plants began some 15,000 years ago and it still dominates the Atlantic coastal landscape of Aquitania in southwest France. A perfectly even, smooth, sandy beach stretches 155 miles (250km) along the coast from the Gironde estuary to the Spanish border. For thousands of years sea currents have deposited sand along the coasts. The sand is blown into dunes by the wind, thereby creating a remarkable landscape between sea and land backed by a succession of enchanting lakes and ponds.

The most prominent natural feature along this breathtaking landscape of beach and constantly shifting dunes is undoubtedly the extraordinary Pyla Dune. It is nearly two miles (2.7km) in length and 1,650ft (500m) wide, stretching along the coast opposite Cap Ferret at the entrance to the Arcachon basin. Reaching a height of around 360ft (110m), it is the highest dune of its kind in Europe and has been placed under special protection as an outstanding natural phenomenon.

Each year, the dune moves about 13ft (4m) inland, slowly submerging the pines in the extensively forested hinterland and burying ancient huts used by resin collectors and pitch ovens, some of which are 400 years old.

On the seaward side of the dunes, there are some indications that the land now covered by the dune was once thickly forested. The oldest layers are around 4,000 years old, while the summit can be fairly accurately dated back to 1860. The dune passes through four so-called paleostrata, i.e., layers dating back to when the ground was forested and later when it was once part of a swamp area.

The silted-up bay

Pyla Dune is the product of one of the last active phases of dune formation in Aquitania. Between 1450 and 1750, when the winds were particularly strong during the so-called "Little Ice Age," two major dune systems gradually began to overlay each other. To begin with, marine currents off the coast began to build up a sandbank known as "Pile." This slowly extended toward the coast and eventually joined up with the shore during the sixteenth century. Further south, a new sandbank was meanwhile emerging from the sea, called "New Pile." During the eighteenth century, the Bay of Pilat was formed between "Old Pile" on the shore and "New Pile" in the sea. The sea winds continued to assail New Pile, driving its sand toward the coast, filling up the bay, and driving it onward to accumulate on the Pyla Dune. There were periods when the dune shifted up to 65ft (20m) inland each year.

In 1855, Pyla Dune was only 115ft (35m) tall. In only 150 years, it has tripled its height. Nowadays, the wind is taking its toll on the Arguin sandbank, adding further layers to Pyla Dune. The island that is left during the ebb tide measures 2.5 miles (four kilometers) in length and 1.25 miles (two kilometers) wide. It is a conservation area, narrowing into the Bay of Arcachon. Wind and waves continue to assault it and its shape is constantly changing. The region is not only a popular destination for water sports enthusiasts, but is also home to one of Europe's largest tern colonies.

During the course of history, Pyla Dune has been known by a succession of different names. For a time, it was called "Le Sabloney," followed by "Les Grands Tucs" or "La Grave." Today, it is generally known as the Pyla Dune, although its older name of "Pilat" is still quite common. The latter derives from its first recorded mention in 1484, when it was initially referred to as "Lous Pilat," until eventually shortened to simply Pilat in 1556.

Several paths lead along the ridge of the dune. Some are well maintained with wooden steps, while others are arduous trails through the sand. The ascent is well worth it, however, as there

are magnificent views from its summit across the vast horizons of the Atlantic Ocean and the Arguin sandbank on one side and panoramic vistas across the green pine forests of the Landes de Gascogne regional park in the hinterland.

The hinterland was once a vast, sandy swamp that dried up in summer to become a steppe landscape, supporting very little other than some sheep grazing. Following a directive by Napoleon in 1801, the region was drained and thousands of square miles were planted with trees, predominantly a species of pine that tolerates hot, sandy conditions. This measure was intended to stop the advance of the dunes and at the same time introduce what was, at the time, a lucrative resin industry. Today, the vast forested area behind the dunes provides a network of cool, shady paths.

Two views of the magnificent Pyla Dune: View over the sandy expanses of the ridge to the sea beyond, with the pine forests in the background (above).

View along the shore toward the slopes of Pyla Dune and the Bay of Arcachon beyond (below)

Vivid mountain landscape

The evolution of France's **LUBERON** region over the centuries

GETTING THERE:
By rail: express train to Avignon, then regional bus connections. By road: A7 from the north, A8 from the south, Aix-en-Provence exit to Pertuis. Airports at Marseille and Avignon

WHERE TO STAY:
Wide choice of hotels, guesthouses, country villas, and farmhouses; campsites

CLIMATE:
Sun shines 300 days a year. Hot summers and mild winters

MAIN ATTRACTIONS:
Hiking trails: botanical trail in the Massif des Cèdres (Cedar forest); ochres trail near Roussillon with ochre quarries. Places to visit: Apt; Lourmarin with visit to Albert Camus' grave and house; Village des Bories (open-air museum); Buoux fortress

"Rustrel Colorado" is the French name for the spectacular limestone cliffs of the Grand Luberon (above)

Pont Julien near Apt is one of the Luberon's oldest cultural sites (below, center)

Vineyards and castle ruins are reminders of the Luberon's turbulent past (below, left and right)

The mountain landscape of the Luberon, the very epitome of Provence, is a myriad of colors including fields of vivid purple lavender, mighty forests in varying hues of green, bright red and orange ochre cliffs, and dazzling white limestone hills. The rugged mountain chain is situated to the east of Avignon, rising over 3,300ft (1,000m) in places and stretching for some 35 miles (55km) between Manosque to Cavaillon. Its highest peak is the Mourre Nègre, which rises to 3,692ft (1,125m). Picturesque villages cling precariously to craggy cliffs while regimented lines of vines and stony limestone fields occupy the slopes leading up to deserted high plateaus. To the north, the mountains descend gently into the Calavon Valley and the plains of Carpentras.

This stunningly beautiful and often mysterious terrain forms part of the Luberon Nature Park, which extends over an area of 640 square miles (1,650km²). It was established to protect not only a unique natural landscape, but also a region with a cultural history in which man and nature have co-existed in mutually influential and adaptive relationships dating back some 1,000 years. Even though the old, traditional farming methods that were geared to fit the peculiarities of the climate, local soils, and mountainous terrain are now just a distant memory in many places, Luberon farmers still practice these traditional farming methods in order to preserve the indigenous plant and animal life.

Early farming practices have created an open landscape. If the growth of constantly sprouting trees and shrubs were not kept down by grazing sheep, many species of plants and animals would lose one of their last sanctuaries.

Grand and Petit Luberon

Situated between the Alps and the Mediterranean, the Luberon is exposed to two climatic systems. The northern and southern flanks of the mountain chain are exposed to the sun and wind, and temperatures fluctuate dramatically due to the differences in altitude between the deeply hollowed out valleys and the high plateaus, producing an astonishing diversity of habitats, which have experienced both help and hindrance at the hands of man.

The Combe de Lourmarin bisects the mountains of Bonnieux and Lourmarin, dividing the mountain chain into the Petit Luberon in the west and the Grand Luberon to the east. The deep ravines, steep cliffs, and dramatic river valleys of the Petit Luberon (Little Luberon) have produced a picturesque landscape of rugged mountains and constitute a refuge for many endangered bird species, such as Bonelli's eagle, the Egyptian vulture, the snake buzzard, and owls. Wild boar and Europe's largest lizards are also found here. The plateau heights support dense Mediterranean garigue vegetation, a dry, sparse landscape of macchia bushes, chestnut oaks, palms, and juniper, interspersed with a variety of herbs including thyme, rosemary, and lavender.

Steep limestone cliffs

Situated between Bonnieux and Cheval Blanc is Europe's largest plantation of Atlas cedars, covering an area of four square miles (ten square kilometers). These trees were introduced from North Africa in 1862 and first planted in the vicinity of Bonnieux village.

Another unforgettable sight are the distinctive ochre-colored cliffs near Roussillon. This unusual rock formation is remarkable for its coloring, which covers virtually the whole spectrum of glowing reds and yellows. Ochre is a mixture of sand and clay. The iron oxide, or rust as it is commonly known, contained within the ochre gives the cliffs their striking hue.

The Grand Luberon is characterized by dazzling, white, limestone crags rising from steep, rocky cliffs. This part of the mountain region is older than its western counterpart. Over the centuries, wind and weather have eroded these mountains to form smoothly rounded hills. Meadows carpet the hilltops and dense woodland clings to the hillsides.

The northern slopes are mainly populated by white oak, whereas the southern flanks are dominated by chestnut oaks and marine firs. The roots of the chestnut oaks create an ideal habitat for truffles, considered the black gold of gourmets everywhere. Truffles were once gathered here in vast quantities for export. Now that they are cultivated, however, truffle-gathering is merely a private pastime.

The land of pink flamingos

The CAMARGUE region in the Rhône delta, a paradise for wild horses and migrating birds, is France's best-known national park

GETTING THERE:
From Arles on Route D35 east of the delta to Salin-de-Giraud, or on Route N570 on the western side of the Camargue to Les-Saints-Maries-de-la-Mer

WHERE TO STAY:
Les-Saints-Maries-de-la-Mer is a tourist resort with a wide choice of accommodation

CLIMATE:
Mediterranean climate

MAIN ATTRACTIONS:
Hiking along the three trails known as "Flamingo Way," "Salt Way," or "Rice Way." Horseback riding on Camargue horses. Bird watching. Places to visit: Arles, St-Gilles, Aigues-Mortes

The amphibious conditions of the Rhône delta resulting from the combination of freshwater, sea, and mud have, over hundreds of years, produced one of Europe's most fascinating, yet most fragile, ecosystems. The Camargue is the alluvial land between the two arms of the Rhône river as it flows into the sea. The 330 square miles (850km²) of land, one of the world's most important wetlands, consist of a spectacular mosaic of lagoons, marshes, ponds, dunes, and beaches, together with an extensive area of steppe landscape that is home to the incomparable, semi-wild Camargue horses. At the heart of the delta is the Lagune Vaccarès, covering an area of 23 square miles (60km²). This body of water is pivotal to the Camargue's entire irrigation system, acting as a water treatment plant for the agricultural drainage water that collects here. Periodic Mediterranean storms whip up the water surface, ensuring the lagoon is always well supplied with oxygen and that micro-organisms are able to convert every last nutrient. This large-scale biological production not only supports 40,000 flamingos, the largest colony of these birds in the Mediterranean, but also countless coots, ducks, snipe, and gulls.

The Camargue is a land of extremes. Very few plants can tolerate its harsh environment and the continual see-sawing between the dry salt desert conditions that prevail during the summer months and the widespread flooding that occurs in winter. The extensive marshes and steppes are primarily populated by saltwort, while dwarf eelgrass is the predominant vegetation in the lagoons. Trees and bushes are uncommon, growing in just a few small pockets on higher ground in the north, mainly as riverine woodland along the banks of the Rhône. A few wind-battered trees also manage to survive on the ancient sand dunes south of Vaccarès. The landscape is dotted with occasional juniper bushes, some of which are said to be more than 500 years old.

The transition zone between freshwater and saltwater

A different situation altogether prevails with regard to the animal life. The Camargue wilderness is in fact home to over 600 species of animal, not to mention 356 varieties of bird, millions of which arrive here in spring and autumn to rest and feed before continuing their journey. Autumn is the ideal time to see

virtually every kind of European wader and, during the winter months, these flooded plains are home to 13 different species of duck. The Camargue is a breeding-ground for eight species of heron, terns, and of course the wonderful pink flamingo. The 35 square miles (90km²) of freshwater and saltwater marshes and the 58 square miles (150km²) of freshwater and saltwater ponds virtually dry up during the summer, but in autumn and winter they provide a source of food for bitterns, mallard, and wagtails.

The flat salt pans, dried in summer and flooded in winter, are overgrown with saltwort, the main diet of the Camargue horses. In spring, they are invaded by wading birds, such as snipe, redshanks, and black-winged stilts.

Most of the mammals, such as rodents, foxes, and wild boar, tend to avoid the open terrain, preferring instead the wooded areas in the southern part of the delta.

On the Mediterranean side, a 12¹/₂ mile (20km) long dike protects the Camargue from the onslaught of the waves. Further west, the dunes perform the same function. To prevent the wind from dispersing the sand, wooden boardwalks have been installed to protect this habitat, which supports a unique collection of vegetation including marram grass, devil's grass, spurge, and narcissi.

Saline pans behind the dikes

The lagoons behind the dikes, surrounded by dunes, are used primarily for salt extraction. The Salin-de-Giraud salt extraction works, covering 43 square miles (110km²), produces around one million tons of salt per year. The Camargue is the product of man's relentless struggle against the river and the sea. It is certainly not the wild, untamed landscape it is often claimed to be. The first dike was completed in 1859 to protect the region from flooding. Ten years later, dikes were also built along the Rhône River to enable farmers to plant extensive vineyards which could be irrigated with fresh water. Meanwhile, rice-growing has replaced wine-growing to a large extent. People eventually realized that if the Rhône no longer supplied the delta with mud, the delicate soils would be deprived of nutrients. Consequently, a rigorous system of water management was introduced. Nowadays, pumps, irrigation, and drainage systems are operated to safeguard this unique landscape and preserve its abundant wildlife.

In spring, autumn and winter, vast expanses of the Rhône estuary are underwater. The Camargue as twilight falls (above, left)

The semi-wild Camargue horses, which roam the river delta in herds, are one of Europe's rarer species of wildlife (above, right)

The elegant pink flamingos are a stunning spectacle. The Camargue boasts Europe's largest colony of these birds (below, left)

Some parts of the delta are still used as agricultural land (below, right)

Mountains of the Cévennes

CÉVENNES NATIONAL PARK
is a region of remarkable scenery

GETTING THERE:
Highway A7 near Loriol/Privas. D104 to Lablachère, continuing along the D104A and D901 to Villefort on the northern edge of the Cévennes National Park. Railway station in Ales. Airports in Montpellier and Rodez

WHERE TO STAY:
Numerous camping sites available. Wide choice of hotel accommodation and private rooms in villages within the Park

CLIMATE:
Between 64° and 70° F (18° and 21° C) in July, with frost in January and lots of snow and storms

MAIN ATTRACTIONS:
Walking, wildlife, and bird watching; Cirque de Navacelles on the River Hérault; Saint Pierre des Tripiers cave with its prehistoric finds; Dargilan and Aven Armand caves; the Tarn Gorge; cliffs at Nimes le Vieux near Veygalier

Situated in the southernmost part of France's Massif Central is one of Europe's most spectacular mountain landscapes, namely, the dramatically chiseled, yet relatively modest mountains of the Cévennes. In reality, this is not a single chain of mountains, but a combination of several mountain groups, wooded hills, extremely dry limestone plateaus and deep gorges, through which some of the Languedoc's main rivers flow toward the Atlantic or into the Mediterranean. This unique landscape with its unusually rich diversity of species and long history of human settlement is protected within a National Park, which extends over 1,250 square miles (3,230km²) and is simultaneously a significant international biosphere reserve. It is the only national park in France that does not lie in high mountain terrain.

Not only are its habitats exposed to a mixture of oceanic, continental, and Mediterranean climatic influences, but the ground is composed of three distinct types of soil, each of which has produced a different landscape supporting an individual diversity of flora.

There are the granite massifs, for example, consisting of erosion-resistant hard rock, namely the Montagne du Bougès Mountains as well as Mont Aigoual and Mont Lozère, the highest peaks in the Cévennes, which rise 5,300ft (1,600m) in height. Their slopes are covered with wet areas of heath énd interspersed with remnants of ancient beech forests.

The extensive limestone plateaus form one of the most impressive and unusual landscapes in the Cévennes. The Grand Causses, as they are known, are famous for bizarre rock formations — typical examples of which can be seen in the Tarn and Jonte valleys and in their spectacular caves.

New species of sweet chestnut

The largest plateau is the Causse Méjean, a harsh, arid area covering 130 square miles (330km²) around 3,300ft (1,000m) above sea level. There is very little precipitation here and the winters are extremely cold and bitter. In spring, however, the steppe-like meadows erupt into a colorful carpet consisting of masses of different flower varieties.

Just a few miles north are a series of valleys, cut in schist and known as the Gardon Valleys. These present a rugged landscape with a milder climate supporting some agriculture, such as the cultivation of sweet chestnut plantations which grow in the thin soils.

Sweet chestnuts have been an important source of food for man and his beasts since time immemorial. In days gone by, around 200 different varieties of chestnut have grown in the Cévennes region, each with its own distinct qualities in terms of size and flavor. Chestnut blight decimated vast areas of woodland starting in 1870. During the 1950s, another fungal disease introduced from America destroyed yet more chestnut trees. Meanwhile, the few farmers who remain within the National Park

are once more cultivating the old stands of chestnut as well as planting new varieties. Even so, the old, neglected chestnut groves still have an ecological role to play in providing nest-holes for nuthatches and green and spotted woodpeckers as well as feeding grounds for deer and wild boar.

Farmers leave the area

The Cévennes area is now regarded as one of the least populated regions in France. As farmers moved away from the region, agricultural areas dwindled, allowing heath land, steppes, and mixed beech and pine forests and oak woods to reclaim the land. This has attracted many animals back to the region, including the black woodpecker, eagle owls, Egyptian vultures and gray herons, as well as mammals such as otters. Around 90 different species of mammal and approximately 200 varieties of breeding birds inhabit the National Park. Red deer, roe deer, mufflon sheep, beavers, capercaillie, and black vultures have been successfully introduced to the area, as well as griffon vultures.

Griffon vultures virtually disappeared by 1940. In 1985, five pairs were released into the wild and by 1999 their numbers in their colony near Le Truel had increased to 180 pairs. These spectacular birds, standing three feet tall with a wingspan of 8ft (2.5m), can no longer find enough food to sustain their numbers and are therefore feed off leftover animal carcasses and offal. The large herds of sheep and cattle that once grazed the Causses and regularly lost occasional animals over the steep-sided gorges are now considerably smaller than they used to be. In any case, dead animals are no longer left lying in the open, but are transported away for disposal.

The Cévennes landscape's biological significance would not be so marked were it not for man's influence. During the Copper Stone Age, hunters and gatherers roamed the Causses uplands, leaving evidence of their existence in numerous places in the form of menhirs and dolmen, some of which are difficult to distinguish among the rock masses.

At the heart of the National Park is a high limestone plateau with vegetation adapted to the arid soils (right)

Lower down, the scrubby terrain is occasionally dotted with ancient landmarks (left)

Glacial splendor in the Alps

The ALETSCH NATIONAL PARK in central Switzerland safeguards Europe's largest glacier

SWITZERLAND

Bern • Aletsch Glacier

Ligurian Sea

GETTING THERE:
By road from Interlaken to Lauterbrunnen or Grindelwald. From various locations between Naters and Fieschan on the road between the Simplon and Grimsel Pass. By the Jungfraujoch railway

WHERE TO STAY:
The entire area around the National Park is geared towards accommodating tourists

CLIMATE:
Sub-oceanic climate on the northern side, sub-continental climate on the southern side. Average annual temperature on the Jungfraujoch is 47° F (8.5° C) and 48° F (9.1° C) at Brig

MAIN ATTRACTIONS:
Jungfraujoch viewpoint; guided walk across the Aletsch glacier; ecological center at Villa Cassel

SPECIAL TIPS:
Mountain climbing or skiing for experienced climbers/skiers only and at their own risk

Europe's largest glacier, the Aletsch Glacier, resembles a river of ice, winding its way down into the Massa valley from the heights of the Jungfrau massif in central Switzerland's southern alpine region. Its melted waters form the source of the River Massa, one of the headwaters of the Rhône. The glacier is more than 12 miles (20km) long and, at its highest point, the so-called Konkordiaplatz, this frozen mass towers to a height of 2,950ft (900m). It is here, some 9,200ft (2,800m) above sea level, that four mighty snowfields converge to supply the glacier with ice and snow, namely the Aletsch névé, the Jungfrau névé, the Eternal Snow névé, and the much smaller Grüneck névé. The valley end of the glacier, or glacier tongue, lies far below the tree line at 5,100ft (1,560m). This mighty glacier, which extends over an area of 34 square miles (87km²), dominates the entire 208 square miles (540km²) of the Jungfrau-Aletsch-Bietschhorn region, a world heritage site comprising what must surely be one of the most awe-inspiring mountain ranges anywhere in the Alps. Visitors have marveled at the mighty, rugged peaks of the Eiger, Mönch, Jungfrau, Aletschhorn, Fiescherhorn, Grünhorn, and Finsteraarhorn for centuries. Not one of these alpine giants measures any less than 13,000ft (4,000m) in height. Together they form the crest of a massive ridge of mountains, which, in turn, forms one of the largest watersheds in Europe. The steep, northern slopes supply the catchment area of the River Aar, a

tributary of the Rhine, which flows into the North Sea. Water from the gentler, southern slopes discharges, via the Rhône, into the Mediterranean.

Textbook glacial activity

The approximately 27,000 million tons of ice comprising the Aletsch glacier is being propelled downwards under its own weight at the rate of some 650ft (200m) a year. Over the millennia, this sea of ice has transformed the surrounding alpine region into a unique landscape, leaving perfect, textbook evidence of the different features of glacial activity in its wake. For example, the U-shaped Lauterbrunnen Valley, scree fields, drumlins, and moraine fields, extends upward either side this river of ice to the 815 acres (3.3km²) of Aletschwald nature reserve.

A walk across this gigantic glacier, passing mysterious, shimmering turquoise crevasses in the ice and deep chasms, running with gurgling melted ice water, is a simply unforgettable experience. The glacier is melting faster than it is forming, however. Up to 2,800ft³ (80m³) of water can flow into the Massa gorge on a warm day. The glacier has been retreating since the mid-nineteenth century, currently at an average rate of 100ft (30m) per year,

and as much as 300ft (90m) a year in the event of a hot summer. It is already nearly two miles shorter than it was 140 years ago.

It is, in fact, quite normal for alpine glaciers to fluctuate in size over the years. Aletsch glacier ice, for example, has left scrape marks on 3,000-year-old tree roots, indicating that the region was still forested at that time. According to medieval sources, the glacier was so huge in those days that this mass of slow-moving ice was actually threatening villages. Nevertheless, today's rate of the glacial retreat far exceeds natural climatic fluctuations.

The fabled Aletsch forest

The moraines pushed aside by the glacier's advance and the drumlins left in its wake start off as barren, inhospitable scree fields. Within a short time, however, the terrain is soon covered with moss and lichen, followed by seed-grown plants. After around 25 years, the first bushes begin to sprout on terrain that was once glacial detritus. The areas that do not support trees are covered instead with alpine herbaceous perennials, such as blue wolf's bane or alpine blue sow thistle, while alpine rhododendron and alpine toadflax occur in drier soils. The dramatic elevation differences that occur in

mountain regions and the changes that glaciers are constantly inflicting on the terrain result in a fascinating diversity of plant and wildlife habitats. Above the tree line, an incredible 529 different species of flowering plants and ferns have been recorded, each occupying their own ecological niche. At the altitudes of 3,000–4,300ft (900–1,300m), the low-lying northern slopes are populated with broad-leaved beeches. Since it is too dry for beeches to thrive on the southern side of the mountain range, this particular zone, with an altitude of 650ft (200m) higher, is populated mainly by pine trees.

The ancient woodland of the lovely Aletschwald forest above the Aletsch glacier consists predominantly of Swiss stone pine, larch, and spruce. In summer, large patches of alpine roses can be seen blooming between the trees. Swiss pine is a particularly interesting type of fir. Its clusters of needles consist of just five needles and its trunk is often strangely contorted. These trees grow exceedingly slowly and consequently live to 800 years old or more. There is evidence of human habitation in this region dating from 3,400 years ago. Archeological finds testify to the presence of Celts, Romans and Alemannians in the area.

The Aletsch glacier sliding down from the heights of the Jungfrau massif through the giant canyon formed by the sides of the Aletsch valley – view of this spectacular natural wonder from the Bettmeralp (above)

Lower down the valley, the glacier reaches the tree line (below, left)

Looking north towards the mountain chain, behind which the ice mass takes shape (below, right); a typical alpine meadow (center, right)

123

The romantic eastern Tyrol

HOHE TAUERN National Park is designed to protect the Grossglockner and Hochalpenstrasse region

GETTING THERE:
Grossglockner
Hochalmstrasse between
Lienz and Kitzbühel;
Tauern railway between
Spittal and Schwarzach

WHERE TO STAY:
Well developed
holiday area with
a wide selection
of accommodation

CLIMATE:
Average annual
temperature is 41° F
(5° C) with heavy
snow in winter

MAIN ATTRACTIONS:
Grossglockner; Pasterze;
Krimml Waterfall;
hiking; winter sports

The dazzling display of flowers in the meadows of eastern Tyrol is unsurpassed (above)

The rugged slopes of the Tauern Mountains give way to gentler woodland in the valleys (below, right)

The Hochalpenstrasse (High Alpine Road), which traverses the Grossglocker region, winds its way in a series of numerous hairpin bends up to an altitude of 8,200ft (2,500m) at the top of the pass (below, left)

The Grossglockner, at 12,470ft (3,800m), is Austria's highest mountain and the majestic heart of Hohe Tauern National Park. This mountain range in southern Austria forms part of the main central alpine ridge in the Eastern Alps. Its impressive succession of steep, awe-inspiring summits, including the Hochalmspitze at 11,025ft (3,360m), the Ankogel at 10,670ft (3,252m), and the Mittlerer Bärenkopf at 11,010ft (3,356m), extends for more than 60 miles (100km) between the Zillteral Alps and Italy in the west and the Katschberg Pass in the east. The Park safeguards some breathtakingly beautiful alpine scenery featuring rugged mountains, vast expanses of glacier, gentle mountain meadows, and rushing water falls.

At the base of the Grossglockner is the glistening, white ice tongue of the Pasterze Glacier, the largest of its kind in the Eastern Alps, stretching over a distance of 5 miles (8km) and measuring 3 miles (5km) across.

The Kriml Waterfall at the foot of Gerlos Pass is yet another unforgettable sight. More than 8,800 gallons (40,000 liters) of water per second tumble over its precipice, to plummet 1,215ft (370m) below into the forested Salzach valley basin in a series of three cascades.

Dazzling display of flowers

The National Park is a region of incomparable beauty, in which the wild, primeval landscape and the centuries-old cultural traditions of mountain farmers complement each other perfectly. The Park is home to 10,000 different species of plant and animal life. A large proportion of these are found in the valley meadows, which are constantly being mown and in the mountain pastures where the livestock grazes all summer long. The mown grass provides a rich habitat for bearded bell-flowers, blue wolf's bane, globe flowers, alpine asters, leopard's bane, orchids, and countless other plants. In spring and summer, the sloping meadows are carpeted with a truly dazzling display of colorful blooms.

Their original habitats are thickly forested valleys, which become less dense as the altitude increases, gravel-covered glacial moraines, and bare, sometimes snow-covered, summits. After the last Ice Age 10,000 years ago, the half-mile thick covering of ice receded from the Alps, and the area became populated by different types of plant from Siberia, the cold Central Asiatic steppes, the Arctic, and southern Europe. It is a harsh terrain, in which only certain, specially adapted species can survive. Many of them are at the limits of their existence since not only do they have to withstand a cold climate with temperatures averaging 41° F (5 ° C), but also incessant winds, high UV radiation, and winter snows several feet thick. High up along the fringes of the tree line, it is mainly only larches that survive, although an occasional, rare Swiss stone pine may be found. (The Swiss pine is a species of fir tree that only blooms once every six to ten years, grows very slowly, and can live for a thousand years.) The gray scree and gravel of glacial moraines and bare rock is highlighted here and there by bright splashes of glacier crowsfoot buttercup and the alpine marguerite.

The dense forests still shelter an occasional, extremely shy brown bear, which stands eight feet (two-and-a-half meters) tall. It is exceedingly rare for these creatures to leave the thick woods and wander out into the high, treeless mountaintops. Lynx, fox, wolves, and badgers are also still found in this alpine region.

A landscape sculpted by rivers of ice

Fortunately, the marmot population is increasing again. These cute, mountain mammals, which grow to 20in (50cm) in length and live in underground burrows, warn each other of

danger by whistling. By 1800, they had completely vanished from the Hohe Tauern after being hunted for their fur and fat. Over the past century, they have been re-introduced into the area and have become a common sight once more.

The Hohe Tauern Mountains were formed 75 to 35 million years ago on the bed of the Thethys Sea, an ocean-sized

precursor of the Mediterranean. As Africa drew nearer to Eurasia 35 million years ago, the seabed was pushed upward. Finally, seven million years ago, at the time the Pyrenees, Carpathian Mountains, and Himalayas were created, the ridge of Alpine peaks was thrust upward into deep folds. The Hohe Tauern did not acquire its present-day appearance until three million years ago, when the rivers of ice forced their way down through the valleys and into the Lower Alps. In the process, they sculpted the valleys into U-shaped troughs and carved out the gentle slopes and terraces that form the fascinating mountain scenery of the Tauern Alps.

The first evidence of human habitation dates from the Bronze Age 4,000 years ago, when copper and tin were greatly prized minerals. Mining in the Hohe Tauern region reached a peak during the sixteenth and seventeenth centuries. Parallel to this, traditional alpine farming methods evolved, which ultimately provided the population with a means of support after the collapse of the mining industry.

White battlements

The rock formations of the **ELBSANDSTEIN MOUNTAINS** are protected

GETTING THERE:
By car from Dresden via the B 172, or from Prague via the E 55 from Lovosice, along the left or right bank of the Elbe. Scheduled flights also fly direct to Dresden

WHERE TO STAY:
Numerous guesthouses and hotels are available in the Czech part of the National Park, and even more in the German section.

CLIMATE:
Pleasant climate from early spring until November. Even winter days can be mild if the weather is clear

MAIN ATTRACTIONS:
Neurathen Fortress nd Königstein Fortress

SPECIAL TIPS:
A paddle-steamer trip from Dresden to Bad Schandau is an unforgettable experience

Artists of the Romantic Period captured it all on canvas: slim pinnacles of rock, flat-topped crags, and ravines reminiscent of North American canyons; veils of mist revealing the outline of a cross on a mountain summit; stone bridges, sculpted by nature and spanning dark gorges. The Elbsandstein Mountains, which lie half in Germany and half in the Czech Republic, comprise some of Europe's most picturesque scenery. The key areas of this region are under stringent protection, as part of the Národni Park Ceské Svycarsko in northern Bohemia and the Switzerland National Park, situated south of Dresden.

This upland region was created by subterranean forces around 90 million years ago, when part of earth's crust, once an ocean bed, was pushed upwards 1,650ft (500m). Sand and chalk from the bottom of the sea bed formed a high sandstone plateau, through which the Elbe River and its turbulent torrents carved dramatic gorges over the millennia. Only occasional areas of harder rock were able to withstand the effects of water erosion, frequently producing a fascinating array of rock formations. The tops of the numerous flat-topped hills are the last remnants of the original, now deeply fissured, single sandstone plateau.

The largest sandstone bridge

If you follow the course of the Elbe as far as Usti nad Labem, formerly known as Aussig, you can see the gradual transition from the rounded domes of the central Bohemian mountains to the more rugged formations that form part of the Elbsandstein range.

The rock walls along the eastern bank suddenly rise almost vertically next to the bizarrely beautiful Schreckenstein fortress, which inspired Richard Wagner's opera "Tannhäuser." A few miles further, the distinctive contours of the two highest table mountains of this sandstone plateau become visible in the west: the 2,383ft (726m) high Decinsky Sneznik (Hohe Schneeberg) mountain and Germany's Grosser Zschirnstein of 1,845ft (562m).

East of the Elbe, not far from Hrensko, ancient river torrents have created what is undoubtedly the largest sandstone bridge in Europe, namely the Pravcická brána, or Prebisch Gate. Around 53ft (16m) or so above ground level, the natural rock

formation arches across a gap of 100ft (30m) from one cliff to another. In the early nineteenth century, it had become such a popular tourist attraction that a hostelry was opened at its base and it now forms one of the sights along the Eisenach-Budapest European hiking trail.

At the border town of Schmilka, the B 1172, which runs parallel to the Elbe, follows a stretch of the so-called "German Dream Route." Right from the outset, sheer rock walls bordering narrow strips of river bank reflect the power and persistence with which the Elbe has cut a path through the sandstone. This dramatic wilderness is known for its characteristic, rectangu-

lar rock formations sculpted by ancient forces. Paddle steamers from Dresden deposit hordes of visitors at Bad Schandau on the right bank of the Elbe.

The Kirnitschtal Railway takes visitors up into the fantastic mountain landscape, popularized by Caspar David Friedrich's paintings. A 100-year old lift also transports hikers 165ft (50m) up to the Ostrau district, an ideal starting point for walks.

Further north, a breathtakingly beautiful walk starts from Rathen up to the 13th century Neurathen Fortress, continuing across the fortified bridge to the famous Bastei Viewpoint, 625ft (190m) above the Elbe. Far below on the right are the tiny-looking rooftops of the town of Wehlen. To the south, around the next bend in the river, is the 1,362ft (415m) high Lilienstein mountain, the most frequently painted and most photographed table mountain in Saxony's "little Switzerland."

Königstein Fortress

Directly opposite is Königstein Fortress, its mighty walls encircling a flat-topped crag 1,180ft (360m) above sea level. Bohemian and Saxon kings began building the fortress around AD 1200. Centuries later, the fortress served as an escape-proof prison. August

the Strong imprisoned Johann Friedrich Böttger, the porcelain manufacturer, in Königstein for his failure to produce artificial gold and Emperor Wilhelm had August Bebel, the workers' leader, incarcerated here.

From the Königstein's battlements, there are splendid views over the small spa town of Gohrisch, the oldest summer resort in Saxony's "little Switzerland," where Adalbert Hauffe, a farmer, is said to have been the first to provide rooms for tourists in 1869. To the north, one can make out the outline of the Elbe town of Pirna. For centuries, this was the main port for shipping Elbe sandstone. Not far from Pirna, the Elbsandstein Mountains drop away to the flatter terrain of Dresden's Elbe valley landscape. To the west, the view extends towards the Erz mountains while, to the east, the horizon stretches as far as the Lausitzer mountains.

Looking down into the gorge from the viewing platform at Neurathen Fortress (above)

Erosion has rounded off the tops of some of the rock formations (center, left)

Near Hrensko in the Czech Republic, the narrow gorge is navigable by boat (below, right)

Rübezahl's mountain kingdom

The **RIESENGEBIRGE** on the Czech-Polish border is well known for its extremely harsh winters

GETTING THERE:
The main highway between Prague and Wroclaw bisects the Park near Nachod. Rail connections between Prague, Göritz, and Wroclaw

WHERE TO STAY:
Wide choice of hotels; mountain cabins also available

CLIMATE:
Mean annual temperature 32°-43° F (0-6° C). Damp changeable climate. Snow to a depth of three to ten feet (one to three meters) in winter

MAIN ATTRACTIONS:
Source of the Elbe; Schneekoppe summit; Adrspach cliffs; Bozkov dolomite caves; water-falls; castles and fortresses; walking and riding

SPECIAL TIPS:
High risk of avalanches from January to March

On the eastern fringes of Central Europe surrounded by the Sudeten mountains lies an insular area of Arctic and Alpine ecosystems, known as the Riesengebirge, Along the ridges of this 4,300ft (1,300m) high mountain massif are the kind of ecosystems that are otherwise only found some 620 miles (1,000km) away in Scandinavia, the Alps, or even Great Britain. The loftiest peaks of the Riesengebirge support an alpine vegetation zone consisting of grasses and lichen that bear a strong resemblance to those found in Arctic tundra regions. Even cloudberries are found here, a plant more typically found in Scandinavian fjäll landscapes. During the colder periods of the earth's history, the Sudeten Mountains formed an important bridge between the northern tundra and the alpine ecosystems typical of the northern Alps, amalgamating a variety of species from completely different ecosystems.

The unique ecological features of the Riesengebirge are protected

by two National Parks. The highest peak in the region rises to 5,256ft (1,602m) and is known as "Schnee-koppe." One of the Parks includes the steep slopes situated on the Polish side of the frontier while the other, on the Czech side, comprises mountain ridges and elongated valleys that drop gently down into

the hilly landscape of Podkrko-nosska Pahorkatina. Together, these Parks cover an area of around 230 square miles (600km²) and are a significant international biosphere reserve, preserving a natural landscape that man has influenced, often to nature's detriment, for the past 800 years.

The Black Triangle

The Riesengebirge is a region of extensive mixed woodland and dense undergrowth. The beech forests that once covered the valleys up to a height of around 2,650ft (800m) have been replaced with dark, sunless plantations of solid fir, although a few remnants of this magnificent deciduous woodland still survive in a few river valleys. In areas where cleared patches of forest have been reclaimed by nature, a rich diversity of new and colorful flora has evolved including orchids, sedges, spring snowflake, and crocus.

The higher elevations 2,600–3,900ft (800–1,200m), once covered with mixed coniferous forest have been replaced by solid fir plantations. Wide tracts of the forested land have all but died off. The Riesengebirge lies within the so-called Black Triangle, in range of major German, Czech, and Polish industrial centers. Emissions from lignite power stations have polluted the soil to such an extent that the trees have been poisoned. Even though air quality has improved drastically since the 1990s, the forests are still dying.

Even so, some fascinating ecological niches still exist in this mountainous region. The summer meadows are carpeted with a brilliant display of flowers including yellow pansies, arnica, and rare species of gentian and campanula, while alpine blue lettuce and various types of butterbur grow beside the Riesengebirge's clear, babbling brooks.

Remnants of surviving tundra

In the Riesengebirge, above the tree line at the fairly low altitude of 3,900ft (1,200m) a few leftover areas of Ice-Age tundra still survive, sporting occasional stands of knee pine often containing trees up to 100 years old. The hollows are filled with sub-arctic peat bogs. The places where this knee pine was once burned away to make room for new pastures are now populated by tough matgrass, which is intolerant of other vegetation.

The region's main ecological treasures, however, are the so-called "cirques." These basin-shaped hollows nestling below the mountain ridges were scoured out by melting Ice-Age glaciers as they flowed down into lower-lying valleys. A spectacularly varied and colorful collection of flora has been preserved over a relatively small area, boasting every species found in the Riesengebirge. The cirques are known as "Rübezahl's Garden" (Krakonosova zahradka, after a mountain sprite), "Schustler's Garden" (Schustlerova Zahradka), or the "Devil's Garden" (Certova zahradka).

The disappearance of mixed forests has had an inevitable impact on the wildlife. Nowadays, only grazing animals such as red and roe deer inhabit the valleys, as well as smaller predators such as foxes, martens, and weasels. The last brown bear was killed here in 1726. By the mid-eighteenth century, wolves too had disappeared and lynxes and wild cats were all killed off by the beginning of the nineteenth century.

Golden eagles and peregrine falcons no longer ride the thermals above the mountain peaks, but lesser spotted eagles and some rare owls have so far refused to relinquish their habitat. Even the endangered black stork still manages to find undisturbed nest sites in the magnificent, majestic mountain scenery of the Riesengebirge.

Schneekoppe is the highest peak in the Riesengebirge mountains (above, left)

Icy winds and heavy frosts produce picturesque snow scenery in winter (above, right)

Mountain cabins provide inviting stopping-off places in summer (below, left)

The Czech name for the Riesengebirge reserve is Krkonossky National Park (below, right)

High in the Carpathian mountains

The **TATRAS** National Park in Slovakia and Poland provides a final refuge for many wild animals

GETTING THERE:
Good rail and road connections from Zakopane. Airports at Krakow and Poprad

WHERE TO STAY:
Wide choice of all types of accommodation

CLIMATE:
Sunny weather in September and October. In January/February, warm in the uplands, cold in the valleys

MAIN ATTRACTIONS:
Sucha Bela gorge; bird and wildlife watching

SPECIAL TIPS:
Some trails only open from 1 July to 30 October

The High Tatras, which stretch for 16 miles (25km) along the border between Slovakia and Poland, are Europe's smallest mountain range. They do, however, have the distinction of being the highest mountains of the 750 mile (1,200km) long Carpathian chain, with 20 peaks reaching upwards of 8,250ft (2,500m) in height. The highest of these is Gerlachovsky Stit, which rises to a height of 8,710ft (2,655m). This mighty ridge of gray granite, running from west to east, forms the frontier between Slovakia and Poland. Numerous steep, secondary ridges branch out from the main ridge, inset by deeply carved valleys. The views from the summits offer stunning vistas across this untamed and dramatic mountain scenery. This incomparable landscape of mountains, valleys, and basins

— including the romantically wild Sucha Bela gorge, equipped with walkways for the benefit of tourists — is unmistakably the work of Ice Age glaciers. These ice fields also left behind 130 or so tarns. Tarns, or water-filled basins in the hollow of a cirque, can descend to depths of 165ft (50m) or more and are filled with crystal clear water that shimmers dark blue or green in the sunlight.

Dense, silent forests of evergreen pine cover the steep slopes of the Tatras. Up to 5,100ft (1,550m) they consist mainly of spruce and fir, interspersed with a scattering of mountain maple. At higher elevations, these are joined by occasional specimens of stone pine with their characteristic, contorted trunks. The sub-alpine or dwarf-tree zone up to 6,100ft (1,850m) is dominated by

gnarled mountain pines. Above the tree line, the terrain is carpeted with alpine meadows, which burst into a dazzling display of flowers in spring and summer.

Remote mountain landscapes

The forests of the Tatras are like an island refuge, providing a home to various relicts from the Ice Ages, such as ring ouzels and three-toed woodpeckers. Other rare species, such as the lesser spotted eagle, peregrine falcon, hazel hen, capercaillie, and black grouse, have also found an undisturbed refuge here amid these vast mountain forests.

This unique and largely inaccessible mountain landscape likewise represents a safe sanctuary for European pine martens, wild cats, wolves, and lynx. Even brown bears are fairly

common here. Most of the time these shy creatures avoid human settlements and trails, but now and then they have been known to rummage through the garbage cans in the local villages.

The high alpine grasslands, pastures, and barren, rocky terrain are home to the Tatras chamois, emblem of the High Tatras National Park. They are preyed upon by lynx, which regularly emerge from the forests to hunt for their next meal. This type of chamois has remained completely isolated since the last Ice Age and has evolved into a separate species of its own. The Tatras marmot, whose whistle is a familiar sound to mountain hikers, is indigenous to the area.

Paradise for tourists

The steep, rugged rock formations surrounding the summits above the mountain meadows and pastures may at first glance appear deceptively devoid of life. These craggy heights nevertheless provide an important nesting site for golden eagles, wall creepers, and alpine accenters, which remain well hidden and scarcely visible among the rocks. Hugging the

scree slopes and nestled amongst the clefts and cracks of dry limestone veins are a number of different varieties of flora, including mountain avens and glacier carnations, all relics from the Ice Age. Rare plants such as the willow-leaved gentian, Tatras larkspur, turk's cap lily, and edelweiss also manage to survive in this inhospitable rocky terrain.

Otters frequent the banks of rushing mountain streams and the numerous waterfalls, constantly on the look-out for shoals of huch, brown trout, and grayling.

Vysoke Tatry National Park in the north of the Slovakian Republic extends over an area of 285 square miles (740km²) and encompasses the Western Tatras, most of the High Tatras, and the Bela Tatras. Its Polish counterpart, Tatrzanski National Park, constitutes just one-fifth of the overall biosphere reserve covered by the two conservation areas.

The breathtakingly beautiful scenery of these wild and magnificent mountains of the High Tatras attracts a steady stream of visitors from home and abroad all year round. In Slovakia, especially, winter and summer tou-

rism play a key economic role. Long, treeless corridors have been cut out of the mountainsides in many places, providing routes for aerial trams and ski-lifts to transport holidaymakers up to the summits. Well-marked trails channel visitors through the landscape, enabling them to experience this spectacular scenery at close quarters, while leaving as much of the region as possible undisturbed. Some areas, which are considered especially sensitive, are kept off limits.

The peaks of the High Tatras tower high above the surrounding landscape (above, left)

This mountain region is dotted with scores of picturesque tarns (above, right)

The hiking trails are punctuated with mountain chalets such as the one shown here (below, right)

An ancient forest undisturbed for almost 500 years

The National Parks **STRADDLING THE BORDER BETWEEN POLAND** and **WHITE RUSSIA** provide a sanctuary for the European bison.

GETTING THERE:
Poland: by road from
Bialystok to Bialowieski
with access into the
Park. White Russia:
by road from Brest to
Kamenets, from where
it is 12 miles (20km)
to the Park

WHERE TO STAY:
Poland: a few hotels
in Bialystok, but
numerous private
rooms. White Russia:
3 hotels and 4 guest-
houses in Kamenets

CLIMATE:
January: 25° F (-4° C);
July 64° F (18° C).
Rarely more than
50 to 60 days of snow

MAIN ATTRACTIONS:
Hiking trails; carriage
trips; museums;
outdoor enclosures.
Poland: trip by
narrow-gauge railway;
nature trails

SPECIAL TIPS:
Most areas of the Parks
are inaccessible,
except in the company
of a licensed guide,
either on foot or
in a horse-drawn
carriage. On the Polish
side, visitors restricted
to groups of 25. Several
nature trails

The inaccessible
forests of Poland's
Bialowieski National
Park and White
Russia's Belovezhskaya
Pusha are home to
many ancient, giant
trees. The deep forest
harbors some 550
bison, living either
side of the boundary
fence (right and
below)

Access to the shores
of the numerous lakes
is barred by piles
of dead wood (center)

Europe's last truly ancient forest, which has remained virtually undisturbed for hundreds of years, straddles the border between Poland and White Russia not far from Bialowieski in Poland and Kamenets in White Russia. The forest, which is both a world heritage site and a significant biosphere reserve, covers an area of approximately 565 square miles (1,460km²), 225 (580) of which lie in Poland and the remaining 340 (880) in White Russia. Right in the midst of this great forest area are the inaccessible National Parks of Bialowieski in Poland and Belovezhskaya Pusha in White Russia.

This vast forest could easily serve as the setting for ancient legends and fairytales. Not a single tree has been felled or any undergrowth cleared for several decades. Even diseased trees are left in peace and any dead wood remains where it has fallen. For centuries now, the forest has been left to renew itself at its own pace. By 1541, the Russian section had already been declared a hunting reserve in order to protect Europe's largest wild animal, the European bison. Strict regulations were introduced in 1557 to control forest exploitation, although tree felling had never figured significantly as the forest was simply too wet and inaccessible.

From 1598 on, only Polish kings were permitted to hunt here, a privilege shared by Russian tsars and tsarinas in 1795. All this changed during the German occupation in World War I when arrangements were made to start felling the forest. The German occupying force even built a special railway for transporting the logs out of the region. During the occupation, the forest ended up sacrificing six-and-a-half million cubic yards (five million cubic meters) of timber as well as its last herd of bison. After this episode, it was once again left to its own devices.

On the watershed

Despite its seemingly infinite vastness, this ancient forest situated on the watershed between the Baltic and the Black Sea is, in fact, only a remnant of what was once a continental forest zone linking the Russian tundra with the Black Sea steppes and the Baltic with the Mediterranean. This explains why some species, which are more likely to be found in southern Europe, are just as much at home here as northern species. Many of the ancient tree trunks are thick with fungi and lichens, indicating an extremely diverse natural history.

On the White Russian side, biologists have recorded 900 flowering plants, while in Poland 630 have been identified, including 26 tree varieties. Spruce

reach a height of up to 165ft (50m), oak, ash, and lime trees reach 130ft (40m) or more. Many of these trees are over 500 years old with trunks around 6½ft (2m) thick. The varying soil types and moisture levels have produced 20 different types of woodland, covering 90 percent of the area in White Russia. These consist mainly of mixed stands of oak, lime, and hornbeam, of pines and spruces, or of a combination of deciduous trees and pines. There are also two distinct populations of bush vegetation, including the hazels bordering the marshland, as well as 13 different bog and meadow habitats. Many of the plants common to this region are endangered species elsewhere in Europe.

Black storks, cranes, and owls

The forest is surprisingly light and bright, having rather less in the way of

undergrowth than one might imagine. An extremely rich variety of animal life thrives in the unique and unspoiled sanctuary which it provides, allowing virtually every European species its own niche. In addition to the 8,000 or so different species of insect that have been identified in the region, the trees and bushes are home to well over 200 different varieties of birds, 120 of which also breed here. These include large numbers of rare black storks, cranes, and many species of owl.

Elk, red deer, roe deer, wolves, martens, badgers, beavers, and otters rank among the most common of the 55 mammals indigenous to the area, but the most significant species found in these Parks are, without doubt, the two impressive herds of free-roaming European bison. Separated by a six-feet-high, barbed wire fence, a 250-strong

herd of these animals exists on the White Russian side of the border, while another herd of around 300 animals lives in the Polish National Park. These are the last of their kind, and it is thanks to the fact that their forest habitat has remained undisturbed that their numbers have recovered since World War I. These herds come from a pool of just 52 zoo animals, 5 of which were selected in 1929 as the basis for a breeding program to begin the return of these animals to the wild. The first small herd was released in 1952. Poland's last wild bison was slaughtered in 1919, White Russia's in 1921.

The last Tarpan horses

Visitors to this nature reserve are unlikely to see any of these magnificent animals roaming wild, for the simple reason that most areas of the National Parks are inaccessible. In addition, the bison is an extremely shy creature. To make up for this, large enclosures have been created on either side of the border, where visitors can get close to some of these large mammals as well as to wolves and other forest animals. One of the enclosures even houses a herd of Tarpans, a small, tough breed of horse that was once on the point of extinction. As with the bison, however, a breeding program has secured its survival.

The Lithuanian Sahara

The **COURLAND SPIT** belongs partly to Lithuania and partly to Russia. Its changing features are protected by a National Park.

GETTING THERE:
Short ferry crossing
from Klaipeda.
By car or bus from
Kaliningrad. Airport at
Palanga near Klaipeda

WHERE TO STAY:
Wide choice of hotel
accommodation in the
holiday resorts of Nida
and Juodkranté

CLIMATE:
Around 63° F (17° C)
in July, with winter
temperatures rarely
dropping below 12° F
(-6° C). Best time
to visit between May
and September

MAIN ATTRACTIONS:
Nida: Thomas Mann's
house, Museum
of Amber, sculptures
on the Hexenberg
in Juodkranté

SPECIAL TIPS:
The conservation area
can only be visited
with special (informal)
permission

**The lagoon stretches
between the Courland
Spit and the mainland
(above)**

**Some parts of the
sand spit are protected
areas. Wooden houses,
like these pictured
here in Nida, are
typical of the region
(below, left)**

**Even today, these great
dunes are still being
driven eastward by the
wind (below, right)**

The shifting sand dunes buried 14 villages before the people living in the area stopped the relentless forward march of the dunes by planting pines, European beach grass, and thyme - all of which acted as windbreaks against the constant sea winds and stabilized the sand with their roots. This 112-mile (180km) spit of land off the Lithuanian coast was populated by a deciduous forest of oak, lime, elm, and birch before the Knights of the Teutonic Order arrived on the scene during the thirteenth century, felling this ancient forest and sparking the relentless erosion of this sand spit separating the Courland Lagoon from the Baltic Sea.

Westerly gales regularly deposit vast quantities of sand in the lagoon and the sand mountains shrink by around three feet each year. Parnidzio Kopa, or the Great Dune, near Nida, in particular, becomes visibly smaller with each passing year.

The Courland Spit is located half in Russia's Kalingrad territory and half in Lithuania. Most of the Lithuanian side is a fascinating and scenic National Park, measuring altogether 102 square miles (265km²). Around 50 square miles (125km²) comprise the underwater kingdom at the bottom of the Baltic, while 16 square miles (42km²) of Park preserve life in the lagoon.

Shifting dunes and pyramids of sand

The chain of dunes that make up the "Lithuanian Sahara" stretches for just over 4 miles (7km), running in a southerly line from Nida to the Russian frontier. These shifting dunes have created a picturesque landscape of elegant waves, grooves, and steep slopes, with softly undulating contours that end abruptly in a sheer, sharp drop. From the summit of the Great Dune, there are panoramic views from which to appreciate the breathtaking color contrasts between the dazzling white sands, green forests, and shimmering blues and grays of the lagoon. At 170ft (52m), it is one of the highest shifting dunes in Europe.

Around Juodkranté, a few, steep-sided, pyramid-shaped dunes have managed to survive. These are unique formations that once stretched right across the sand spit in several places. From the top of the 130ft (40m) high Schafsberg, outstanding vistas extend across the lagoon, sand spit, and Baltic Sea. A few significant remnants of original forest have also survived in the area, including some impressive 200-year-old oaks and pines. These small, dense pockets of ancient forest are home to ermine and elk, while ospreys nest deep in the interior.

This peninsula was formed around 13,000 years ago, when the last Ice Age glaciers retreated. Deep underwater currents transporting sand from south to north collided with submarine ridges on the sea floor, blocking their flow and causing a build-up of sand. This sand barrier grew in height until it eventually broke the surface of the Baltic Sea around 5,000 years ago. A sand dune developed that drifted steadily from north to south, gradually forming this spit of land that is still moving slowly eastwards.

Over 60 miles (100km) of sandy beach

This eastwards shift continues to this day. Its progress can best be observed from the summit of the Vecekrugas Dune near Pervalka. This elevation, with its pine-clad slopes rising to a height of over 220ft (67m), is the highest in the National Park.

At its widest point, the Courland Spit is only 2.5 miles (4km) wide. Its western shore is lined with over 60 miles (100km) of idyllic and uninterrupted beach bordering on the Baltic, 165ft (50m) wide in places. Hidden in the fine, white sand are precious pieces of amber, petrified lumps of prehistoric resin from long-vanished, prehistoric pine trees. Where the beach meets the foothills of the dunes, the shifting sands are home to some rare species of plants including vetch and sea holly. Numerous sandy paths wind through the shady pine and birch forests that carpet these great dunes, helping to anchor them in place.

The shifting dunes take no notice of frontiers, however, and continue their forward march as far as Morskoje. These vast, primeval, and remote forests on the Russian side of the border are traversed by the original post road to Königsberg. In the region of Rybatschij, it passes near to one of the oldest ornithological centers in the world. Many of the 600,000 birds that pass over the sand spit and lagoon on their spring and autumn migrations are ringed here.

The floodplains of the Volga

The Volga delta is home to a unique, amphibious environment protected by the **ASTRAHAN** Nature Park

GETTING THERE:
To Astrahan: Airport.
By rail from Pawelezer
station in Moscow.
By road from Volgograd
and Elista. Volga ferry
services from the Baltic
and from Moscow
(package trips)

WHERE TO STAY:
Hotel accommodation
in Astrahan; cruise and
club hotels in the river
arms of the delta;
campsite

CLIMATE:
In July up to 113° F
(45° C); in January as
low as -40° F (-40° C)

MAIN ATTRACTIONS:
Ship and boat cruises
and excursions from
and to Astrahan; canoe
trips; bird watching;
fishing

SPECIAL TIPS:
Large areas of the Volga
delta only accessible
by boat

Vast fields of water plants carpet the waters of Astrahan National Park (above)

Surrounded by reed beds, the profusion of waterways in the delta are lined with white and French willows (below)

At the end of a journey of some 2,250 miles (3,600km), the waters of Europe's longest river, the Volga, deposit their mud content in a unique delta landscape of marshy river meadows on the northeastern shores of the Caspian Sea, the world's largest inland lake. The Volga delta measures almost 125 miles (200km) across. The town of Astrahan, which in the eighteenth century was a scattered community straddling 11 islands just off the coast, now lies 56 miles (90km) inland from the Caspian Sea. Extending over 7,300 square miles (19,000km²), an area roughly the size of Slovenia, this intricate network of lakes, ponds, and flowing streams with channels of saltwater, brackish water, and freshwater is dotted with innumerable islands and islets. On the mainland, deserted dry steppes and semi-deserts stretch far into the North Caspian interior.

Life in this amphibious kingdom is not only affected by the extremes of temperature, ranging from -40° F (-40° C) in winter to 113° F (45° C) in summer, but it is also affected by vast fluctuations in water level to which the Volga is subject. In spring, melted ice from the upper reaches of the river inundate many of the lower lying islands and vast tracts of the cattle-breeding areas in the north. At this time of year, water levels rise by an average of 5ft (1.5m), producing a landscape characterized by scores of shallow bays and lakes.

Rare species of willow

During the periods of low water in summer and autumn, new marshes emerge, only to be submerged again during autumn and winter flooding.

Along the coast is an area of 3,100 square miles (8,000km²), generally regarded as one of the world's significant wetland areas. The numerous tributaries in the heart of the conservation area are lined with white and French willows. Tamarisk and red-leaved dewberry bushes thrive in the transition zone where these waterways give way to broad shallows, while the open expanses of still water are carpeted with various types of reeds, water lilies, water chestnuts, and flowering rushes. In the summer months, once the melted ice has drained away and water levels have dropped again, the delta puts on a breathtaking display of lotus flowers. Alt-

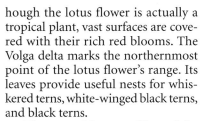

hough the lotus flower is actually a tropical plant, vast surfaces are covered with their rich red blooms. The Volga delta marks the northernmost point of the lotus flower's range. Its leaves provide useful nests for whiskered terns, white-winged black terns, and black terns.

These nutritious mudflats of the Volga delta provide an ideal breeding ground and resting place for millions of water birds. Around 150 species reside here, including cormorants, glossy ibis, gray heron, and spoonbills, as well as ospreys and herring gulls. The balloon-shaped nests of tiny penduline tits dangle precariously from the outermost tree branches while waders converge on the sand and mud banks that are exposed during the summer months. This deserted delta area is one of a handful of sanctuaries remaining for the rare Dalmatian pelican and pygmy cormorant.

European otters, minks, and muskrats

Hoopoes, blue rollers, great gray shrike, and lesser gray shrike are the

most common species populating the vast landscapes north of the delta, while demoiselle cranes rear their young in the dunes and dry steppes.

More than 30 types of mammal roam the islands or hunt for food in the water or along the shores, the most common being raccoons, wild boar, mink, and muskrats. The shy European fish otter and beaver also reside here as well as some of the rarer species include the Saiga antelope and European lynx.

All of these animals are largely dependent on the incredible abundance of fish available in the largest wetland area in Europe. The most common species are catfish, pike, and zander. When the spring floods arrive, many fish lay their eggs in the shallows. Even wild carp can sometimes be found in inundated areas. This is the season when the sturgeon set off from the Caspian Sea, heading for their breeding grounds in the upper reaches of the river. All too often, they fall victim to the nets of poachers wanting to exploit the valuable caviar market.

Man has always exploited the natural riches of this fruitful Volga delta and also helped develop the surrounding 385 square miles (1,000km²) of land into an international biosphere reserve. Along with the traditional pursuits of fishing and birding, reed gathering has also provided an important source of income. The higher-lying islands have always been ideal for grazing cattle and now rice and vegetable-growing have also become important aspects of the economy.

The seals of Lake Baikal

The National Park surrounding the world's largest freshwater lake is a refuge for many rare animals and plants

In eastern Siberia, surrounded by mountain ranges towering over 6,600ft (2,000m) in height, is Lake Baikal, which holds the largest volume of freshwater of any lake in the world. It contains approximately 5,518 cubic miles (23,000km²) of water, or 20 percent of the world's total freshwater reserves. Even to a depth of 130ft (40m), its waters are crystal-clear because they contain only half as many minerals as other lakes. The numerous rivers that tumble down from the steep, barren mountains in the west and east transport very few sediments into the lake.

Covering an area of 12,000 square miles (31,000km²), Lake Baikal is virtually the same size as Belgium, measuring 395 miles (636km) in length, yet only 50 miles (80km) wide. Twenty-five million years ago, the continental plates here began to shift, thereby creating the East Siberian rift system, a series of deep troughs. During the course of time, the 365 mountain rivers and streams filled up this system of troughs, which is drained by a single river, the Angara, in the south. Even now, the east and west shores are still drifting apart at the rate of approximately half to three-quarters of an inch a year, creating space for yet more water.

The lake bed is divided into three deeper basins. The northern basin is geologically younger. The mighty, underwater Akademiker ridge separates it from the two southerly depressions which are, in turn, separated by a barrier of sediment deposited by the Selenga River, the largest tributary to empty into the lake.

Lake Baikal, descending to depths of 5,370ft (1,637m), is the world's deepest and oldest inland lake. Not only is it of enormous geological significance, but it is unusual because it represents a veritable Aladdin's cave for ecologists and evolutionary biologists alike. For this reason, Lake Baikal has been designated a world heritage site.

Even the vegetation covering the slopes on either side of the lake varies considerably. The western side is populated by coniferous forest and mountain steppes, while the eastern slopes are covered with stone pine forests.

The home of the Barguzi sable

Along the northern shore, the western flanks of the Barguzinski mountains are covered with thick larch woods, interspersed with rhododendron thickets. This mountainous region around the 9,320ft (2,841m) summit of Mount Baikal gives way higher up to an alpine belt of lichen vegetation and barren mountain tundra, forming a protected area known as the Barguzinski National Park.

It is a remote and unique environment, in which around 40 types of mammal and more than 240 species of bird — including ospreys and capercaillies — can live virtually undisturbed by man. The forests are inhabited by large numbers of brown bears, wolves, foxes, otters, elk, Siberian roe deer, and white-tailed deer. The renowned Barzugi sable has also become a common sight once more after having been hunted almost to extinction on account of its thick pelt. Luckily, the area was declared a National Park in 1916. Since then, its numbers have recovered well.

Underwater wildlife paradise

The greatest and most surprising diversity of flora and fauna is to be found in the waters of Lake Baikal itself. So far, between 1,500 and 2,500 species of animal have been identified in the lake. Eighty percent of these are endemic, occurring here and nowhere else. The most famous of these are the rare Baikal ringed seals, one of the few species of freshwater seal in the world. It is possible that they made their way to Lake Baikal from the North Sea during the Ice Age along the Jenisej and Angara rivers, or perhaps they swam up the River Lena. Lake Baikal boasts a population of around 3,000 of these wonderfully graceful swimmers, although they are being placed increasingly at risk from environmental pollution and waste water draining into the lake from local timber factories.

One of the most surprising evolutionary processes to have occurred over the course of millions of years involves Lake Baikal's freshwater shrimps, of which there are more than 255 species and sub-species. They have adopted a variety of feeding methods in this unusual habitat. Some of them search for plankton in the open water, others populate the plant life growing in the bays, and yet others have transformed themselves into parasites. Several of them have developed a specialized dependence on the unusual sponge reefs existing in the shallower bays of Lake Baikal. As in the case of coral reefs in the ocean, they also provide a unique ecological niche for a whole host of other creatures specifically adapted to life in such a habitat.

GETTING THERE: International airports at Irkutsk and Ulan Ude, with connecting flights to Moscow three times a week. The Trans-Siberian railway also stops in Irkutsk

WHERE TO STAY: Baikal is a popular tourist destination. Several fairly basic hotels

CLIMATE: -13° F (-25° C) in winter, rising to 64° F (18° C) in summer

MAIN ATTRACTIONS: Ivolginsky Dazan theatre and Buddhist temple in the capital of Ulan-Ude. Hot spa and thermal springs in the Schumak region. Flora and fauna in the Sajan mountains

View over the conservation area on the eastern shore of Lake Baikal with Barguziski National Park (above)

Many rivers, springing from the surrounding hills, empty into the lake (below, left)

These traditional, wooden houses are typical of the region (below, center)

Between the lake and the distant hills lies an expanse of steppe (below, right)

The plains of the Puszta

HORTOBÁGY National Park in Hungary preserves a cultural landscape that has produced a unique set of natural habitats

Hortobágy/Puszta

Budapest •
HUNGARY

Adriatic Sea

Mediterranean
Sea

GETTING THERE:
Highway 33 to
Hortobàgy. Rail links
between Debrecen
and Füzesabony. Visitor
access to the Park by
horse, carriage, cycle,
or by foot.

WHERE TO STAY:
Luxury and middle-range
hotels in Hortobàgy

CLIMATE:
Moderate continental
climate with severe
winter and warm
summers. Windy

MAIN ATTRACTIONS:
Bird-watching; walks
along nature trails;
riding; cycling;
shepherd's museum

SPECIAL TIPS:
Much of the Park
is closed to visitors

Beneath the vast skies of eastern Hungary, the Hortobágy Puszta, or 'plains,' form a table, stretching across an apparently endless expanse of grassland between the Tisza River and the town of Debrecen. Currently 290 square miles (750km²) of this unique cultural landscape are under protection and the region has also been designated an international biosphere reserve. Its marshes and lakes are among the world's most significant wetlands. The Park consists of a mosaic of canals, marshes, moors, fishponds, and forests — an endless expanse of continuous wetland, relieved only by occasional patches of grassy terrain on higher ground and a few stands of woodland.

This fascinating landscape is the product of hundreds of years of agricultural and domestic livestock farming and has given rise to a variety of unique natural habitats. The low-lying areas were once the floodplains of the River Tisza, which punctually burst its banks twice a year. It was thickly forested and its lowest-lying sections consisted of impassable marshland. The Tisza River meandered its way in a series of broad curves right across this area. During the Middle Ages, the forest was cleared and a thriving farming community began to flourish on this fertile soil, which provided a livelihood for the inhabitants of the 50 or so villages that the Puszta once comprised. Remnants of some of the loveliest woodland ever to thrive on these flood plains are still seen near Ároktõ and Tiszacsege. Islands located in the midst of these open waters support mixed woodland consisting of oak, ash, and elm, while poplars and willows grow on the wooded peninsulas.

When the farmers moved away

The farming community left the area during the fifteenth century when the country was under Turkish rule and the grasslands were left as grazing ground for native Nonius horses, Hungarian gray cattle, and the famous Racka sheep with their long, curly horns.

This breed of sheep was much sought after for its meat throughout medieval Europe. The shepherds drove their herds into Western Europe, Poland, and Turkey, in order to sell them.

In 1846, efforts got underway to tame the Tisza River and canalize it. The damp pastures dried out and the land dried up. It was not until irrigation canals were introduced much later that the plains became agriculturally viable again. Nowadays the grasslands are home to grazing animals such as cattle and semi-wild herds of horses, which roam the steppes accompanied by shepherds wearing traditional costume.

Although these animals no longer have a great deal of economic significance, they nevertheless play a major role in preserving this immensely important habitat with its great diversity of rare flora and fauna. They are also key factors in ensuring the genetic continuation of traditional breeds of domestic animal, in preserving Hungary's traditional forms of land use and animal breeding, and in serving, not least, as a tourist attraction. By the end of the Second World War,

this breed of gray cattle had all but vanished. Fortunately, it has been possible to build up the herds again, thanks to modern breeding methods and material from gene pools.

Plans for reclaiming the dried up, saline grasslands had been under consideration since the nineteenth century, but it was not until 1915 that prisoners-of-war began building the first fishponds. Over the years, this collection of ponds has become the largest artificially created system of fishponds in the world, extending over an area of 23 square miles (60km²). They are fed by water from the Tisza River, channeled to them via a network of canals.

Unspoiled landscape

Only 10 of the original 17 fishponds are still in use. The banks of the abandoned ponds, like other areas of open water, have become overgrown with dense reeds and reed mace, while white and yellow water-lilies, floating hearts, and water nuts bloom in profusion across the surface of the water. The surrounding reed-beds are home to bearded reedlings, water rail, and small coots. This relatively untouched steppe and wetland landscape is also one of the main refuges and last retreats for numerous rare birds, including several species of heron such as the gray heron, purple heron, and great white heron. It is home to egrets, cormorants, black storks, and several types of geese and also boasts the lar-

gest colony of rare spoonbills in central Europe, numbering around 250 breeding pairs.

Many relatively uncommon warblers also breed here, including sedge warblers and tamarisk warblers. Hortobàgy is also home to a population of 3,500 great bustards, the biggest of all steppe birds, while staker falcons, imperial eagles, and ospreys circle majestically in the skies above.

One of the most exciting experiences for bird-watchers is witnessing the annual bird migrations in spring and autumn, particularly the spectacular crane migration. Around 95 percent of these magnificent birds, which cross Hungary en route to Finland or the Sudan, break their journey here, feeding on these rich marshlands to build up their strength for the rest of their flight.

The draw-well has become the symbol of the Puszta (above, left)

Horse racing was once one of the major pastimes of Puszta dwellers (above, right)

Large parts of this conservation area are still inaccessible swamps (below)

Water cascades over limestone ridges into the valley below

The **PLITVICE LAKES** in the heart of Croatia were created as the result of an unusual combination of natural circumstances

CROATIA Zagreb
Plitvice
Lakes
Adriatic Sea
Mediterranean
Sea

Crystal-clear water plunges down from one lake into another through a series of foaming waterfalls. Almost hidden in the fine spray, the bare limestone crags separating the cascading water are carpeted with thick, bright green mats of moss, hanging like curtains from the glistening wet rocks. Incorporating the mighty slopes of Licka Pljesevica, Mala Kapela, and Medvedjak mountains, Plitvice National Park in Croatia was established as a conservation area to preserve this fascinating, foaming water landscape with its bizarre cliffs, grottoes, and dense, silent forests.

The 16 crystal-clear Plitvice lakes were formed as the result of the interaction between a number of unusual biological and chemical processes, which even now are continually altering the direction of water flow, reshaping the lakes, and creating new basins and cataracts. The 12 upper lakes in this karst basin are dammed by natural barriers formed by soft calcium carbonate deposits, which continually increase in height. Certain varieties of moss, as well as algae and water bacteria, extract calcium carbonate, or travertine, from the water and encrust it around their roots. By accumulating one layer on top of another, these organisms are gradually raising the height of the limestone barriers, which dam the river upstream and create a constantly changing succession of new cataracts, some of which have now reached 260ft (80m) in height. Travertines, extremely brittle and delicate calcium structures, continue to grow at the rate of approximately one-third of an inch a year. Occasionally, sections of these soft calcium barriers are broken off by the force of the water, which then finds fresh routes down to the nearest lake.

As the mosses get older

Young mosses are green and soft because they have not yet accumulated any travertine. After about a year, however, when they have encrusted the first calcium deposits around their roots, they become darker in color. Older moss is yellowish, completely covered in calcium, withered, and rock hard.

The biochemical relationship between minerals and organisms is extremely sensitive. Above all, the water must be extremely clean and pure. Even the tiniest amount of pollutant or even fertilizer is enough to destroy the delicate balance. Just below the bridge spanning the Korana River at the end of the park, where one can discern the beginnings of new lakes and cascades, the travertine build-up ends abruptly due to the large amount of organic material entering the river at this point. It is partly for this reason that visitors to the Park are asked to follow long wooden walkways around the lakes and waterfalls.

The four lower lakes were created in a completely different way. These were formed where karst caves collapsed. Much of the water in the upper lakes drains away through the porous limestone ground, hollowing out giant subterranean caves en route. Approximately 20 such caves exist near the lower lakes. When their ceilings collapse, the hole quickly fills with water and becomes a lake.

Hidden refuge for bears and wolves

Plitvice Park is constantly changing. Visitors will only get a snapshot impression at any given moment. The scene may look quite different in a several years' time. In just 35 years, for example, the water level in some of the lakes has risen by 20in (0.5m), resulting in some major changes to its outline and the contours of the cascades.

Although this large National Park covers 115 square miles ($300km^2$), only a fraction is comprised of lakes and waterfalls. The dense, dark forests and surrounding karst landscape are also protected since without such extensive forested areas, the wind and weather would quickly erode the Dolomite cliffs. Boulders and gravel would accumulate in the lakes and destroy the fragile travertine cataracts.

Conifers, hornbeam, and forests of mixed beech and fir grow on the Dolomite terrain around the upper lakes and springs. The conifer and beech woods on the limestone ground around the lower lakes are carpeted with bracken, rendered almost impenetrable by the maple and heather undergrowth. Bears and wolves still inhabit this area, although they are rarely seen at a close range. Brown bears are more likely to be found rooting through the garbage cans in the parking lot at the main entrance to the Park.

The water plunges in a series of cascades from lake to lake. To avoid possible contamination, a system of wooden walkways renders the area accessible to visitors (left)

Young mosses seem to act as a water filter. They retain traces of calcium, encrusting this around their roots, and turn themselves into petrified plants (above, right)

There are many drowned trees among the lakes (center, left and below)

143

The underwater kingdom of the Kornati islands

Off the coast of Dalmatia, a submarine National Park preserves the underwater life around the **KORNATI ISLANDS**

GETTING THERE:
Only accessible by boat. Day trips from Vodice, Biograd, and Zadar

WHERE TO STAY:
300 guesthouses on different islands. Camping not permitted

CLIMATE:
Mediterranean climate. The moist, warm, Jugo wind off the sea often bring rain; the Bora wind off the mainland usually brings good weather

MAIN ATTRACTIONS:
The 6th-century Toreta Tower near Tarac; ruins of an Illyrian settlement near Pedinka; Roman fish vivarium on Piskera

SPECIAL TIPS:
Only one food store near Piskali. Provisions available from local fishing boats during the summer

One of the Mediterranean's richest underwater kingdoms is hidden beneath the azure blue waters of the Adriatic Sea off the coast of Croatia. It is home to sea scorpions, gilthead sea bream, great shoals of other Mediterranean fish and dolphins. Lying approximately 9 miles (15km) off the Dalmatian coast within Kornati National Park, it is an area popular with divers.

Extending over 115 square miles (300km^2), this cluster of 140 small, closely-packed islands, shallows, and reefs forms a unique landscape, not found anywhere else along the Mediterranean coast. Eighty-nine of the islands lie within the National Park, named after the main island of Kornat, which covers 12^1/$_2$ square miles (32.5km^2). There are two main groups of deeply fissured, rugged limestone islands strung out over a length of 15^1/$_2$ miles (25km) along the coast. The islands of Pasman, Vrgada, and Murter form the boundary of this 8 mile (13km) wide archipelago on the mainland side, extending as far as Dugi Otok Island in the

northwest and the Zirije Islands in the southeast.

Wave action, tides, and constant sea winds have, over thousands of years, eaten away at what was once a single, continuous plate of soft limestone to create this unique labyrinth of channels and rocks. Wherever you look, steep cliffs rear up out of the sea, such as the sheer, 260ft (80m) high cliff near Klobucar. Local residents call these cliffs "crowns," from which the Kornati Islands presumably derive their name (kruna = corona). Breakers have cut deep furrows and clefts into these rocky islands and, along the coast of Mona, the sea has carved deep rocky overhangs around the base of the island.

Remains of ancient cisterns

These islands have examples of numerous other fascinating geological formations: for instance, the multi-colored geological strata visible on Kornat, with their intricate patterns of concentric circles. The southern end of the main island, measuring 660–990ft (200–300m)

across and over 4 miles (7km) long, also has its hidden treasures, namely a single huge boulder towering 360ft (109m) in height and known as the "Opat."

The Kornati Islands were covered in forest until the Romans started felling trees to use in ship-building, thereby robbing the islands of their green vegetation. The Romans also deepened the shallow straits between the islands of Kornat and Dugi Otok by six feet to allow big ships to pass through. Near Mala Proversa, ruins of ancient rainwater cisterns and a vivarium, in which fish were kept to provide fresh food for sailors, testify to the presence of these early settlers.

During winter, the Kornati Islands are uninhabited. They are owned by a number of families, most of which reside on Murter. The archipelago only comes to life in summer when tourists converge on the 300 or so guest cabins and the owners come to tend the olives groves thriving on some of the islands. The olive groves are interspersed with grasses and bushy

brome-grass and the steep slopes are home to patches of Dubrovnik centaury, a protected species that is only found in the Kornati Islands. Dubrovnik centaury is the original form of the yellow centaury commonly found in garden rockeries.

The islands provide grazing for a few sheep, which favor the ancient patches of meadow surrounded by natural stone walls. The skies are home to herring gulls and birds of prey, circling over these largely barren, dry, and dusty islands.

A world of algae

The most precious of the region's natural treasures lies mainly underwater, as three-quarters of this National Park of 86 square miles (224km²) protects a submarine environment. The water is so clear and still that sunlight filters down to depths of 260ft (80m). The labyrinth of stones, crevices, and caves is home to at least 436 species of maritime plants and algae, including 222 types of red algae alone. Nearer to the shore are mats of algae, consisting of 72 species of brown and 51 species of green algae. This nutritious environment is home to 300 different animal species, including sponges, cave-dwelling creatures, crabs, invertebrates, echinoderms, and other varieties of tunicates.

The vast labyrinth of caves shelters huge numbers of fish as well as octopi waiting for their next meal. Schools of dolphin are often seen out in the open sea. Since fishing is completely prohibited in the area, this National Park area provides a safe habitat for altogether 65 species of fish. The open waters are consequently populated by large numbers of striped barbel, dentex and gilthead sea bream, drumfish, large and small scorpion fish, brown wrasse, and even sea eels. The shallow, sandy bays are a perfect starting-point for snorkeling expeditions to explore this fascinating underwater kingdom.

Settlements like the village of Vrulje are rare in the Kornati Islands. Note the typical stone walls, parceling up the land (above)

Evening across the Bay of Telascica (below)

MONTENEGRO
Durmitor
Podgorica

Adriatic Sea

Mediterranean Sea

GETTING THERE:
Zabljak can be reached from the road running between Sarajevo (Bosnia-Hercegovina) and Podgorica. By road or bus from Mojkovac (railway station). Summer helicopter flights from coastal resorts

WHERE TO STAY:
Zabljak is an up-and-coming holiday resort with several new hotels

CLIMATE:
In July, 68°–84° F (20°–29° C); cooler at higher altitudes. Around 50° F (10° C) in winter, with frost and snow at higher altitudes

MAIN ATTRACTIONS:
Mountain climbing; hiking; white-water rapid trips; skiing. Ddjurdjevica Tara Bridge with views over the Tara gorge; Tmora with views across the valleys and villages; ice caves above Zabljak

SPECIAL TIPS:
The National Park can be explored only on foot

The silent mountains of Montenegro

The **DURMITOR MASSIF** is not only a National Park, but also a biosphere reserve

Traversed by some of Europe's deepest gorges, the sheer, jagged limestone peaks of the mighty Durmitor massif tower in the northeastern corner of Montenegro almost seem to touch the sky. Some of them are pointed pinnacles, while others resemble vaulted domes. Deep grooves have been carved out of the summits of Mount Savin Kuk and Mount Sljeme, while the pin-point summit of Uvita Greda is scored like a screw and that of Obla Glava rounded. The peak of Medvjed appears dramatically white against the green forests and the Crvena Greda shimmers in a variety of different colors depending on the sun's position. A total of 15 majestic mountain peaks dominate the 125 square miles (320km²) of Durmitor National Park. The highest of these is Bobotov Kuk at 8,275ft (2,522m).

Ice Age glaciers have carved deep valleys out of this mountain massif, leaving behind a legacy of 16 breathtakingly beautiful, tranquil glacier lakes dotted throughout this rugged karst mountain range. They gleam like eyes, sparkling amid the depths of the dark forests. Some of them benefit from special protection, while others exhibit some unusual features. For instance, the National Park's largest lake, Crno Jezero, simultaneously feeds two different rivers, the Tara and Komarnica, otherwise known as the Piva River. Water flows out of the lake into the River Tara, while water also simultaneously seeps through cracks in the lake bed, flowing through the Durmitor massif via an underwater drainage system and feeding the Komarnica River.

Mighty, rushing torrents such as the Tara, one of Europe's last wild and untamed rivers, have carved dramatic ravines in the soft rock. At the bottom of Europe's deepest canyon, nearly 4,300ft (1,300m) in depth, the Tara River swirls and surges around giant boulders before crashing into the valley below in a series of breathtaking cascades.

Rivers, lakes, dry karst landscape

This spectacular National Park is a designated world heritage site and part of a large, international bios-

phere reserve, covering an area of nearly 700 square miles (1,800km²). Rivers, lakes, dry karst, and dramatic differences in altitude within a comparatively small area have all contributed to form a wide range of habitats and climates. The Durmitor Mountains are influenced by two climatic zones, namely the Mediterranean and alpine. This unique combination of environmental conditions accounts for the exceptional diversity of species occurring in this spectacular landscape.

Dense, deciduous forests grow throughout the valleys and along the rivers. The high plateaus support alpine heath land dotted with subarctic vegetation, while the wetter areas are covered with marshes. Impenetrable Mediterranean pine forests cling to the steep slopes, while the bare summits of the sub-alpine zone are covered with small beech and dwarf pines. The gently rising scree slopes in the foothills of the mountains are interspersed with numerous untouched alpine mea-

dows, which explode into a stunning array of colorful flowers in summer. Along the fringes of the Tara valley, the last stretches of unspoiled black pine forest grow in soil that would more typically support beech woods.

Eagles in the sky

This diverse, yet silent, mountain kingdom is home to many plants that thrive only here, such as various forms of mullein, gentian, and campanula. A total of 37 different species have so far been identified in the biosphere reserve, of which 6 are exclusive to the National Park. Biologists have recorded more than 1,500 different species of plant within the National Park.

Rainfall and streams wash a large quantity of minerals, along with organic material, leaves, and the remnants of plant material from fields and forests, down from the mountains into the lakes. These materials contain considerable quantities of nutrients and consequently support

a dense population of broad-leaved pond weed, which floats just beneath the water's surface.

Brown bears, gray wolves, wild boar, wild cats, and chamois still roam these forests. These shy creatures are rarely glimpsed by visitors. Various species of eagle circle overhead, soaring on the thermals above the mountains, while black grouse and rock partridge can be heard rustling through the bushes or grassy

undergrowth. More than 130 different bird varieties populate these silent forests or build their nests in the shelter of rocky, inaccessible crags.

From the holiday resort of Zabljak on the Park's northeastern border, this majestic natural landscape, a kind now rarely seen in Europe, can be explored by means of a network of some 1,250 miles (2,000km) of marked trails.

The foothills of the Durmitor massif with its mighty mountain ridges, where farmers graze their sheep, resemble alpine pastures (above)

The mountain forests reveal occasional glimpses of glistening lakes (below, left)

View into a valley near Lake Skutari (below, right)

ROMANIA
Danube delta
Bucharest •
Black
Sea

Islands in the stream

A **UNIQUE NATURAL LANDSCAPE HAS EVOLVED** in the Danube estuary

GETTING THERE:
By rail, bus, or road to Tulcea and from there by minor Route 222 as far as Mahmudia in the direction of Murighiol. Only waterways in the delta region itself.

WHERE TO STAY:
Campsites. Hotels as well as private rooms available in small villages. Houseboats

CLIMATE:
Best time to visit is late spring to autumn. Summer temperatures around 75° F (24° C)

MAIN ATTRACTIONS:
Bird watching; canoe trips; fishing; old church at Leta

After journeying 1,771 miles (2,850km) through nine different countries, the Danube, Europe's second longest river, finally empties into a huge, flat, fan-shaped delta and into the Black Sea. The Danube delta extends across an area of 1,740 square miles (4,500km²) from Tulcea to the coast 50 miles (80km) away in the northeastern corner of Romania on its Ukrainian border. This unique landscape includes 110 square miles (280km²) of National Park and enjoys world heritage status.

The Danube splits into three arms as it approaches Tulcea. To the north, the Chilia Veche arm flows along the border, dividing yet again near Periprava and forming its own small delta. The central arm, known as the Sulina River, which has been partially straightened, flows straight into the sea. It is a main shipping route, carrying passengers and freight upriver to Austria and Germany. To the south, the Sfantu Gheorghe river arm meanders its way 70 miles (112km) to the small town of Sfantu Gheorghe, where it finally discharges into the Black Sea.

The Danube delta constitutes one of Europe's most significant wetlands and presents a landscape that is constantly changing. The result of the inexorable struggle between land and water is a constant succession of new islands, rivers, sandbanks, ponds, and marshes which wash away as soon

they are formed. The contours of the area alter from one year to the next and even from one season to another.

All three arms of the river carry enormous amounts of mud along with them, which they deposit as they approach the delta. Each year, the Danube delta deposits another 80–100ft (24–30m) into the sea. The Chilia arm carries the largest volume, 63 percent, of all the Danube's water of water. The Sulina arm carries around 16 percent. This fan-shaped delta area is peppered with a large number of lakes, some of which are overgrown with reeds or water lilies, not to mention hundreds of canals and inaccessible swamp areas.

Reed beds cover 660 square miles (1,700km²) of delta as far as the eye can see, possibly the largest single area of its kind anywhere in the world.

Explosive reed roots

The root system of these reeds forms the basis for a very unusual type of floating vegetation in the delta, known as plaurs. The decomposing organic material gives off a potent mix of gasses. Occasionally, these explode among the submarine thickets of reed roots, blasting apart large sections of decaying vegetation to the surface to become floating islands. These in turn have become home to a unique ecosystem of plant life, even providing a foothold for trees. Plaurs can remain anchored

to the sea bed or become floating islands that sometimes block the waterways.

The vast reed beds disguise the fact that the delta is actually home to an extremely rich diversity of bog and water plants, including white and yellow water lilies and floating ferns. Various carnivorous plants, such as bladderwort, commonly occur here. The strips of terra firma and sandbanks, or "Grinduris" as they are known, are generally covered in steppe grasses and dotted with patches of woodland.

Lianas and tamarisk

One such woodland area lies near Padura Letea. A unique environment has evolved here, which has been left undisturbed for centuries. The 500-year-old oaks, willows, elms, and lime trees are draped with lianas and interspersed with sub-tropical Mediterranean plants, such as tamarisk and whitethorn.

This vast labyrinth of ponds, rivers, canals, and marshes attracts millions of birds. Some 300 species occupy this amphibious landscape, 176 breed here. These latter include around 2,500 pairs of pygmy cormorants, more than 60 percent of the world's population of this rare bird. Alongside the cormorants are flocks of pink and Dalmatian pelicans, which can be seen flying across the horizon in spectacular formations if not strutting through the shallow waters in search of food.

Herons are likewise attracted to these floating islands and reed beds. Nearly every species of heron has been recorded here: gray, silver, the purple heron, night heron, and little egret to name but a few. Mute swans, graylag geese, teal duck and moorhens paddle contentedly over the open water and between 30 to 40 ospreys circle majestically in the skies above.

Ancient Greek settlement and small museum on Lake Sinoe near Cetatea Istria; boat trips from Tulcea along the Sulina or Sfantu Gheorghe river channels; short boat trips from Mahmudia

Reed fences help protect the villages in the Danube delta from flooding (above)

Local fishermen still use traditional fishing methods, such as the fish traps shown here (below, left)

Floating island or solid ground? Willows under water (below, right)

BULGARIA
Sofia
Pirin   Black
Sea

Mediterranean Sea

Majestic fir trees

PIRIN NATIONAL PARK in southern Bulgaria is the last refuge for many European animals

GETTING THERE:
Trains from Sofia to
Septemvri; from there
by narrow-gauge
railway to Bansko. By
car along Route E 73

WHERE TO STAY:
Small hotels; hunting
cabins; private accom-
modation in villages
around the Park

CLIMATE:
Long, cold winters
in higher regions, with
snow for five to eight
months of the year

MAIN ATTRACTIONS:
Vihren cabin and climb
to the summit

Bulgaria is home to southeast Europe's highest mountain chains,
stretching virtually untouched right
across the country. Situated just 75
miles (1.20km) south of Bulgaria's
busy capital city, Sofia, is one of the
country's most impressive ranges: the
Pirin massif. It is the second highest
in the land, characterized by majestic,
jagged peaks and sheer rock walls.
Numerous sparkling lakes hollowed
out by glaciers nestle in deep valleys.
Silver ribbons of surging rivers wind
their way through the valleys, fed even
during the summer months by water
melting from snow on the summits.
They plummet from valley to valley
in a succession of countless, breathtakingly beautiful cascades.

Pirin is part of Bulgaria's southern
chain of mountains, incorporating
both the Rodopi and Rila ranges.
Forty-five of Pirin's peaks exceed
8,500ft (2,600m), most of them resembling three-sided pyramids or multi-
sided structures with sharp, jagged
edges. They are remnants of a 25-mil-
lion-year old plateau that disintegrated when the mountains were forced
upward into folds approximately 10
million years ago. Vihren, at 9,565ft
(2,915m), is the highest and the
second highest peak in Bulgaria. Its
northern aspect consists of an almost
sheer 1,500ft (450m) rock face, which
can be seen for miles around.
Pirin People's Park, as Bulgaria's
National Park is commonly known,

protects the high-lying regions between the Strouma and Mesta rivers. It
covers an area of around 155 square
miles (400km²) and is a designated
world heritage site.

Karst limestone regions

Although the mountains mostly
consist of granite and slate, a remarkable karst limestone area also exists
between the twin peaks of Vihren
and Kaminitza as well as in the central sections of the Park, abounding
in karst caves and overhangs. Near to
the summit, there are several patches
of areas of snow that have never tha-
wed completely, even in summer.
These are the early stages of new glaciers, which are form slowly over the

years as the snow partially thaws, refreezes, then acquires a fresh, additional layer. As yet, these incipient glaciers measure only a few thousand square yards in area and are just a few yards thick.

Thanks to its remote location, the Pirin mountain massif is an ideal refuge for rare plants and animals. Whereas dense, mixed, broad-leaved and coniferous woodland extends around the base of the mountains, the precipitous slopes are covered with dark fir forests and interspersed with an occasional granite or dazzling white, limestone cliff. Along the tree line is a broad band of mighty, windswept Bosnian pines. These trees grow nowhere else on earth. The Baiouvi-Doupki-Djindjiritsa Reserve is home to stands of 250 to 300-year-old trees that have been placed under special protection. These include what is probably Pirin's oldest tree specimen, the 1,200-year-old Baikousheva's Mura, a particularly impressive white fir.

The tree line here starts at just 6,600ft (2,000m), as a result of tree-felling in the past. Only in a few places does it extend any higher to around 7,200–7,600ft (2,200–2,300m). Above the tree line are glorious alpine meadows, full of different varieties of plants nestling between rocky cliffs, scree, and bare rock. A profusion of flowers, a combination of alpine, Balkan, and Mediterranean varieties, transform the bare, grass-covered terrain into a dazzling sea of color, particularly in summer. Peonies, alpine azaleas, yellow globeflowers, spring gentian, forget-me-nots, poppies, and crocus form a strikingly beautiful, floral carpet that is unequalled in its diversity anywhere in Bulgaria.

Well marked trails

Glowing, red Pirin poppies peep from among the rocks, while delicate edelweiss flowers are occasionally glimpsed among the scree. Around 70 of the plants found here are unique to Bulgaria. Many of these are glacier varieties, survivors of geologically ancient times provided with a last refuge by these mountains.

The Park is also home to many species of animal, particularly invertebrates, which are endemic to this region. The dark forests surrounding the lower lakes have, since prehistoric times, been the haunt of numerous wolves, brown bears, and lynx, magnificent creatures pushed to the brink of extinction elsewhere in Europe. Eagles, falcons, and kites circle overhead, while quail, partridge, and pheasant can be heard rustling through the undergrowth.

Despite the remoteness of this mountain location and the dearth of visitors that make their way to the magnificent and matchless landscape, there are nevertheless many well-marked paths and cross-country ski trails, most of which are not at all difficult and lead to several idyllically situated hostels offering overnight accommodation. At 6,400ft (1,950m), the Vihren cabin is only a two or three day hike from the summit, but is also accessible by car.

Well-run mountain hostels, such as this one on the slopes of Mount Vihren, help make the National Park accessible to visitors (above, right)

Tree trunks are used to bridge the many mountain streams (above, left)

The cliffs of Cinque Terre

The rocky coastal cliffs of Liguria have retained their own natural rhythm of life despite the many summer visitors

GETTING THERE:
The regional railway from Montorosso passes through all five villages. Verona-La Spezia-Genoa Highway

WHERE TO STAY:
Cinque Terre is a very popular tourist resort with a wide choice of accommodation

CLIMATE:
Mediterranean climate: June/July 86° F (30° C); November/December rarely drops below 50° F (10° C)

MAIN ATTRACTIONS:
The five coastal villages; coastal footpath; Roman port of Porto Venere at the mouth of the Gulf of La Spezia; San Pietro church on the Arpaia heights; trips to the islands

SPECIAL TIPS:
Car access not impossible, but inadvisable in view of the extremely narrow, steeply twisting streets. Very few parking facilities. Better to use electric buses

A 10 mile (15km) stretch of coastline runs between Punta Mesco in the north and Cala di Montenegro in the south, encompassing an area of around 15 square miles (39km²) along Italy's Ligurian coast. Cinque Terre, a designated world heritage site, offers a unique coastal landscape, which man has been trying to shape for centuries. Cinque Terre takes its name from the five villages of Montorosso al Mar, Vernazza, Corniglia, Manarola, and Riomaggiore.

This breathtaking mountainous scenery of multi-colored sandstone was formed over 25 million years ago during the Tertiary period. Wind and rain have gouged deep valleys, sheer cliffs, and scores of little bays and promontories out of the soft rock. The area is unsuitable for major roads or settlements as the slopes are much too precipitous. The houses in these five villages are huddled tightly together, clinging to the sheer rocks, or perched on the crest of mountain summits. Over the centuries, farming families have turned the mountainsides into a spectacular succession of tiered terraces, some of which are no more than a yard wide. The soil needed to grow olive trees and cultivate vineyards had to be brought in from far away. To create each square yard/meter of cultivatable land, approximately one cubic yard/meter of sandstone was required to build a one-yard/meter length of dry stone wall, 20in (50cm) wide and often over 6½ft (2m) high.

Wines worthy of princely palates

At 330–495ft (100–150m) above sea level, the terraces become so narrow that laboring among the vines is a grueling task. It is these higher altitudes, however, that produce the best grapes, which are used in the production of the internationally renowned and highly desirable Sciacchetra wine. Even back in the Middle Ages, the wines of Corniglia and Vernazza enjoyed an outstanding reputation. Not only were they greatly prized in Rome itself, but by the late Middle Ages were also being supplied to the princely courts of France and England.

For hundreds of years, these five villages could only be reached from the sea or by narrow paths twisting steeply up the cliff face. When the railway reached Cinque Terre in the late nineteenth century, many impoverished farm workers seized the oppor-

tunity to abandon the area and move to La Spezia. More and more land was left uncultivated and the dry stone walls, built with so much effort, disintegrated, causing whole terraces to fall away. Mediterranean vegetation was quick to reclaim the abandoned terraces. Maritime pines and chestnut oaks quickly gained a foothold and the soil filling these sandstone terraces, brought in at such great pains to increase the cultivatable area, became overgrown with arbutus, tree heathers, and broom.

Meanwhile, the unique character of this coastline has been recognized and efforts are underway to preserve it. Crumbling terraces are being rebuilt and, thanks to the incentive of state support, many farmers are returning to traditional wine-growing methods in the region.

Wildlife has never stood much of a chance in this terrain. Only wild boars trample paths through the

dense woodland that has taken over the higher ground in these sandstone mountains. Hikers frequently mistake these wild boar paths for proper trails, following them until they end up well and truly lost.

One footpath, leading along the coast from Montorosso al Mar to Riomaggiore, offers breathtaking and magnificent views across the terraces, villages and far out to sea. Parts of the trail have been carved precariously out of the rock face while the cliffs fall away in a sheer drop to the sea.

Three offshore islands

Just opposite Porto Venere to the southeast are the three picturesque islands of Palmaria, Tino, and Tinetto. Palmaria is the closest to the mainland. Rising to a height of 610ft (186m), it is a popular destination for locals and tourists alike. Tino is a military base and only open to visitors on 13 September, the Festival of

the Holy Venerio. The body of this saint is said to have lain on the spot where the ruins of San Venerio monastery now stand. Tinetto is only 120 square yards (100m²) in size, but nevertheless once boasted a double-naved church and monastery. The ruins of the church, the oratory, and the monks' cells are well preserved.

The sea off Cinque Terre is a marine conservation area. The submarine cliffs, rocks, and innumerable shallows provide an ideal habitat for a rich diversity of sea creatures, including brightly colored sea fans (Gorgonia flabellum), which flourish in numerous shades of yellow, red, deep burgundy, orange, and pink. There are also clumps of dazzling white funicella verrucosa, a species of sea fan, which has become increasingly rare in the Mediterranean region. Even in the shallows, there are impressive coral formations, including the extremely rare black coral.

Magical colors: The village of Vernazza perches on a rocky promontory surrounded by water (above)

Halfway up the cliff, a path leads from one village to the next (below, left)

Montorosso is the Italian name for these rocks lying just off the coast (below, right)

The fertile valleys of the Monti Lattari mountains

The Amalfi coast with its picturesque hillside villages and the **COSTIERA AMALFITANA** boasts some of Italy's most spectacular natural scenery

GETTING THERE:
Airport at Capodichino/ Naples. Good road links

WHERE TO STAY:
Well-developed tourist resort

CLIMATE:
Mediterranean

MAIN ATTRACTIONS:
Pompeii; Herculaneum; Duomo di Sant'Andrea in Amalfi; numerous churches and cultural monuments

SPECIAL TIPS:
Photography is not permitted in some churches and museums

The Costiera Amalfitana is probably the most scenic coastal road in all of Italy. The gentle, green hills of the Monti Lattari, literally "Milk Mountains," extend between the Sorrento peninsula and the coast of Amalfi further south. These mountain slopes run down to a wildly romantic stretch of coastline, dotted with small holiday resorts, many of which appear to be clinging to the steep rock faces in a series of terraces. The villages are surrounded by extensive olive plantations and vineyards, their rich harvest of fruit shimmering with a silver sheen in the autumn sunlight. All this visual beauty is heightened by the all-pervading perfume of citrus trees, for which the Amalfi coast is so famous.

Dense chestnut forests still grow in many areas along the coast, interspersed with cypress, cedars, and dense thickets of almost impenetrable Macchia scrub. These are all that is left of a forest that once covered large areas of the peninsula. Over the past few centuries, much of it has been felled to make room for the cultivation of citrus fruits, nuts, and vineyards. The high plateau up in the hinterland is now used mainly as grazing land. In many places along the coast, indigenous shore vegetation has been forced to give way to major new building projects. Even so, a few native plants can still be found here, including rock samphire and a species of bird's foot trefoil.

World heritage site

As in many parts of Italy, wild animals suffer greatly from hunting. Birds especially, particularly the huge numbers of migrants, tend to be the main victims. Larger mammals are no longer found in the region, although occasionally lone birds of prey, including buzzards or falcons, may be seen riding the thermals above these steep cliffs. The rocks, which heat up during the day and give off their store of warmth at night, provide a perfect habitat for lizards and snakes, harmless as well as poisonous. Scorpions also lurk under some of the stones.

The Amalfi landscape has been affected by man and it is for this reason that the peninsula has been awarded world heritage status. It is situated within a region of major geological activity, most powerfully illustrated by the presence of Mount Vesuvius, which rises to a height of 4,190ft (1,277m) north of the Amalfi coast.

This is one of the world's most thoroughly researched volcanoes and Europe's most active continental volcano. Like Mount Stromboli, it is a stratovolcano, built up of sheets of lava and ash with just one central chimney.

Here, along the western coast of Italy, the lower parts of the South Apennine chain are below sea level. A grid-like network of active volcanic rents in the earth's crust have determined the coastal landform, from which the Sorrento peninsula rises in the form of a mountain ridge extending out to the Isle of Capri.

Volcanic rumblings

Deep within the earth, there are still unmistakable rumblings of volcanic activity along a fault line running through the Bay of Naples. The town of Pompeii at the foot of Vesuvius became tragically famous after being buried in ash and destroyed during an eruption on 24 August, AD 79. The excavations at "Pompeii Scavi" offer the visitor a remarkable, though uncomfortably real, glimpse of Roman life at the time of the eruption.

The ancient volcanic rock, now covering the original rocks that once rose from the sea bed, forms the bedrock for the chain of famous coastal towns which have sprung up all along the Amalfi coast: Positano, Praiano, Furore, Amalfi, Ravello, Minori, Maiori, and Cetara.

The small Italian town of Amalfi on the Gulf of Salerno was originally built in AD 320 by soldiers of the Roman Emperor Constantinus after they were transferred here from Melphe on the Adriatic coast. During the tenth century, the town became one of the most powerful maritime republics in Italy, rivaling Genoa, Pisa, and Venice as a naval power in trade with the Orient. Amalfi's maritime code, the so-called "Tavola Amalfitana," or "Table of Amalfi," regulated shipping throughout the entire Mediterranean region and was still recognized until well into the sixteenth century.

The full beauty of the Amalfi coast, however, is perhaps best appreciated by getting acquainted with the hidden charms of the Amalfitana. To do so, the visitor is advised to follow the tracks of travelers from centuries past and explore the region on foot along winding mule paths and up and down rocky steps, bordered with fragrant citrus trees and yellow broom. Such paths lead you away from the busy coastal highway, enticing you into peaceful valleys and past precipitous rock formations. The most famous hiking trail along the Amalfi coast is called the "Sentiero degli Dei," or "path of the gods." This two-hour walk starts at an altitude of 1,640ft (500m) from the village of Agerola Bomerano and passes through remote and magnificent coastal scenery high above the sea.

Amalfitana became famous in the nineteenth century as a rather exclusive tourist resort. It is reached along the Costiera Amalfitana coastal highway, which hugs the coastline high above the sea (left and below, right)

Wolves of the south

ABRUZZO NATIONAL PARK is a sanctuary for a growing population of brown bears and Apennine wolves

ITALY
Rome • Abruzzo
Mediterranean Sea

GETTING THERE:
Not far from the highway between Rome/Naples and Bari. Bus services from Rome, Naples, and Avezzano to Pescasseroli. Railway station in Avezzano

WHERE TO STAY:
Abruzzo National Park is a popular tourist center. There is a wide choice of accommodation in the small mountain villages

CLIMATE:
Mediterranean climate; cool at higher altitudes with snow in winter

MAIN ATTRACTIONS:
Hiking; European black pine forest; Mancino Castle and viewpoint overlooking Pescasseroli from Trail BN1; Lake Vivo; Barrea

When Abruzzo National Park was established in southern Italy, it represented the last hope for Italy's brown bears, the Abruzzo chamois, and the Apennine wolf. Brown bears once roamed all over the Central Apennines, from the Alps to Abruzzo. New settlements and forest clearance to make way for fields in central Italy meant that the bears' natural habitat dwindled proportionately. By 1500, they had already become restricted to the North Italian Alps and the Abruzzo region of southern Italy.

Four hundred years later, the two populations had shrunk to fewer than 100 animals and were on the verge of extinction. Most of the surviving bears in the Abruzzo occupied an area of just two square miles (five square kilometers) within the royal hunting grounds, where they remained safe from persecution by local farmers and shepherds. In 1923, when the National Park was created, this small area formed the heart of what is now a national reserve covering 170 square miles (440km²) between Salerno and Barletta in central Italy.

The Park preserves a rugged, harsh mountain landscape, with summits rising on either side of the Sangro River valley to heights of 6,600ft (2,000m) and more. It is separated by narrow ravines and broad valleys and dotted with a handful of picturesque villages.

Black pine forests

Two-thirds of this breathtakingly beautiful mountain region is covered with deep, dense forest, consisting mainly of beech, interspersed with plane trees, maples, and a species of sorbus or mountain ash trees. Silent forests of solid beech line the Cervara Valley, while Villetta Barrea, another lateral valley, is home to a wonderful, dark forest of European black pine, a habitat now very much a rarity in Europe. Above 6,300ft (1,900m), the only trees that grow are mountain firs and, above the tree line, bushes and shrubs struggle to survive on the bare, inhospitable scree and rocky ground.

This terrain nevertheless supports well over 200 different plant varieties, which have remained largely unaffected by the traditional farming that in and around the five villages in the Park. On the contrary: it is the farmers sending their goats and sheep into the upper pastures to graze during the summer and wintering them in the valleys each year that has resulted in the stunning variety of flowers that bloom each spring and summer to carpet the meadows with a dazzling display of color. Some of the flora species are now quite rare: for example, the lady's slipper orchid, a striking species that only blooms properly once every two years or so.

Shy brown bears

It was some time before farmers and shepherds could bring themselves to accept the brown bears as fellow inhabitants of the region. After all, these awesome predators, weighing some 440lb (200kg), would occasionally make off with one of their goats or sheep. The situation was eased to some extent by the National Park authorities offering compensation payments in the event of any losses incurred as a result of wild animal damage. Hikers are unlikely to catch a glimpse of this shy creature, but will frequently come across rocks that have been rolled aside, a sure indication of a bear having passed that way in its search for worms and insects

Not only has this unique National Park provided a sanctuary for 100 or so Abruzzo bears, it also represents a refuge for the Apennine wolves, which teetered on the brink of extinction a few decades ago. Their numbers have since swelled to such an extent in this forested mountain region that they are now found right across the Apennines as far as the Southern Alps.

The Abruzzo chamois once faced a fate similar to that of the bears. Though related to the Alpine species, the Abruzzo chamois is an individual species in its own right. The National Park is home to the sole surviving herd, now numbering over 1,000 animals. Hikers occasionally catch a glimpse of these magnificent creatures, with distinctive black and white markings on their throats and spectacular horns, standing on scree slopes either in splendid solitude or in groups of several animals.

In order to restore the fauna to its former glory, roe and red deer were introduced and now roam the forests throughout the mountainous parts of the National Park. Even a few otters, once hunted for their pelts so relentlessly that they all but disappeared, frolic and swim once more in some of the Park's remoter streams and lakes.

Panoramic view of the Sangro river valley that bisects the National Park (above)

Lago Montagne Spaccata on the fringes of the Park is a popular attraction for visitors (below, left)

The village of Anversa degli Abruzzi, 6 miles (10km) to the north of the Park, is regarded as the gateway to this nature reserve (below, center)

The harsh winter climate and strong winds have left many trees misshapen (below, right)

In the shelter of the dunes

The shifting dunes of **DOÑANA NATIONAL PARK** in southern Spain are a paradise for bird life

Where the Guadalquivir flows into the sea, numerous freshwater lagoons provide an ideal habitat for several rare bird species (above, right)

In the hinterland, pine forests give way to a steppe-like landscape (above, left)

A rare sight among the large numbers of birds is the peacock, seen here displaying its plumage (below, right)

On the rare days when the wind is still and the sea becalmed, light bounces off the Atlantic like the reflection off a mirror, illuminating the gently undulating white dunes along the coast in its dazzling glare. Along this stretch of coastline, known as "Costa de la Luz" because of this intense luminosity, lies Spain's Doñana National Park.

This Park, situated at the mouth of the Rio Guadalquivir, was established to protect Europe's largest complex of shifting dunes and is exceptional in that the landscape combines such a variety of different ecosystems, ranging from dunes, lagoons, and cork oak forests to marshland. This nature reserve with a core zone of around 190 square miles (500km²) is also an international biosphere reserve and, as one of Europe's largest and most significant wetland areas, has been awarded world heritage site status.

Just beyond the last houses of Matalascañas, a handful of wooden posts mark the boundaries of the National Park. To the west of this seaside resort, there are over 20 miles (35km) of unspoiled sandy beaches, strewn with shells. The gathering of shells, or "coquinas," for use in traditional handicrafts is one of the few human activities permitted within the heart of the Park. The tough young men of the area fish the coquinas out of the cold Atlantic Ocean, while the older men sort the catch according to size and variety. The quantity of the catch is restricted. Each "coquinero" is only permitted to take a maximum of 18lb (8kg) of shells home per day.

Along the freshwater lagoons

A belt of dunes, about half a mile wide and reaching 100ft (30m) high in places, stretches along the beach. The Atlantic winds drive the grains of sand relentlessly before them, pushing these "dunas móviles," or shifting dunes, away from the shore at the rate of 6–15ft (2–5m) a year. The seaward side of the dunes is swept bare and plants find it virtually impossible to gain a foothold. On the landward side, however, hollows supporting plant growth gradually fill with sand, causing any trees and vegetation there to die off. The dead vegetation eventually decomposes to provide the organic material needed to support the next generation of trees, which will spring up here in 50 to 100 years' time once the dune has passed over the area.

Wooden walkways lead across dry, sandy heath land and stable dunes to the pine forests and freshwater lagoons of the hinterland. Here are several thatched hides, from which the abundant bird life can be observed all year round, an absolute paradise for the large numbers of visiting birdwatchers. Doñana Park boasts no less than 365 different species of birds. Traveling further inland, the pine forests give way to dense, shrubby vegetation including cistus and juniper, known as Vera. This Medi-

terranean steppe region is home to several rare birds of prey, such as the booted eagle, Imperial eagle, and snake buzzard. It is also a last refuge for the endangered Iberian lynx. Adjoining this shrubby landscape are groves of cork oak, behind which are the wet marshlands of the Marismas. These extend about 135 square miles (350km²) to the natural boundary of the Rio Guadalquivir.

Storks in trees

During the winter months, the marshes are ankle or even knee-deep in water, a veritable paradise for millions of water birds including the purple gallinule, which is seldom seen elsewhere. More than 150 species of birds observed in and around Doñana National Park breed in these marshes, some of the most spectacular being perhaps the dense colonies of nesting herons.

In addition to the resident birds, around 150 migrants also break their journey here en route to

and from Africa. December and January witness the arrival of more than 600,000 birds eager to feast on the rich pickings of the Marismas wetlands. For some species, like the wild geese, this area is the most important wintering site in Europe. Storks also nest here. The skies above the aptly named "stork hill" on the eastern edge of the National Park are filled with dozens of circling storks. The marshes dry out in springtime, leaving only barren, dry vegetation in their wake and the trees are densely packed with breeding pairs. Only the Lucios, the small ponds, still retain a little brackish water at the end of a hot summer.

The abundance of wild life in Doñana and its largely unspoiled condition is thanks to Spain's King Alfonso who declared this deserted, thickly forested region a royal hunting ground in 1262. The region was named after a Castilian duchess, Doña Ana, who had built an isolated palace here.

In the lee of the mild Atlantic trade winds

The cool, moist climate on the Canary Island of Gomera has produced extensive evergreen laurel forests

On a raft made from inflated goatskins, Jonay sailed across the 22 mile (35km) channel every day to meet in secret with Princess Gara, whose parents strongly opposed any marriage between their daughter and this peasant boy. He crossed the channel between Tenerife and La Gomera, the home of his beloved, until the lovers were discovered by villagers, whereupon they fled to the highest point on the island and speared each other with lances made of laurel wood.

It is from this legend that Mount Garajonay derives its name. On a clear day, its 4,880ft (1,487m) high summit provides magnificent panoramic vistas across the glittering blue Atlantic Ocean and the other Canary Islands of El Hierro, La Palma, Tenerife, and Gran Canaria. The densely forested heights of the rest of the island unfold beneath it. The wooded vegetation occupying the drier southwestern and southeastern flanks consists mainly of sweet-willow and tree heather or brier, which can grow to over 50ft (15m) in height. Because of its high silicic acid content, the roots of a briar tree will not burn. Brier wood is therefore frequently used to make pipes.

The northern and northeastern mountain slopes are covered by laurel forest whose trees bear large, robust, shiny, dark green leaves, just like those used in ancient times to make the victor's crown.

Jungle of ferns

The National Park was established in 1981 and is now a designated world heritage site. Almost three-quarters of its area of 15 square miles (40km²) are covered with laurel forest.

Walking through this evergreen forest on a hot day is a delightful experience. The air is moist and pleasantly cool. Even at the height of summer, the leaves are constantly dripping with moisture. There are no streams or waterfalls bubbling beside the trails, but every now and then the forest opens up into a clearing, where enough light penetrates to allow various rare flowers to grow, such as Tabaiba spurge with its profusion of yellow flowers, or the white rockrose and orange bellflower. In other places, the forest floor is covered with tall ferns which form an impenetrable jungle. Surrounded by 65ft (20m) high tree trunks, thickly covered with moss and festooned with long strands of old man's beard dangling from gnarled branches, it is easy to imagine oneself in the middle of an enchanted forest. All the more so when dense veils of mist swirl between the trees, assuming mysterious, gnome or elf-like shapes.

When the clouds build up

This lush, green vegetation in an otherwise a dry region is entirely due to the northeast trade winds. These Atlantic trade winds bring a constant supply of rainfall to the northern and northeastern slopes of La Gomera. As the rain-bearing clouds collide with these slopes, they deposit their moisture in the form of drizzle or wet mists. This natural phenomenon is crucial for the island's water supply since most of its drinking water is acquired in this way.

Of the 450 species of plants on La Gomera, several are indigenous, including various tree species such as Canary Mahogany, Canary Ebony, and the Tilo tree. Similarly, several species of fauna are also exclusive to this island. During the Tertiary period, laurel forests were widespread throughout large areas of North Africa and Southeast Europe. The climatic changes induced by the Ice Age, followed much later by man's influence in the form of forest clearance, have almost completely eliminated them. The rainforest in Garajonay National Park represents one of the greatest surviving remnants of continuous laurel forest in the world — a living fossil.

The rocks beneath this primeval forest also date back to the Tertiary period. Five to 15 millions years ago, volcanic eruptions spewed basalt and ash to the earth's surface, which was deposited in horizontal layers. Later, streams of hot lava burned their way through these basalt strata and ash fields. On the fringes of the gently sloping central heights of La Gomera gray, heavily eroded volcanic dikes and domes known as "roques," rear up from the ground. Nearby, the terrain drops steeply away into a series of deep ravines or "barrancos," deep cuts that run from the coast to the very heart of the island.

GETTING THERE:
To Reina Sofia Tenerife Sur airport on Tenerife or by ferry from Cadiz to Tenerife. From Tenerife, take a high-speed ferry to La Gomera. The Park can be reached along a mountain road

WHERE TO STAY:
Holiday Island has a wide choice of accommodation. Package tours

CLIMATE:
Mediterranean climate with no extreme temperature fluctuations. Fair amount of rain in winter

MAIN ATTRACTIONS:
Hikes; guided tours; Garajonay summit

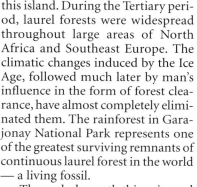

Farmers have cultivated terraced steps on the slopes of Fortaleza Table Mountain on Gomera (left)

View from Gomera across to Tenerife (center, above)

Gran Rey Valley is one of the island's loveliest valleys (below, center)

The root systems of Gomera's mighty eucalyptus trees are an impressive sight (right)

The laurel forests of Madeira

The **LAURISILVA** covering the island's northern slopes is protected within a National Park

ATLANTIC

PORTUGAL
●Lisbon

● Laurisilva
laurel forest

GETTING THERE:
International airport
at Funchal. Package
holiday destination.
The laurisilva forests
can only be accessed
on foot

WHERE TO STAY:
Madeira is a popular
holiday island
with a wide choice
of accommodation

CLIMATE:
Average January
temperature 61° F (16° C),
rising to 70° F (21° C)
in July. Warmer in the
south, with frequent
rainfall

MAIN ATTRACTIONS:
Walks through the
laurisilva forests
and along the
"levadas," or canals;
botanical garden;
Funchal Ecological
Park; Ribeiro Frio and
Queimadas forest parks

SPECIAL TIPS:
Some sections
of the Park are
closed to visitors

Rearing up out of the Atlantic some 370 miles (600km) off the coast of Morocco is the volcanic island of Madeira and its three satellite islands. Like the Canary Islands, Cape Verde Islands, and the Azores, Madeira is part of the Macaronesian island group. These islands still support what is left of a habitat that evolved between 20 and 2 million years ago, long before the great Ice Ages of the Tertiary period.

In the days when the earth's climate was warmer and wetter than it is now, vast forests of laurel, or laurisilva, blanketed large tracts of southern Europe and north Africa. When the last Ice Age laid its cold mantle over the continents, most of this type of woodland was killed off. The Macaronesian islands with their own distinct Atlantic climate are the only place that these laurel forests have managed to survive until the present day. While the smaller, neighboring islands support nothing more than a few sparse remnants of this unique type of forest, Madeira itself is still generously populated by laurisilva. The northern slopes of all its ancient volcanic mountains, the entire northern half of the island, its deep valleys, and inaccessible gorges are all still covered with dense laurel forests. Ninety percent of the area is thought to be original forest, untouched by human influence.

On Madeira, the laurisilva forms a lush green belt of vegetation around the mountain slopes between altitudes of 990–4,290ft (300–1,300m). The areas are similar to tropical rain forest areas because the northeast trade winds are constantly driving moist sea air onto the islands, hitting the north-facing slopes and forming rain clouds over the course of the day.

Water, water everywhere

Inevitably, the discovery of this densely wooded island in 1419 by João Gonçalves Zarco Madeira, a Portuguese navigator, soon led to vast numbers of hardwood trees being felled to provide timber for the ship-building industry. On top of this, large tracts of forest were burned in order to make room for sugarcane plantations.

Despite these depredations, around 80 square miles (200km²) of irreplaceable forest has managed to survive. A nature reserve and designated world heritage site now protects 60 square miles (150km²) of this unique forest, an area equivalent to 16 percent of the island.

Wherever you are in the laurisilva, there is water: running, gurgling, and flowing down into the valleys from the mountain uplands, or tumbling over scores of spectacular waterfalls. The laurisilva forests also have a key role to play with regard to the island's water supply. On the one hand, they preserve the humus layer, thereby ensuring the ground's capacity to filter and store water. Furthermore, the forest prevents the topsoil from being washed away. Without the stabilizing force of the forest, rainwater would flow straight down the resulting bare mountainsides and drain straight into the sea.

Early settlers on Madeira devised and built an extremely clever system of canals along the mountain slopes, catching the valuable water deposited in the northern part of the island and channeling it down into the fields in the south. Footpaths run alongside these so-called "levadas," enabling present-day visitors to experience Madeira's remarkable scenery first hand and to penetrate deep into the rainforest itself.

The dense, leafy canopy on these wet, northern slopes is most commonly populated by the Azores laurel, tilo tree, and Canary mahogany. Some of these specimens are 500-year-old giants and their trunks are frequently thickly overgrown with mosses and lichens, likewise endemic to the region. The forest floor is home to ancient ferns, which evolved some 20 million years ago and have become extinct elsewhere. The drier, southern slopes support a variety of trees including Canary ebony, tea trees, and olives.

Paradise for ornithologists

More than 150 plant species thrive in these laurel forests. Although many are also present on the other Macaronesian islands, 66 varieties are endemic to Madeira. These include the Madeiran blueberry and a species of tree heather that can top 20ft (6m) in height, as well as numerous orchids such as the large-leaved rattlesnake plantain.

In sharp contrast to the profusion of plant life, animal life on Madeira is relatively scarce, though no less diverse. The altogether 500 or so species of fauna consist mainly of invertebrates, insects, and spiders.

The profusion of bird life, including species such as sparrow hawks, swifts, Madeira chaffinches, and the rare Cape Verde petrel, attracts many birdwatchers to the island — often to the detriment of the birds themselves. Consequently, there are only 20 to 30 breeding pairs of the seriously endangered, soft-plumaged petrel left in these misty, mountain forests. Additionally, the breeding pattern of the species is not particularly fecund. The female lays only one, single egg after successfully pairing. During the breeding season, these nocturnal birds now have to be protected from overly intrusive bird-watchers.

Madeira's damp marine climate has helped the gnarled laurel trees in this unique primeval forest to survive the ages. They thrive only in damp conditions (above)

View across the laurel-covered mountain slopes on Madeira's northern coast where the valleys are often veiled in mist (below)

Where Iceland's glaciers are protected as historic monuments

SKAFTAFELL NATIONAL PARK protects a natural landscape fashioned by volcanic fire and ice

ICELAND
Skaftafell
Reykjavik

North Sea

ATLANTIC

GETTING THERE:
Iceland's Ring Road
passes the entrance
to the Park. Bus service

WHERE TO STAY:
Hotel with additional
bunks available
for visitors with their
own sleeping bags;
two guest houses;
guest rooms in three
farmhouses; camp site

CLIMATE:
Oceanic climate with
mild winters; 32°-59° F
(0°-15° C)

MAIN ATTRACTIONS:
Walks along numerous,
well-signed trails across
Skaftafellsheidi up to
Vatnajökull or along
the sand flats and
glacier tongues.
Svartifoss Waterfall
and Sjónarsker
viewpoint

SPECIAL TIPS:
No vehicles permitted
in the Park

Having crossed the long bridge across the endless, black, sandy expanses of Skeidarársandur, the green mountain ridge of Skaftafellsheidi stands out like an oasis in between the desert and the ice. It traverses the 660 square miles (1,700km²) Skaftafell National Park, located in southern Iceland, the so-called land of glaciers, at the foot of Vatnajökull Glacier. Covering an area of well over 3,100 square miles (8,000km²), the Skaftafellsheidi is the third largest glacier in the world. It is three times the area of Luxembourg and its white peak is prominent above nearly every mountain panorama in Iceland. The mighty glacial tongues of Skeidarajökull, Morsárjökull, and Skaftafellsjökull penetrate deep into the National Park, pushing moraines of sand, gravel, and boulders before them. The great glacial rivers of Skeidará, Morsá, and Skaftafellsá spring from these glacial tongues.

In 1996, a volcano erupted beneath the gigantic Vatnajökull Glacier, melting the ice from beneath. Enormous quantities of water built up underneath the glacier, finally bursting out and flowing along the course of the Skeidará River to the sea. Approximately two million cubic feet of water rushed along the river, tearing up everything in its path. The trail of devastation is still visible.

Ice tunnels and glacial lakes

Surrounded by tongues of ice, inset with greenish shimmering ice tunnels and caves and bright blue glacial lakes harboring the occasional floating iceberg, rugged cliffs, and wildly rushing glacial torrents, the region supports a a rich and abundant diversity of flora rarely seen in Iceland. Even forests, a rarity on Iceland, thrive here, providing shelter for countless rare birds. The birches of Bæjarstadaskógur Forest, which populate the slopes of Skaftafellsheidi, are taller here than anywhere else on Iceland.

Skaftafell National Park is a protected area on the lee side of Iceland's Öræfajökull Mountains. Mount Hvannadalshnúkur, the highest summit, rises 6,956ft (2,120m) from a landscape fashioned by fire and ice. A microclimate prevails here, making it warmer and sunnier than anywhere else on this otherwise bleak island. The modest birch fo-

rests provide a glimpse of how Iceland looked when Ingólfur Arnarson, the explorer, first set foot on the island in 874 with his companions near Skaftafell. Until the fourteenth century, Iceland's climate was so mild that vast, dense forests covered the mountains and broad fertile meadows stretched along the coasts. The early settlers even managed to plant cereals and the glaciers were much smaller than they are today. Ancient tree trunks and the remains of roots in the Skedarádur and Skaftafellsá testify to the fact that the land now covered by glaciers was once covered by green forest 600 years ago.

Arctic willow herb

The area was declared a National Park in 1967. Since it can no longer be used for grazing, many different types of vegetation have gained a foothold in the region. Apart from numerous varieties of heather and crowberry, widespread throughout Iceland, a fascinating diversity of vegetation has evolved here, including angelica, spring vetch, and the beautiful, pink flowering Artic rose bay wil-

low herb that is rare in Iceland. During the midsummer weeks when the nights are short and the days long, vast numbers of brightly-colored butterflies flit among these stunningly colorful flowers.

More than 300 species of bird nest on the wooded slopes, including redwing, snipe, meadow pipits, and wrens. The sand flats of Skeidarársandur are also an important breeding area in the Atlantic for the Great Kua and falcons and ravens build their nests on its inaccessible cliffs and rocks.

At the end of a narrow gorge that cuts into Skaftafellsheidi is the 25ft (8m) high Svartifoss Waterfall, which plunges over a precipice in a curtain of spray, surrounded by a semi-circle of polygonal black basalt pillars that bear a strong resemblance to organ pipes. Although this is not one of the most spectacular waterfalls in existence, it is undoubtedly one of Iceland's most picturesque. The best view of the cascade and across the Skaftafellsheidi ridge is from the Sjónarsker viewpoint above the waterfall.

Aerial view of the Skaftafell volcanic peaks (left)

Svartifoss Waterfall plunges down into the valley through a narrow ravine (above, right)

Inland glacier lakes are dotted with innumerable ice floes (below, right)

The Tuareg desert

TÉNÉRÉ NATIONAL PARK in Niger lies in the middle of the Sahara

L'Air et du Ténéré

NIGER

Niamey

Golf of Guinee

GETTING THERE:
Flights from Niamey to Agadez; bush taxis; lifts in trucks. Landing strips for light aircraft within the National Park

WHERE TO STAY:
Camping in the bush in tents or under the stars; two basic rest houses in Iférouane

CLIMATE:
Hot all year: around 86° F (30° C), rising to 122° F (50° C) between March and June

MAIN ATTRACTIONS:
Trip through the sea of sand dunes in the Ténéré desert; rock pictures; dinosaurs' graveyard south of the Aïr massif

SPECIAL TIPS:
Taking a guide with you reduces the risk of armed attacks

Caravan traveling through the desert (above)

The desert sands stretch for hundreds of miles (below, right)

Rock pictures in the Aïr mountains (below, left)

Ténéré, this vast expanse of sand, gravel, and stones in the central Sahara, is bounded by the Tibesti, Hoggar, and Aïr mountain ranges and referred to by the Tuareg nomads as the "empty land." Endless miles of seemingly flat, barren desert stretch into the distance, where the wind has sculpted some of the Sahara's most beautiful dunes out of a "sea of sand." To the west, where their progress is halted by the forbidding Aïr massif around Arakao and Temet, their soft, almost erotically curving shapes tower upwards to heights of around 1,000ft (300m).

The Aïr massif rises out of the desert plain in the west like one single, mountainous mass, punctuated by individual peaks towering up into the sky, their improbable shapes sculpted by thousands of years of erosion by wind and sand. The unmistakable outline of Mont Greboun in the north, for example, rises to a height of 6,560ft (2,000m). Note also the shimmering blue, cobalt-rich Montagnes Bleues mountains.

Relics of the Mediterranean

The desert is truly alive. Here, and in the Aïr mountains, biologists have identified 350 different varieties of plants, 40 different mammals, 165 different types of birds, and 18 reptiles, including many endangered species. The National Park, created to protect this unique natural environment, encompasses half the Aïr massif.

The desert is shifting above an ancient metamorphic plate, formed around 500 million years ago. It became a sea bed 280 to 300 million years ago and later supported a wet, tropical rainforest.

The Aïr mountains were created when volcanoes erupted from the plains 65 million years ago, forming one of the largest volcanic ring systems in the world. It comprises nine individual massifs, measuring up to 50 miles (80km) across and stretches 340 miles

(550km) from the former sultanate of Agadez to the Algerian border. Arguably the most spectacular of these is the Arakao caldera, encircled by giant sand dunes in the northeast of the massif.

The plants found in these gray-black mountains and sandy plains grow around the oases, or burst into life in the event of one of the region's infrequent rain showers. They are relics of Sudanese and Mediterranean species, from which they have been separated for thousands of years. Zachun trees and horizontally growing Arak trees, the nearest relatives of which are found in the Sudan, are two such examples. Acacias and tamarisks grow in the mountain valleys, while the moister regions above 3,300ft (1,000m) also support various varieties of fig, similar to those found in Mediterranean regions. Above 4,950ft (1,500m), the wild olive, an internationally endangered species, has also managed to establish itself.

Similarly, any animals living here were separated from their ancestors thousands of years ago. These include relatively large numbers of endangered hoofed animals that have managed to survive the hazards of hunting, poaching, and growing tourism. The population of the rare Addax or Mendes antelope, similar to a red deer in size with long, slender corkscrew horns, has increased from just 15 animals in the late 1970s to around 100 today. The 12,000 Dorcas gazelles are likewise more numerous following the creation of the nature reserve and several successive years of rainfall.

Protected area for antelopes

At the heart of the National Park is a large protected area, closed to visitors, which provides an undisturbed sanctuary for the rare Mendes antelopes, as well as around 70 olive baboons and 500 Patas monkeys. This special reserve extends over some 5,000 square miles (13,000km²).

Reminders of the region's prehistoric occupants can be seen in the dinosaurs' graveyard along the road to Bilm, which skirts the southern side of the Aïr mountains. Along this 95-mile (150km) stretch of road are the fossilized remains of numerous dinosaurs, whose bones have survived in the desert sand for thousands of years. It was here in 1998 that a complete skeleton of a previously unknown spinosaur was discovered, later christened Suchomiomus tenerensis.

The Aïr mountains contain many ancient rock carvings including 20ft (6m) high images of giraffes, which date back some 30,000 years and bear testimony to the earlier occupation of this region.

Where the White Nile tumbles over a thundering waterfall

MURCHISON PARK in Uganda, a paradise for hippos and giraffes, is at last witnessing the return of other big game

Murchison
UGANDA
Kampala

GETTING THERE:
By ordinary vehicle to the Park, which will provide you with a four wheel drive vehicles. Five hours from Kampala, along partly metaled roads. Landing strips at Paraa and Rabongo for light aircraft

WHERE TO STAY:
Several lodges in all price categories; the historic, luxury lodge of Sarova Paraa, situated right by the waterfall; several camping sites

CLIMATE
Pleasant all year round, does not exceed 84° F (29° C). Best time to visit: January to March (low season)

MAIN ATTRACTIONS:
Murchison Falls; Nile boat trip; Buligi Peninsula circuit; Rabongo rainforest

Bisecting Uganda's biggest nature reserve from east to west, the White Nile River, (also known as the Victoria Nile), flows through the center of Murchison Falls National Park and empties into Lake Albert. Before reaching this lake, however, it drops in a sequence of spectacular cascades and waterfalls into the East African Rift Valley. At the Falls, the Nile forces its way through a 20ft (6m) wide cleft in the rocks and plunges 140ft (43m) with a deafening roar and a great cloud of spray into two more sets of rapids before eventually ending up in a foaming pool. For the final 20 miles (30km) or so of its journey, the broadening river flows sedately towards the lake, rippling gently. This waterfall, also known as the Kabarega or Kabalega Falls, is by far the most spectacular to be found anywhere along the entire 4,185 miles (6,735km) length of the Nile. The water thunders down into the gorge at a rate of 66,000–132,000 gallons (300,000–600,000 liters) per second. The resulting curtain of spray forms a huge, dense cloud of mist between the rocky cliffs, which appear to tremble under the sheer weight of water. The most impressive view of the waterfall is undoubtedly from the top, looking down over the plummeting torrent of foaming water to the calmer, lower stretch of river in the distance, winding its way around sand banks and small wooded islands. A path leads from the top of the Falls all the way down to the swirling pool at the base of the waterfall. From here, there are fascinating views of the foaming waters rushing into the narrow ravine.

Hippos all the way

Over the course of a boat trip from the Falls to Lake Albert, every bay seems to be filled with hippos in their hundreds, snorting and blowing as they wallow in the water while, in their midst, huge crocodiles bask on the sand banks. When the first Europeans explored the Nile during the mid-nineteenth century, the whole river teemed with these armored reptiles. However, they have since retreated to escape the intrusions of man and motor boats and now only inhabit the more remote, upper reaches of the Nile. Its well-stocked waters provide them with an abundant supply of giant fish, such as the Lake Albert or Nile perch, which can grow to around 7ft (2m) in length and weigh 440lb (200kg). The varied landscape of the Rift Valley supports a wide range of different habitats and consequently a rich diversity of animal and plant life. Dense, primeval rainforest covers the higher terrain in the southwest. The Rabongo rainforest south of the cascades is home to various species of primate, including several families of chimpanzees.

To the north, on the far side of the river, the landscape unfolds into gentle, rolling savannah, interspersed with occasional Borassus palms. Vast herds of buffalo, antelope, waterbuck, bushbuck, and reedbuck make their way through the long waving grass which camouflages the lion following hot on their heels.

Breathtaking bird life

The shores of the Nile River, the vital artery traversing Murchison Park's 1,480 square miles (3,840km²), are a natural magnet for numerous groups of elephants. Majestic and dignified Rothschild giraffes patrol the forest perimeter, stripping the occasional leaf and fresh shoots from the treetops.

The main focus of interest in Murchison Park, however, is the bird life, a major attraction for ornithologists and amateur bird lovers alike. Seldom can so many varieties of African birds be observed in such close proximity to one another. Around 450 different species have been identified in the Park. Egyptian geese, pelicans, hornbills, and cormorants are usually seen along the broad sweep of the river below the waterfall, conducting their courtship rituals along the bank while keeping an eye out for likely prey. With patience and a little luck, you might catch a glimpse of one of the rare shoebills among the papyrus stems. These birds are quite capable of snapping a baby crocodile in two with their mighty bills.

The rich diversity of bird species can almost certainly be traced to the impact of the civil wars in the 1970s and 1980s, during which poachers and warring factions all but destroyed the huge herds of ungulates and elephants. Reduced grazing pastures have resulted in a regeneration of the forests, which have become denser and more impenetrable as formally rare plants re-establish themselves. These changes in environmental habitat have benefited the birds and small mammals. The population of larger animals has increased substantially since hostilities ceased.

Giraffes regard the riverine woodland along the Nile, as well as the palm-studded savannah, as their personal larder (left)

With its foaming torrents and numerous cascades, the river is the region's main life-giving artery (below, right and above)

Where lions laze in trees

The scenic landscapes of **QUEEN ELIZABETH NATIONAL PARK** in Uganda are a paradise for wildlife

UGANDA

•Kampala
Queen
Elizabeth Park

Red Sea

INDIAN
OCEAN

GETTING THERE:
Five to six hours by
car from Kampala, on
mostly metaled road;
landing strips for light
aircraft in Kasese and
near Mweya Safari
Lodge; bus connections
from Kampala and
within the region

WHERE TO STAY:
Luxury lodges; a simple
guesthouse in Mweya
belonging to the
Research Institute
for Ecology; several
camp sites

CLIMATE:
Best to visit after
the rainy season
in October/November
and March/April

Queen Elizabeth National Park is a popular reserve, being regarded as one of the jewels in Uganda's ecological crown. It lies nestled in one of the most beautiful landscapes in East Africa, the West African Rift Valley. The Rwenzori Mountain rises 16,400ft (5,000m) on its northern boundary. To the northeast, the Park is almost completely surrounded by the marshy, wet hinterland of Lake George while the southeastern portion is characterized by savannah and forest extending as far as the Congo border on the shores of Lake Edward. The Kazinga Canal, which connects the two lakes, splits the Park into a northern and southern sector.

Grassy savannah, open bush, tracts of forest, rainforest, marshland, lakes, streams, and to the north

of the Kazinga Canal, a bizarre crater landscape, provide distinctly different habitats that support an extraordinary diversity of flora and fauna. It is hardly surprising that the Park is on UNESCO's list of the world's major biosphere reserves and Lake George is on RAMSAR's list of primary wetland ecosystems.

Home of the hippo

Since Uganda's independence, many national parks and lakes have changed their names several times. For many years, Queen Elizabeth National Park was known as Rwenzori National Park, before reverting to its former, royal, colonial name. Both names are current, however, which can lead to confusion with the more recently established Rwenzori Mountain National Park,

a reserve that only protects the high mountains on the border with the Congo.

Queen Elizabeth National Park is home to about 100 species of mammal and 606 varieties of birds. The Kazinga Canal boasts the largest concentration of hippos on earth. A boat trip will bring you face to face with hundreds of them, jostling for a position among the papyrus along the banks, snorting noisily or yawning hugely. And there are always the elephants that congregate here to drink and bathe.

A boat trip is an ideal and comfortable means of observing the animals at close quarters and it is certainly the best way to see the numerous birds in their individual habitats of open water, marshy riverbanks, or dense forest: black bee-

eaters, shoebill storks, over eleven different species of kingfisher, falcons, and whole colonies of pelicans and cormorants.

Lake George, north of the two other lakes, is actually a landscape where open water, permanent marshland, marsh vegetation, swamp, grassland, and forest merge imperceptibly with one another. This shallow lake averages a depth of 8ft (2.4m) and is 13ft (4m) at its deepest point.

Storybook jungle

In the middle of the vast, dry savannah on the Park's northwest boundary is the Kyambura gorge. It is somewhat surprising to encounter here a dense, lush, verdant green jungle, of the kind you read about in storybooks, with a dense canopy and thick lianas dangling down to the forest floor. It is home to several families of chimpanzees, which chatter and crash about excitedly in the treetop branches.

Elephant, buffalo, giraffe, and bushbock graze peacefully among the waving grasslands, which are also home to Uganda's very own signature animal, the deer-like cob antelope with its amazingly long, coiled, S-shaped horns.

Naturally enough, the predatory leopards, hyenas and lions are never far behind. The lions occupy the southern part of the Park and exhibit a rather unusual behavioral characteristic, namely a penchant for tree-climbing. They drape their bodies along a branch and lie dozing with all four paws dangling. Such behavior is unique to these "tree-climbing lions," as they are known locally, and is not found in lion populations elsewhere.

Tourists are few and far between in this region as the Park's tourist and administrative center is situated on Mweya Peninsula, which juts out into Lake Edward and lies on the far side of the Kazinga Canal. Some distance north of here, the terrain becomes a lunar landscape punctuated by numerous volcanic craters. Many of these are now crystal-clear lakes, attracting attract thousands of flamingos.

Queen Elizabeth National Park is just beginning to recover from the depredations of civil war. The poachers have been driven out, thereby guaranteeing the animals' protection from further persecution. In fact, the Park seems to have become something of a sanctuary for elephants, which find their way here from the neighboring Congo where they are still hunted by poachers.

Dried up lake in Queen Elizabeth National Park, situated in the west of Africa's Great Rift Valley (above)

Several large groups of baboons populate one particular area of the Park (below)

The land of the Masai

Kenya's **MASAI MARA** game reserve is home to the largest herds of animals anywhere in the world

GETTING THERE:
Main road route via Narok, approximately five hours by car from Nairobi. Two daily flights from Wilson Airport in Nairobi to Narok. Four landing strips for light aircraft in the Park

WHERE TO STAY:
A choice of lodges in all price ranges. Around 25 camp sites in the reserve – not all are shown on maps

CLIMATE:
Cooler, dry season from July to October. Temperatures rarely rise above 86° F (30° C) and seldom fall below 59° F (15° C)

MAIN ATTRACTIONS:
The great migration of wildebeest, zebra, and antelope. Hot-air balloon trips. Masai village near Narok

SPECIAL TIPS:
A native driver/guide recommended, especially if driving off-track. Night driving not permitted

Vultures feeding off animal carcasses

Many seasoned safari travelers, travel writers, documentary film makers, and researchers refer to Masai Mara as one of their favorite landscapes in East Africa. The vast expanse of sky above the open savannah, the immense amount of game, and the annual migration of huge herds of gnu, zebra, and antelope entice them back time and time again. Many people also come to see the Masai themselves, the warrior nomads who have roamed these plains since the seventeenth century — not as hunters, but as herdsmen, killing wild animals only in self defense.

The Masai people still dress in traditional red robes and proudly carry traditional weapons: a spear, bow and arrows. Their lifestyle is linked so closely with the savannah and its game and so rooted in the soil that they are the only tribe permitted to graze their herds of goats and cattle within the confines of this national reserve. Nowadays, the Masai's actual dwellings, consisting of round, brown huts made of clay and cow dung, lie outside the boundaries of the reserve. As a defense against lions, cheetahs, and leopards, a family's group of huts is ringed by a high thorn fence. Each village comprises several groups of huts encircled in this way, as well as cattle enclosures similarly protected by a ring of thorn bushes.

Prey and predators

The Masai Mara is a vast savannah of gently rising hills, scattered woodland, and occasional acacia trees. Its vital arteries are the Mara and Talek Rivers, which supply the area with water all year round. To the south, the hilly terrain unfolds into the vast, virtually endless plains of the Serengeti in Tanzania. On the western boundary, the high plateau of the Oloololo Escarpment towers looms on the horizon. Throughout the year, the base of this mountain is a popular gathering place for large numbers of animals, especial-

ly zebras and antelopes as well as their predators.

Herds of wildebeest frequent the lush grasslands and scattered acacia woodlands along the Mara River, while the rhinos, including the rare black rhino, prefer the privacy of the thick vegetation found eastwards in the sandy Ngama Hills. The vast central plains, interspersed with a few scattered bushes and boulders, are the best place to see the "big nine" of African game: buffalo, elephants, leopards, lions, rhinos, cheetahs, zebras, giraffes, and hippos.

A trek to the Mara River

In April, the rains arrive and the parched savannah is transformed into a fertile, green paradise. This is the signal for the start of one of nature's most breathtaking spectacles. Millions of wildebeest and other hoofed animals begin their journey from the seemingly endless vastness of Tanzania's Serengeti plains to Masai Mara. They are followed by 7,000 giraffes and 1,000 elephants, trailed of course by the savannah's own predators, 3,000 lions, along with leopards, cheetahs, hyenas, and jackals. Around the end of July and beginning of August, the migration crosses the Mara River whose shores provide the setting for some of nature's most dramatically breathtaking, if somewhat gruesome, scenes. Crocodiles lie in wait ready to fall upon their prey as they try to cross the river. Lions, cheetahs, hyenas, and jackals pounce on any animal that shows the slightest hesitation at the dark, swirling river water or staggers out on the other side, weak from its exertions. By the time these enormous herds reach Masai Mara, some of them will have covered around 620 miles (1,000km) on their hazardous journey. They will be joined by another 100,000 wildebeest, which migrate here from the Loita Mountains in the east.

This season also marks the arrival of many different varieties of birds in Masai Mara for whom the steppe is a rich source of food. Pairs of Verreaux's eagle owls build their nests together, while crowned cranes display their singular courtship dance and ostrich families lay up to 70 eggs in communal nests.

But they too are only temporary visitors to the Masai Mara. Before the dry season begins again in October and November, they will again be gone, along with the wildebeest, antelope, and zebra.

The rainy season transforms the savannah into a velvety green paradise. Vast numbers of zebra migrate to this area from the south (above)

Many hoofed animals, including huge herds of wildebeest, visit Masai Mara park (below, center)

The herds of zebra and antelope must cross great rivers like Sand River, where cheetahs, crocodiles, and other predators lie in wait for a meal on the shore (below, right)

The red soil of the savannah

TSAVO NATIONAL PARK in southern Kenya is one
of East Africa's most spectacular wildlife sanctuaries

GETTING THERE:
Two-hour car trip
from Mombasa; three
hours from Nairobi.
Six landing strips
for light aircraft in the
south of the National
Park; 13 in the north.

WHERE TO STAY:
Lodges and tents to suit
all budgets and tastes

CLIMATE:
Warm all year round.
Best time to travel
is during either of the
dry seasons in January
(high season, around
86° F/30° C) or June to
September (around 82°
F/28° C)

MAIN ATTRACTIONS:
Herds of elephants
and other wild animals;
Mzima Springs;
Lugard's Falls;
Crocodile's Point;
Yatta Plateau

View from one of the
lodges across the red
earth of the savannah
to the Chyulu
Mountains in the
distance (above)

While elephants
congregate during
the dry season around
the few water holes
(below, right),
marabous gather
in the tree-tops of the
savannah's gnarled
trees (below, left)

The story of the two man-eating lions of Tsavo is still a prominent part of local folklore. In 1898, or so the story goes, they killed 135 laborers working on the railway line between Mombasa and Lake Victoria. Aside from the fact that it was actually "only" 28 men, there was something very distinctive about the appearance of these two male lions: they had no manes.

Lions like this still live in Tsavo National Park in southern Kenya, an area half the size of the Netherlands. While it is usual for two or three male lions to be in charge of a pride of six females, Tsavo lions will not countenance rivals and have even bigger harems, numbering around eight lionesses. Biologists believe that they possess more sex hormones than others of their species in the rest of Africa, which explains their aggressiveness and lack of mane, the lion equivalent of baldness.

The Park is bisected by the Nairobi-Mombasa highway and railway line, splitting it into a west and east section. The endless expanse of savannah in Tsavo East with its thorn-bush vegetation still evokes the atmosphere of an untamed Africa. The only landmark rising abruptly from these flat plains is Mudanda Rock, a miniature replica of Ayers Rock in Australia.

The water hole attracts large numbers of wild animals at its base. Hundreds of elephant, buffalo, and hyena congregate here during the dry season. From its summit, there are panoramic views for miles, right across to the mountains in the east as far as Kilimanjaro and across the plains to the west, dotted here and there with green strips of forest along the shores of rivers and streams, helping to break the monotony of the landscape.

Elephants and their uses

The Galana River with its dense growth of palm trees along its banks is home to a large number of hippopotamuses and giant Nile crocodiles. Its source is 375 miles (600km) away in the mountains of Mount Kenia, from where it flows straight across Tsavo East before emptying into the Indian Ocean under the new name of the Sabaki River. The best place to observe the river wildlife is from Crocodiles' Point and from beneath the magnificent Lugard's Falls, where the Galana thrusts its way through a narrow gap in the rocks in a series of rapids.

At the start of the rainy seasons in March and October, things start happening in the soil of the Aruba plains to the east of Voi. Dung beetles, or tumblebugs, measuring 2 inches (5cm) across, start emerging from their holes in the ground in search of elephants, whose dung they roll into tiny pellets. They begin mating after just three weeks and the females disappear back into the ground, where they excavate holes the size of a shoebox and fill them with the dung pellets in which they have wrapped their eggs.

Tsavo West is much smaller, but its landscape is much more diverse thanks to its mountains, volcanoes, rivers, and water holes. Baobab trees are plentiful, but make it more difficult to get close to the animals.

Along its eastern border is the Yatta Plateau. It is 180 miles (290km) in length, making it one of the longest lava flows in the world. It originated as a lava flow from the Chaimu Crater just over 200 years ago. It is intersected by trails leading up to viewpoints offering incomparable vistas over the bright red soil that is typical of this broad expanse of African bush savannah.

Oasis in the steppes

This soil is also responsible for the coloring of the famous pink elephants, which are a common sight in Tsavo West. The animals "spray" themselves liberally with this red laterite dust, which acts both as a sun-screen and keeps irritating insects at bay.

The jewel of the Park is undoubtedly the Mzima Springs, where crystal clear water bubbles up out of volcanic rock in the middle of a bone-dry steppe landscape, creating a fertile oasis of abundant life in the barren wilderness. Each day, 40 million gallons (190 million liters) of water that percolates through the porous lava in the Chyulu Hills 25 miles (40km) away and flows from a subterranean river into three large lava basins. These springs also supply drinking water to Mombasa by pipeline.

The luxuriant green vegetation of papyrus, fig trees, date, and rare raffia palms with their extra long fronds surrounding these springs make it a paradise for crocodiles, hippopotamuses, lions, baboons, and several species of antelope, as well as turtles. Green guenons swing through the trees and an abundance of colorful birds can be heard among the leaves and fronds, including snake neck birds that are only found in a few places in Kenya.

A land of lush grass

SERENGETI'S vast savannah provides some of the best grazing grassland in Africa, making it a paradise for big game

Serengeti

Dodoma●

TANZANIA

INDIAN OCEAN

GETTING THERE:
By car via Arusha. Regional airports in Moshi and Arusha, with several landing strips in the Serengeti

WHERE TO STAY:
Comfortable lodges available in the Serengeti suit all pockets. Camping is also permitted

CLIMATE:
Temperatures warm, but pleasant all year round thanks to the higher elevation. Rainy seasons: October-November and April-June

MAIN ATTRACTIONS:
Guided safaris

SPECIAL TIPS:
Many roads are temporarily impassable after heavy rainfall

Storm over the Serengeti (above)

The tall, dense grass of the savannah provides predators like the lion (below, left) and the cheetah (below, right) with ideal hunting grounds

Unperturbed by their presence, elephants congregate around the water holes during the dry season (below, center)

Who can possibly resist the magic of the Serengeti plains whose vast sea of grass waves gently in the breeze beneath the hot, African sun? The animals integral to this awe-inspiring scene have no boundaries or frontiers. They obey only the call of the wild.

The habitat that has survived in the Serengeti is one of the oldest ecosystems on earth. Together with the neighboring Ngorongoro Reserve to the east and the Masai Mara Park in Kenya, it forms one of the largest, intact migration areas for hoofed animals anywhere in the world.

When the brief rainy season in October and November turns the steppes green with fresh growth, it is the signal for 1,500,000 gnus and hundreds of thousands of zebras and gazelles to begin their great migration. They descend from the northern hills and drop down into the Serengeti Plains in the southeast. They are driven by a primeval instinct, which overcomes any familial bonds. If a calf can no longer follow its mother, it is simply left behind, an easy meal for lions, cheetahs, and jackals.

The return journey

After the heavy rainfall between April and June, the main wet season, the herds set off return home by different routes. Nothing, not even deep gorges or crocodiles lurking in the rivers, can distract them from their chosen route home. Humans also pose hidden dangers. Not only do the animals' migratory routes involve crossing state frontiers, but they can also lead the animals away from the safety of the reserves.

Since time immemorial, man has shared the savannah with animals. Over three million years

ago, as evidence discovered in Ngorongoro reserve has testified, this part of the world formed the cradle of mankind. Today, the proud Masai continue to drive their herds freely across the plains of the savannah. They are the only people permitted to graze their cattle within the Park.

When Ngorongoro's now dormant volcanoes erupted two to four million years ago, they ejected lava and ash far and wide across the area now known as the Serengeti Plains. Salts contained within this debris seeped into the earth, forming an impermeable, rock-hard layer no more than 39in (1m) below the surface. It is too hard for even the toughest tree roots to penetrate, which is why the Serengeti remains virtually treeless.

Subterranean saline barrier

This very same salt barrier creates perfect growing conditions for the various grasses, ensuring that any rainwater remains close to the surface, promoting the growth of luscious pasture for all the grazing animals. What is more, the animals themselves actually help regenerate this lush grassland by feeding on it. The shorter they crop the grass, the quicker it grows and the more moisture it contains.

The frequently dried-up riverbeds are lined with strips of riverine woodland, providing unique and rare habitats within the Serengeti. These rivers fill up so much during the two rainy seasons that enough water is retained in the ground over the dry months to support this dense woodland with its own microclimate.

Strange-shaped kopjes

This microclimate is home to numerous orchids peeping out of the lush greenery. Climbing plants entwine themselves around the trees, enveloping them and creating a perfect habitat for the innumerable insects that populate the forest floor and tree canopy, including great swarms of stalk-eyed flies. The prolific bird population includes osprey, mouse birds, bee-eaters, and owls.

Up above in the canopy, colobus monkeys and shy bush babies frolic from branch to branch. On the forest floor, African monitor lizards, measuring from 39–78in (1–2m) in length, forage for food or lie sleeping in the undergrowth. Elephants, buffalo, hyenas, and lions come seeking the cool shade of the forest.

The Grumeti and Mara Rivers, which almost never run dry, are home to the mighty hippos which stand up to their necks in water and, during the dry season, amicably jostle giant crocodiles for space in the dwindling, greenish waters of the shrinking water holes.

The vast plains are interspersed with the bizarre shapes of kopjes, silhouetted against the skyline. The water table in the vicinity of these rocky outcrops is usually higher than out on the open savannah. As a result, hundreds of different plant species, which do not occur anywhere else in the surrounding grasslands, have established themselves around these kopjes.

In the clefts and niches, favored by lions as safe hideaways for their young, a small, unique animal kingdom has evolved, consisting of lizards, snakes, mice, and hyrax — small mammals resembling portly and extremely shy guinea-pigs.

The cradle of civilization

NGORONGORO CRATER provides lush grazing for big game

When a volcano dies, the whole lava cone collapses inward, leaving behind what is known as a caldera, a ring wall encircling a flat area at the bottom of the volcano. This is how the Ngorongoro Crater originated in northeast Tanzania to the west of the Kilimanjaro massif. It may not be the world's largest volcanic crater, but it has the distinction of being the largest to have so well withstood the passage of millions of years.

There is a simply breathtaking panoramic view from the rim of the crater across the 12 mile (20km) wide valley basin with its steep, wooded slopes. Its real treasure, however, lies nearly 2,000ft (600m) lower on the floor of the caldera. Its 100 square miles (260km²) have become home to one of the most fascinating concentrations of African big game. Its lush, short grass provides a rich supply of fodder for a permanent population of 25,000 animals. Herds of ungulates including gnus, zebras, gazelles, buffalo, eland, and hartebeest graze here, drifting from one water hole to another. Hippopotamuses inhabit the marshy areas. Lions, leopards, and cheetahs have an abundant choice of prey.

Ngorongoro Crater offers the visitor a unique opportunity to catch sight of one of the 20 to 30 black rhinos, a species that has been almost wiped out in Africa by poachers. Nowhere else can one see so many lions in such a compact area. Five prides, numbering altogether 100 or so animals, have divided up the crater floor into individual territories, each with its own small lake.

Constant changes

Many visitors are surprised by the fact that the elephants that regularly descend into the crater are all males. The herds of cow elephants and their young apparently baulk at making the steep descent and strenuous climb back up, preferring to remain around the forested rim of the crater.

One of the highlights of the Ngorongoro Crater's bird life is the spectacular sight of vast flocks of pink flamingos, which sometimes fly in from the nearby soda lake.

When the great migration season gets underway, herds of zebra, gazelle, and gnu leave the crater to join the procession of animals heading for the adjacent Serengeti. When drought strikes, transforming the fertile crater basin into a dust-blown savannah, many animals seek greener pastures in the mountainous areas beyond the crater. If a mighty deluge of rain occurs, causing the lakes and marshes in the valley to flood, they return. Consequently, the face of the Ngorongoro Crater changes from month to month and year to year.

The Masai also graze their herds of cattle in Ngorongoro. No one knows precisely how many of these nomadic people pass through the country; there are possibly 25,000, or even 40,000. They migrated here some 200 years ago and have virtually become part of the landscape of the Ngorongoro mountains.

Fossil footprints

Man is believed to have originated in this area some 3,600,000 years ago. The volcanoes were still active when an upright, humanoid creature left a clear footprint in a soft lava field near Laetoli, not far from the Ngorongoro Crater.

Even more corroborating evidence was discovered in the Olduvai Gorge. This gash in the solidified lava forms a ravine nearly 300ft (90m) deep, which runs for about 30 miles (50km) towards the Serengeti.

The first discovery was made by the German entomologist, Kattwinkel, who came across the bones of a long extinct, three-toed species of horse whilst searching for new species of butterfly and took them back to Germany with him. When Louis Leakey, a Kenyan-born archaeologist, saw the bones in Berlin, it prompted him to organize an expedition in 1931 to research the discovery more closely. His wife, Mary Leakey, found the 1,750,000-year-old remains of a hominid, *Australopithecus boisei*, in the Olduvai gorge in 1959. *Australopithecus boisei* is nicknamed "Nutcracker man" because of his extremely powerful jaw. The gorge has since yielded the remains of 50 specimens of prehistoric and early man, including *homo habilis* who bears strong similarities to us today.

Herds of gnu
and zebra grazing
in perfect harmony
on the pastures
of Ngorongoro
Crater (above)

The big game within
the crater includes
the rhinoceros, which
finds ample fodder
here to rear its young
(below, right)

After the rains, some
lakes in the marshes
of the crater basin
retain their water
for a long time,
providing an ideal
source of water
for numerous animals
(below, left)

White-capped mountain

Mount **KILIMANJARO'S** remarkable flora

Kilimanjaro
Dodoma●
INDIAN
TANZANIA
OCEAN

The volcanic massif of Kilimanjaro is a prominent landmark punctuating the seemingly endless plains of the savannah in northern Tanzania, rising over three-and-a-half miles (5.8km) into the tropical African sky. Kibo, the highest of its volcanic peaks, is frequently encircled in a ring of cloud. And although its white glaciers glitter in the sun, the Equator is only three degrees' latitude away.

When Johannes Rebmann, a German missionary, returned home to Europe in 1848 and related what he had seen, scholars scoffed at his story. It was not until ten years later that they finally realized their mistake. A veritable stampede to the volcano ensued, but it was not until 6 October 1889 that Hans Meyer, a Leipzig professor of geography, and Ludwig Purtscheller, an Austrian mountaineer, conquered the Uhuru summit on the Kibo rim which, at 19,340ft (5,895m) above sea level, is the highest peak in Africa.

A panoramic view

Kibo is actually not difficult to climb. Mountaineering skills are not essential, although some people may find they are affected by the thin air at higher altitudes. If you are gasping for breath at around 13,000ft (4,000m) on the third day and your progress is becoming slow and cumbersome, you are almost certainly experiencing symptoms of high altitude sickness, for which the only cure is to turn back.

On Mount Kilimanjaro, however, the trail is a goal in itself. Every turn reveals a series of unforgettable vistas across the rolling expanse of the steppes surrounding the base of the volcano. Over the course of just a few days, you will also pass through the entire spectrum of different climate zones. The lower slopes of Kilimanjaro, up to 4,000ft (1,200m), are heavily populated with people, mainly small-holders, whose numerous dwellings are virtually hidden beneath the green canopy of coffee plantations. Countless creeks spring up out of the volcanic rock, providing local farmers with ample water for their intensive small-scale farming.

On the edge of the forest mists

As the trail approaches Marangu Gate, the main entrance to the park situated at around 5,900ft (1,800m), the route begins to wind through eucalyptus and pine trees. Beyond the Gate, these become a dense forest. A further 650ft (200m) higher, where the protec-

ted area technically begins, the vegetation gradually thickens into a heavily misted, impenetrable forest belt. Giant lycopods and mossy ferns line the route, tree branches are heavily draped with old man's beard, and small orchids provide an occasional splash of color in the deep green depths of the jungle.

Between 9,200 and 9,900ft (2,800–3,000m), the terrain opens up quite abruptly into the broad, gently rising slopes of Afro-Alpine grassland and upland moor, characterized by dry heaths and boggy, deep-cut valleys. Nature has a number of special surprises up her sleeve at this level, such as varieties of heather growing to 39in (1m) in height, giant groundsel 16 1/2ft (5m) tall, and a giant species of lobelia that reaches a height of nearly 10ft (3m).

From 13,000ft (4,000m) upward, plant life becomes increasingly sparse until it eventually gives way to an alpine zone of dry gravel and barren stone. The lichen clinging to the rocks is the only sign of life up here on the saddle between Kibo and Mawenzi.

Above 16,000ft (4,900m), on the rim of the Kibo crater ring, only one single type of lichen survives, growing at the rate of just 0.04in (1mm) per year and reputedly living for several hundred years.

The thawing ice

The glaciers surrounding the summit of the volcanic cone extend down as low as 16,400ft (5,000m). The largest of these is the Penck Glacier. In 15 to 30 years, however, the ice and snow will all have disappeared. One third of this glacial ice has already melted in the past

12 to 15 years alone. The loss of this melted ice water will make it difficult for the farmers at the foot of the mountain to water their crops.

The outer rim of the crater at Kibo's southern end measures 6,500ft (2,000m) in diameter and descends to a depth of 1,000ft (300m) inside the crater. From the floor of the crater rises another volcanic cone within the first, measuring 2,600ft (800m) in diameter and exhibiting at its center a 400ft (120m) high tapering cone of ash. It seems that Kibo is just dormant for the time being, for its crater is constantly venting gasses from the earth's core.

Situated east of Kibo and the high desert saddle is Mawenzi, a rugged and deeply fissured volcano. Older than Kibo, its caldera wall has long since been eroded away. Its battered summit is all that remains of the lava core.

Kilimanjaro's highest peak is 19,340ft (5,895m) in height. The extensive slopes of this mountain massif have been designated a conservation area. The summit is frequently shrouded in cloud (above)

From Kenya's Amboseli National Park in the north, there are stunning views of Kilimanjaro's snow-capped summit. The reserve accommodates several herds of elephants (below)

Forest giraffes of the Congo

The **OKAPI RESERVE** in the central African rainforest is home to many rare species of wildlife

Okapi Reserve
•Kinshasa
REPUBLIC OF CONGO

INDIAN OCEAN

GETTING THERE:
Private care hire from Bunia or Isiro, but very poor roads.
It is recommended that travel and trekking be arranged through authorized agencies

WHERE TO STAY:
Basic accommodation available

CLIMATE:
Hot and humid all year round: 75° F–88° F (24° C–31° C). Dry season: December–March

MAIN ATTRACTIONS:
Treks through the Park; okapi breeding station; taking part in a traditional pygmy hunting expedition

SPECIAL TIPS:
Heed any travel warnings as Ituri is still considered a particularly unsafe area

In the northeastern corner of the Democratic Republic of Congo between the Ituri and Nepoko Rivers lies the Ituri rainforest, which has flourished here for well over one million years. This region remains largely unexplored and no doubt still harbors many secrets. One of its best kept ones came to light only recently. In the beginning of the twentieth century, the world's biologists thought they knew about every kind of African big game that existed. In 1901, however, during a visit to a pygmy settlement, a British colonial official noticed two skulls and a complete animal skin that he was unable to identify. He sent the latter to London, where experts established that it was from a member of the giraffe family. It was another six years before European eyes rested for the first time on a living example of this species: an okapi calf.

The most striking characteristic of the okapi is the horizontal white striping on its hindquarters and haunches. The rest of its coat is a glossy, dark chestnut brown and its head, sporting small, backward sloping, furry horns, is gray. In contrast to its savannah cousin, this forest giraffe, with its short legs and short neck, stands just shoulder-high at 5–5¹/₂ft (1.5–1.7m). What it does have in common with its taller relatives, however, is its 16in (40cm) long tongue, which it uses to strip the leaves and fruit off trees.

Okapis are exceptionally timid animals, living exclusively in the depths of the rainforest in the northeastern part of the Congo where the forest floor is firm and dry.

There are around 30,000 of these animals in the wild, 5,000 of these in the Okapi reserve. This conservation area covers approximately 5,400 square miles (14,000km²) and, in turn, comprises around one-fifth of the Ituri rainforest.

Hunted by poachers

The reserve was originally established as the logical accompaniment to a breeding station set up in 1952 in Epulu to supply zoos all over the world with captive-bred okapis. Okapis also became a popular gift given to foreign heads of state on official visits.

Since then, the reserve itself has come under threat and, along with all conservation areas in the Congo, now features on UNESCO's list of endangered nature parks. During the civil war of 1997–1999, the forests of central Africa served as popular hiding places for the rebel armies, who hunted local game to excess. In their wake followed an influx of gold and coltan (columbite-tantalite) prospectors from the neighboring, densely populated region around Kisangani, who constructed dams, cut down areas of forest for fields, and poached the animals.

Following the ceasefire in 1999, however, many international organizations have become actively involved in supporting local authorities' efforts to regain control over the reserve and help Nature reclaim her own.

The Ituri rainforest can still spring a few more surprises, however. The Congo is one of 25 countries with the highest rate of endemism and the greatest diversity of species. Around 15 percent of all plant and animal species are exclusive to this region. One such example is the African mouse deer that, despite any resemblance to a piglet, is, in fact, a species of deer. It inhabits the wetter areas of the forest close to rivers and

streams. Biologists have identified 52 different kinds of mammals, including giant ground pangolin, African crested porcupine, rare species of meerkat, and red colobus monkeys, as well as more species of Duiker, a deer-sized antelope with short horns, than are found anywhere else in the world.

Rare Congo peafowl

Among the profusion of birds was one that persistently eluded detection by the white man. It was not until 1935 that a visiting ornithologist came across the feathers of an unknown type in a pygmy elder's headdress. This bird turned out to be the Congo peafowl, for which a new zoological family had to be created. Not only does this violet and green bird have all the characteristics of a peacock, it also has those of a guinea fowl.

So far, 329 different types of bird have been recorded in the Ituri rainforest, including long-tailed hawks, plumed guinea fowl, black guinea fowl, and various species of rail.

This enormous diversity of fauna is matched by the flora. The 22 acres (9 hectares) of mixed forest that botanists have so far researched have revealed 302 different tree varieties and 130 types of liana. The crown of this forest is a light leaf canopy 100–130ft (30–40m) above the ground, through which a few individual trees rise to even greater heights. Many parts of the region are covered with Mbau forest, which has a uniform canopy and little undergrowth, while the numerous rivers and streams are bordered with swamp forest. Dense secondary forest has reclaimed previously felled areas.

Okapis are extremely shy creatures which require a tropical rainforest habitat where the ground is firm and dry (above)

The great whirlpool in the steppes of Africa

National Parks flank the Zambezi River on either side as it plunges over the VICTORIA FALLS

ZAMBIA
Lusaka
Victoria Falls Harare
ZIMBABWE
ATLANTIC OCEAN
IINDIAN OCEAN

GETTING THERE:
By air via Harare to Victoria Falls or via Lusaka to Livingstone. Train or express bus links between Harare and Lusaka via Victoria Falls and Livingstone. Excellent roads from Harare, Bulawayo, and Lusaka. Problem-free border crossing at Victoria Falls

WHERE TO STAY:
All categories of hotel, as well as lodges and campsites

CLIMATE:
Rarely exceeding 77° F (25° C) in winter, cool at night – ideal for animal watching. Wet season February to May – best time for viewing the Falls at their most spectacular. Seldom above 86° F (30° C) in summer

MAIN ATTRACTIONS:
Rainforest and bank below the waterfall; the Victoria Falls National Park; Hwange game reserve (Zimbabwe); and Mosi-oa-Tunya (Zimbabwe) National Park. Best views of the waterfall from the Livingstone Statue, Knife Point (Zambia), bridge, and Victoria Falls Hotel garden (Zimbabwe)

SPECIAL TIPS:
Pay heed to travel warnings in Zimbabwe

As David Livingstone, the famous Africa explorer, was drawing near these mighty waterfalls in the middle section of the Zambezi River on 16 November 1885, he initially believed the noise he heard to be the roar of a bush fire. What he eventually saw and heard two hours later took his breath away: a wide curtain of water, plunging 330ft (100m) with a noise like thunder over a broad precipice into the depths of a narrow transverse gorge, no more than 165ft (50m) wide. He had discovered "Mosi-oa-Tunya," i.e. "the smoke that thunders," which he renamed "Victoria Falls."

His discovery coincided with the end of the dry season, during which water tumbles over the Falls at a rate of 2–3 million gallons (10–15 million liters) per minute. During the rainy season from February to May, this increases to 100 million gallons (500 million liters), which crash down over this mile-wide precipice into the narrow ravine below, creating the widest curtain of falling water in the world. There is so much resulting spray that the surrounding landscape is barely discernible. This fine mist rises up from the gorge to a height of 1,300ft (400m) and its glistening aura above the barren low veldt savannah is visible from 20 miles (30km) away.

This fine moist spray brings life to this high, dry plateau in the form of a narrow strip of riverine jungle straddling both shores of the Zambezi. This rainforest habitat, which includes ebony, teak, fig, and wild olives, supports a rich diversity of plant species.

A paradise for animals

The water and humidity also attract huge numbers of game from the strange, dry mopane forests of the high plateau savannah. Giraffes, elephants, rhinos, buffalo, zebras and various species of antelope, klipspringer, leopards, and lions are frequent visitors to Victoria National Park (Zimbabwe) and Mosi-oa-Tunya (Zambia), which straddle the frontier

between Zimbabwe and Zambia. The variety of bird life is also breathtaking. Up to 400 species have been identified in nearby Hwange National Park in Zimbabwe. The adjoining ravines provide nesting sites for rare species such as the Taita falcon and Verreaux's eagle. The basalt river bed, along which the one-and-a-quarter mile (two km) wide Zambezi makes its slow and stately progress toward the precipice, was formed 150 million years ago during the Upper Jurassic period. Movements within the earth's crust occasionally caused the river to change course, washing away the soft sandstone between the basalt and consequently carving out a successive series of ravines running south to north. The edges of the zigzag-shaped clefts below the waterfall chart the movement of its seven predecessors. A new channel is currently being eroded, signaling the formation of a ninth set of falls. A few thousand years from now, the wide expanse of waterfall in its present form will have disappeared.

One hundred years of tourism

The full extent of this magnificent natural wonder can really only be appreciated from the air in one of the so-called "Angel Flights" available by helicopter or small plane. These can be arranged in Livingstone or Victoria Falls and derive their name from the words that the Scottish explorer and missionary wrote in his diary, namely that "scenes so lovely must have been gazed upon by angels in their flight."

The news of Livingstone's discovery soon began to attract tourists to the area. The year 1898 saw the construction of the first encampments and lodges on the Zambian side. In 1905, a 430ft (130m) high bridge was built across the gorge, adding a further picturesque attraction for the growing stream of visitors. The town of Livingstone was built on the Zambian side of the Falls, opposite the "Victoria Falls Hotel" in Zimbabwe, which in turn soon spawned a settlement by the same name. "Vic Falls," as it is fondly known, grew into a modern tourist resort during the 1970s and today is a center for all kinds of adventure sports, such as bungee jumping off the bridge, white water rafting, and free climbing.

Livingstone has remained more sedate. Its pace of life is slower and its hospitality more genuine. From this

side, steep narrow paths lead down to the base of the waterfall, where you can look straight into the yawning depths of Boiling Point, a swirling witch's cauldron into which the torrents cascade before disappearing into the narrow Batoka gorge. This jagged ravine, which the river has carved out of the basalt plateau over the past 500,000 years, is 60 miles (100km) long and 400–800ft (120–240m) deep.

Solitary trails along jungle paths in a rainforest nurtured by a fine mist of water droplets enable visitors to experience nature at its wildest and most unspoilt. The path along the river above the Falls provides panoramic vistas of the savannah and its animals. It is advisable to keep one's distance from the riverbanks, however, as crocodiles can spring like lightning out of the water without any warning.

View from the ravine of the basalt plateau precipice with the waters of the Zambezi cascading over it

Amid the thunderous spray of Victoria Falls: a deluge of water plunging 330ft (100m) into the depths (above)

This aerial view shows the huge gash the Zambezi River has cut in the landscape (below)

River delta in the desert

Botswana has declared the OKAVANGO BASIN and MOREMI RESERVE a conservation area

Okavango Basin
BOTSWANA
Gaborone
ATLANTIC OCEAN
INDIAN OCEAN

GETTING THERE:
Mainly roads
from Francistown,
Windhoek, Bagani,
or Livingstone/Kasane
to Maun. Charter
flights from Gabarone
and Francistown.
The delta area
is accessible by light
aircraft, canoe,
or on foot. Only very
experienced drivers
of four wheel drive
vehicles should
venture onto the limited
number of tracks in the
Moremi reserve. Large
choice of Safari tour
operators in Maun.
Apart from in Maun
itself, no fuelling
stations for hundreds
of miles.

WHERE TO STAY:
Hotels and camping
sites in Maun. Plenty
of lodges and campsites
in and around the delta,
ranging from luxurious
lodges to basic tent
accommodation.
Off-site camping
is prohibited

CLIMATE:
Dry season is from July
to October. Most
animals move into the
delta from the Kalahari
during this time.
Wet season is
November/December
and is very hot
and humid

MAIN ATTRACTIONS:
Moremi Game Reserve;
lodge accommodation;
guided canoe safaris;
light aircraft flights
over the delta

Originating in the highlands of Angola, a river known as the Cubango springs from the Bié Plateau south of Vila Nova. It flows generally southward before turning east, at which point it becomes the Okavango River, flowing along the border between Angola and Namibia. Measuring nearly 1,000 miles (1,600km) in length, it is the fourth longest river in southern Africa. It does not empty into the ocean, however, but discharges its waters into a vast delta in the middle of the Kalahari, one of the world's greatest deserts. The Okavanga Delta extends over an area of 6,600 square miles (17,000km²) and is unquestionably Africa's largest oasis situated in the middle of the parched wilderness of the Kalahari.

After crossing the narrow Caprivi Strip, the river gradually broadens, eventually dispersing its waters into a maze of lagoons and immense labyrinths of innumerable waterways connecting small, and sometimes not so small, islands of palm and savannah. The southern edge of this fan-shaped area of saturated sand and water is approximately 150 miles (240km) long.

Only three percent of the water that the river feeds into the plains flows out again. It accumulates instead in the southern swampland surrounding the diminutive Lake Ngami or continues for another 185 miles (300km) through the Kalahari Desert to Lake Xau on the Makgadikgadi Pan to the southeast. This small outflow is nevertheless sufficient to remove the salts that would otherwise be deposited when the water evaporates. Without this small outflow, the delta would be a lifeless salt pan.

The Kalahari was once a lake

The Okavango Delta is remnant of a vast lake that once filled the Makgadikgadi Basin. Its waters and swamps covered a large part of the central Kalahari. It is probable that the Okavango, Chobe, Kwando, and upper Zambezi rivers converged at one time to form a single, mighty river that flowed through the central Kalahari across the Limpopo and into the Indian Ocean.

Each year, the Okavango deposits around two million tons of sand in the delta, creating sand bars that regularly block the river's natural flow. This forces it to keep switching directions, resulting in an ever-changing pattern of channels and waterways across the delta plain. Dense thickets of papyrus reeds, growing just a few inches under water, can also cause the channels to become blocked. Only a handful of waterways are deep enough to be navigable by canoe. The Okavango Delta is consequently an outstanding example of an ecosystem that has achieved an extremely dynamic, natural balance, while constantly changing. As a result, this island in a sea of arid desert supports a surprising variety of habitats and an abundance of plants and wildlife. For the great migratory animals of the Kalahari, the delta represents a natural, virtually trackless reserve and one huge watering hole.

Impenetrable papyrus thickets line the river and waterways cross the expanse of floodplains. Mopane woodland and palm trees surround the higher-lying islets, affording a shady refuge for the larger animals. Beyond the forest, the landscape unfolds to reveal the drier expanse of the savannah where elephants and antelope roam, trailed by lions, cheetahs, hyenas, and wild dogs. About 30 percent of all wild dogs, whose numbers are declining throughout Africa, are thought to live here. After dark, the hippopotamuses trample broad paths through the papyrus on their nightly forays. By day, these pathways enable the antelope to move from one island to another.

Water for the elephants

Altogether, a total of 1,060 species of plants and 32 large mammals have been recorded here. The area is also

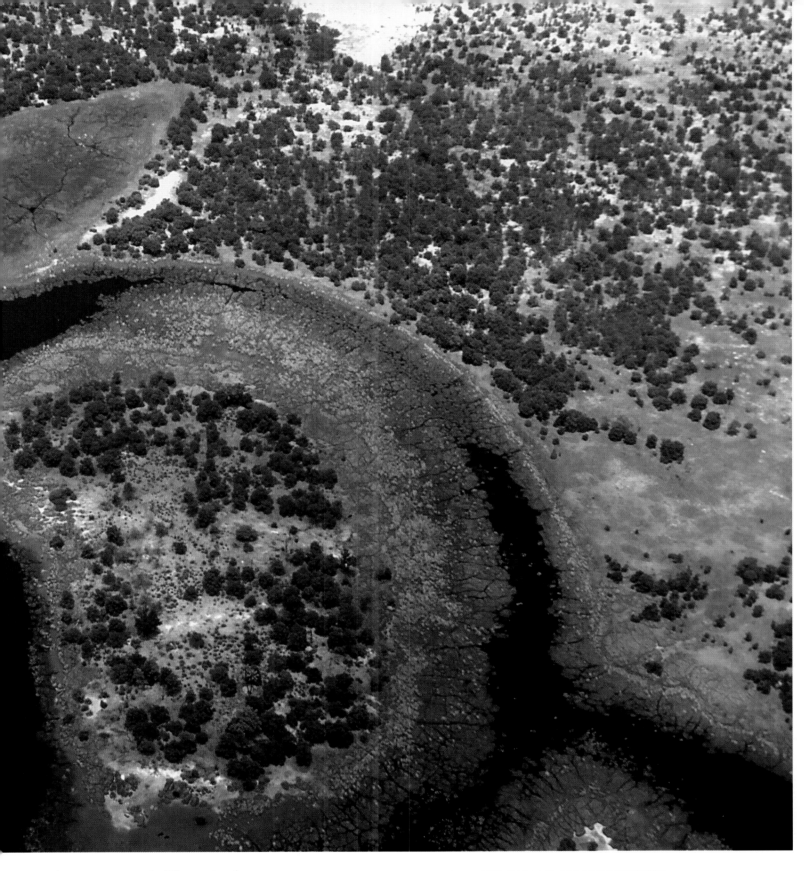

home to around 650 spectacular varieties of brilliantly colored birds, which flock here from all corners of equatorial Africa. These include storks, ibis, herons, cranes, and weaver birds.

In the eastern sector of the delta is the Moremi game reserve, an area covering 1,930 square miles (5,000km²) and comprising around 20 percent of the Okavango Delta. It is a combination of mopane woodland and acacia forest, floodplains, and lagoons.

It is the only area that visitors can penetrate without too much difficulty. Large herds of elephant congregate here particularly during the dry season, but the area is also a magnet for buffalo, giraffes, zebras, and all the other African animals that come to slake their thirst at the numerous pools.

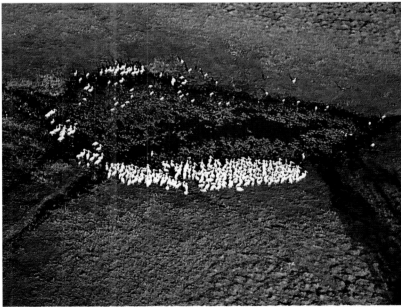

This aerial photo of the Okavango Delta illustrates how quickly the river could change course on this floating bed of sand (above)

Pictured below is a colony of pelicans

Where elephants roam the streets

CHOBE NATIONAL PARK in northern Botswana is home to the largest elephant herds on earth

Almost no other national park in southern Africa can boast an abundance of wildlife to compare with that found in Chobe National Park in northern Botswana. This reserve is particularly noted for its huge elephant population, numbering over 70,000, and it is not uncommon to come across herds of 100 or more animals. Sometimes, these gray giants can even be seen wandering inquisitively through the provincial town of Kasane and its nearby encampments.

These elephants form part of what is probably the largest single concentration of this mammal left in Africa, a population estimated at around 120,000 extending over the whole of northern Botswana as well as northwest Zimbabwe. Their numbers have gradually increased from just a few thousand animals that survived the extensive poaching prevalent during the civil wars in the 1970s and 1980s. The Chobe elephants are migratory. During the dry season, they move north where they congregate around the Chobe and Linyati Rivers. During the rainy season, they return to the lowlands in the southeastern part of the National Park, traveling approximately 125 miles (200km) each year.

Although the Chobe elephants are among the largest in Africa, their tusks are very brittle and often in a lamentable state. It is rare to find an animal with a good, strong pair of tusks.

A trip by riverboat

It is not just the elephants that make Chobe National Park so special, however. Visitors find the magnificent African landscape equally enthralling. This area covering 4,000 square miles (10,000km²) of African soil is characterized by four distinctly different ecosystems and supports an astonishing variety of different habitats. In the extreme northeast around the Chobe River is the Serondela region with its lush plains and dense forests, while the hot, dry savanna nestles between the fertile Savuti marshes in the southwest and the Linyanti swamps in the southeast.

If you want to experience something really special, it is worth taking a boat trip on the Chobe River to observe the teeming wildlife. Herds of elephant can be seen trampling the banks, while hippopotamuses wallow and snort in the muddy shallows, sur-

veyed by crocodiles lying in wait for their prey. Otters can be glimpsed darting into the undergrowth, while large herds of buffalo, giraffe, antelope, and zebra warily lower their heads to drink, knowing that lions, cheetahs, and hyenas are not far away.

In the far northwestern corner of the reserve lies the virtually forgotten and seldom visited Linyanti Swamp, which covers an area of nearly 350 square miles (900km@) adjacent to the river after which it is named. It flows into Lake Liambezi, at which point it becomes the Chobe River. During the dry season, animals such as elephant, buffalo, and zebra congregate here. The trees and vegetation along the riverbank are filled with an overwhelming cacophony of sound from large numbers of birds sporting a dazzling array of colors. Even the pelican, a rarity elsewhere, can be seen here.

A network of waterways

The Mababe Depression to the south of the Park is all that remains of a large lake that once covered the whole of northern Botswana. These flat and inhospitable Savuti lowland marshes are mainly frequented by elephants, but lions, wild dogs, and hyenas are also regular visitors. It is rare nowadays to see herds of impalas, gnus, buffalo, zebras, and antelope occurring in vast numbers. The three main rivers of southern Africa — the

Okavango, Chobe, and Zambezi — are in fact closely interlinked. The Selinda Spillway connects the Okavango via the Linyanti and Chobe Rivers with the Zambezi. The spillway branches off eastwards at the start of the Okavango Delta, forming a link with the Linyanti Swamp in Chobe National Park. When the Okavango Delta is flooded, a small amount of water also flows along this channel into the Linyanti Swamp, the Chobe River, and into the Zambezi. When water levels are low, the swamp empties again. A rise in the water level of the Zambezi completely reverses the direction of flow in the Chobe River, flooding the area around Lake Liambezi. There used to be another canal linking the river system in Moremi National Park in the south with the Savuti marshes in the south of Chobe National Park. However, the Savuti Canal, which was intended to link these two great swamps, is something of an enigma. It meanders over 60 miles (100km) through the swamplands, its waters bringing life to the Mababe Depression. In 1888, it dried up completely, then suddenly, in 1957, its waters reappeared and remained until 1979, (with the exception of the drought-stricken years of 1966 and 1967,) and has since dried up again. It is possible that this phenomenon may be caused by subterranean movements in the earth's tectonic plates.

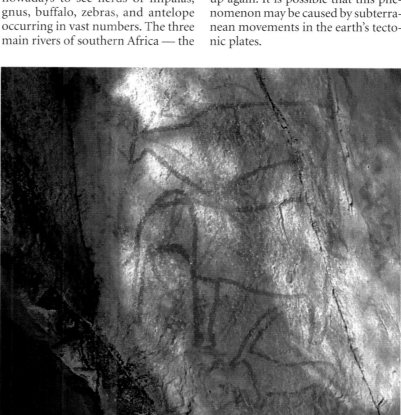

GETTING THERE:
Local airfield in Kasane. By car via Kasane, Maun, or four-wheel drive vehicle via Ngoma Bridge (Caprivi/Namibia). There are no service facilities between Kasane and Maun. Four-wheel drive vehicles are essential in the Park, and it is advisable to travel with two vehicles

WHERE TO STAY:
Lodges available throughout the Park in various price categories, plus several camp sites with toilet and shower facilities. Booking several months in advance is essential

CLIMATE:
Best time to travel is April to August, when the climate is fairly pleasant and the animals remain close to the water holes. Wet season starts in November, when it is hot and humid and the roads are often impassable

MAIN ATTRACTIONS:
Boat trips on Chobe River, Linyanti Swamps, and Savuti marshes in the Mababe Depression

SPECIAL TIPS:
Exceptionally good infrastructure

Chobe National Park boasts a variety of different habitats. The Savuti marshes are currently dried up (above, left)

Hippos live happily alongside crocodiles in Chobe's waterways (below, left)

Rock pictures in Allen's Camp reveal the artistic skills of early inhabitants (below, right)

Spectacle of the salt flats

The wildlife of **ETOSHA NATIONAL PARK** in northern Namibia has survived intact despite numerous onslaughts

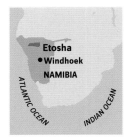

The harsh glare of white salt stretching as far as the eye can see. Dust, heat, and burning sun. The Etosha salt pan in northern Namibia may well seem one of the most inhospitable places on earth to humans, yet it is nevertheless home to 114 mammals and around 340 species of birds. Even some endangered species like the black rhino and sable antelope have found a refuge here.

The central pan itself occupies an area of 1,850 square miles (4,800km²) at the heart of Etosha National Park, which in turn extends over some 8,500 square miles (22,000km²) and supports one of the largest concentrations of African game, including lions, elephants, giraffes, antelope, zebras, and springbok. Cheetahs and leopards can also be glimpsed occasionally, although they prefer to remain hidden in the thick grass. The diversity of bird life reaches a peak during the rainy season, when flocks of flamingos and vast numbers of wading birds fly in from afar to join the vulture, hawks and eagles.

At one time, Etosha National Park covered nearly 40,000 square miles (100,000km²) and was the largest national park in the world. Under South Africa's apartheid regime, however, the Park was reduced in 1967 to well under a quarter of its original size as part of the government's homeland policy.

Twelve million years ago, the Etosha salt pan began as a lake bed, fed by the Kunene River as it flowed southward from Angola and filled this large depression with its waters. Later, the river altered course, turned westward, and discharged its waters straight into the Atlantic Ocean. The water evaporated, the lake dried up, and all that remained was the salt pan. During the rainy season, however, a number of otherwise dried-up rivers, which follow an almost parallel course down from Angola in the north, channel so much water into the area that large parts of the Etosha Pan can be waist-deep in water.

Inhospitable saline soil

Plants do not grow in this saline soil. Only in places where the ground remains damp is there evidence of some algae and bacteria, which cast a green sheen over this salty desert. Grass, rushes, and a few stunted trees may be found on the low-lying islets, which are only submerged when water levels are high.

Beyond the rim of the salt pan is the savannah with its low-growing scrubby vegetation, which in turn gives way to the fertile soil of the extensive grasslands, providing abundant fodder for gnus, zebras, and springboks. In the western sector of the Park, where the soil is brackish and chalky, the sparse vegetation consists mainly of savannah thorn-scrub. To the east, however, is a savannah populated by gnarled mopane trees, figs, and date palms. A mixed dry forest of camel thorn palms and purple pod cluster leaf trees covers the northern sector.

The entire Park is surrounded by a strong, 10ft (3m) high electric fence intended to keep the animals in and poachers out. This inevitably disrupts the natural annual migration cycle of the herds but artificial routes have been created to replace them. Water is fed through pipes to the numerous watering holes in the park and the flow is turned on and off at certain times to encourage the herds to migrate.

When gravels roads were first built to accommodate visitors to the Park, it almost caused a disaster. The quarries, from which the gravel was extracted, filled up with water in which salts dissolved. This produced a perfect breeding ground for the baccillae that cause anthrax. Because of the particular susceptibility of many herbivores to this disease, the hartebeest population dropped in just 30 years by 90 percent and the number of zebras fell from 15,000 to a mere 5,000. The Etosha lions, however, remained immune and their numbers rapidly increased.

Sick lions – elsewhere

In contrast to other Africa game reserves, the big cats of Etosha are free of the FIV virus, the big cat equivalent of the HIV virus in humans. As a result, Etosha lions are often relocated to build up numbers in other wildlife parks. In the Kruger National Park, 83 percent of the big cats are affected by FIV and the figure is 79 percent in the Serengeti.

In order to avoid disturbing the animals and upsetting the natural balance, a special protected area for endangered species has been established in Otjovasandu in the western section. Around 20 percent of Etosha National Park is open to visitors— more than enough, certainly, to enable a close encounter with Africa's animals in this magnificent natural setting.

A herd of springbok congregating at a water hole (above, left)

Just a few months later, the same spot is overgrown with dried grasses (above, right)

A herd of zebra visit another watering hole (center, right); gemsbok, whose horns can grow to over 39in (1m) in length, graze on the dried grasses of the savannah (below, right)

The greatest game reserve

South Africa's **KRUGER NATIONAL PARK** becomes Limpopo Park

Kruger
National Park
Pretoria
SOUTH AFRICA
ATLANTIC OCEAN
INDIAN OCEAN

GETTING THERE:
Daily flights from
Johannesburg to
Hoedspruit; private
charter flights also
available to Timbavati
in Kruger Park.
Excellent roads
from Johannesburg
and Harare

WHERE TO STAY:
Wide choice
of accommodation
in South Africa;
camping and luxury
lodges available
in Zimbabwe
and Mozambique
outside the park
boundaries

CLIMATE:
Warm all year round.
Best game-watching
season is during the dry
months from October
to March, although
veldt temperatures
are often very high
at this time

MAIN ATTRACTIONS:
Site of the Iron Age
palace of Thulamela;
ruins at Pafuri and
around Mpumalanga.
Guided wilderness
hiking trails in Kruger
Park (book well
in advance!)

SPECIAL TIPS:
Heed any travel
warnings in respect
of Mozambique
and Zimbabwe

**View from a hill
looking down into the
Olifant River Valley,
which traverses Kruger
National Park from
west to east (above)**

**Lions, leopards,
and the distinctively
spotted puma are
the most dangerous
predators of the
savannah. They prey
mainly on antelope
and other ruminants
(below, left and right)**

South Africa once had plans to erect electric fences around its borders to keep illegal immigrants out of the country, but now even the simple wire fence constructions separating Mozambique, Zimbabwe, and South Africa are being dismantled to accommodate what will be the largest nature reserve in the world.

This new reserve, the Great Limpopo Transfrontier National Park, extends over the triangle where the three countries meet and straddles the Limpopo River, which forms the border between South Africa and its two northern neighbors. This enormous park, an amalgamation of the former Kruger National Park in South Africa, Limpopo, Zinave, and Banhine in Mozambique, and Gonarezhou in Zimbabwe, already encompasses an area of 13,500 square miles (35,000km²). This will expand in time, as more and more areas are placed under protection, and will eventually comprise around 38,600 square miles (100,000km²) of territory, an area far larger than Portugal.

In this way, a rich diversity of African habitats will be united under the aegis of a single reserve, ranging from the dry, flat savannah terrain of Kruger National Park, the wet, humid landscapes and lakes of Mozambique, to the spectacular sandstone cliffs of Gonarezhou. The new arrangement will be a blessing for the former Kruger National Park, enabling it to better accommodate some of its elephants and other grazing animals, which have multiplied to such an extent that they are in danger of destroying the very habitat on which their survival depends. They will now find a new home north of the Limpopo River, along with hundreds of zebras, blue wildebeest, impalas, and other low veldt animals from the Kruger National Park's savannah plains. Sixteen years of civil war in Mozambique and Zimbabwe, not to mention the great drought during the 1980s, have brought many species of large mammals there to the verge of extinction.

Lost cultures

Limpopo National Park is not only designed to protect Africa's animals, but also intended to safeguard the ancient cultures of the Shangaan-speaking tribal communities of Makuleke in South Africa, the Shingwedzi and Limpopo peoples of Mozambique, and the Sengwe and Chiredzi tribes of Zimbabwe. Visitors have the opportunity to experience unfamiliar cultures, observe their tribal dances and handicrafts, and even learn something about the skills of traditional healers.

There is a great deal of evidence to suggest that the land within this triangle of countries has been inhabited since the Stone Age. Some of its earliest inhabi-

tants were the San, who left a legacy of wall paintings in the sandstone caves. They were followed over the course of about 800 years by the Bantu and by the time the first Europeans arrived in the early sixteenth century, some remarkably civilized cultures had developed here, the impressive ruins of which can still be seen today.

Kruger National Park, as it was formerly known, offers the ultimate in Safari tourism. The "Big Five" African game animals can be spotted with relative ease. Buffalo, lions, elephants, rhinoceros, and leopards have become accustomed to the safari vehicles, ferrying tourists along the approximately 3,100 miles (5,000km) of well-built roads that criss-cross the flat, dry plains of the savannah. Cheetahs, giraffes, hippos, and herds of different species of antelope also seem unperturbed by this attention.

Dramatic cliff formations in the savannah

Despite the highly developed tourist infrastructure of Kruger Park, its network of roads, rest camps, and lodges still comprise only 3 percent of its overall area. The remainder belongs to nature. In addition, there are a number of large, privately owned game reserves bordering the Park, offering a high concentration of African big game combined with luxurious accommodation and even so-called "eco safaris," on which guests can accompany experienced biologists, vets, and rangers on their patrols. Less well-known is Gonarezhou National Park, a little gem among Africa's nature reserves situated in the remote northwestern section of Limpopo Park. Gonarezhou National Park encompasses dramatic rock formations such as Chilojo Cliff, which is visible from a distance of 30 miles (50km), rearing up out of the vast expanse of untouched savannah grasslands and magnificent baobab forests. The elephants in this region are the largest and heaviest anywhere in Africa. Since very few visitors find their way here, many of the park's trails are overgrown or have been swallowed up by the sea of savannah grassland.

Here too, civil war and drought have left their scars on the land. By the mid-1990s, however, when the park re-opened after the ravages of war, the elephant population had recovered to such an extent that 750 animals could be transferred to other parks.

Visitors to this region, which covers an area of just 2,000 square miles (5,000km²), will be entranced by the great sense of peace and tranquility that reigns here, far away from the well-trodden tourist track. The resident animals are still very wary and far less accustomed to man than their counterparts in some of the other, more famous parks.

Alpine landscapes on South Africa's high plateau

The DRAKENSBERG and ROYAL NATAL nature parks protect a wide diversity of flora and fauna

A mighty mountain chain, 620 miles (1,000km) in length and forming a series of deep geological folds, forms the eastern boundary of South Africa's vast high plateau area, where it drops away steeply to the low-lying coastal region. The alpine section of this escarpment, which lies some 9,850ft (3,000m) above sea level, is located in the province of KwaZulu-Natal, along the eastern border of the Kingdom of Lesotho. From the main highway between Johannesburg and Durban, 15 access roads lead into the Park, where the visitor can choose accommodation ranging from cabins and lodges to tents and even caves.

Deeply fissured mountains rise steeply to towering summits, sheer rock faces of black basalt loom over light-colored sandstone, unspoilt river valleys, and rocky ravines. Such natural scenery presents a breathtakingly stunning panorama. Raging mountain torrents have carved deep gorges out of the terrain, cascades of water crash their way down through narrow canyons, and mushroom-shaped peaks sprout up in the midst of sweeping valleys. This entire area is protected by a combination of the Royal Natal National Park, the Drakensberg/Ukhahlamba Park, three additional nature reserves, a wildlife reserve, and six state-administered forests.

In the far north of the Park is the so-called "Amphitheater," a 5 mile (8km) long and 1,650ft (500m) high vertical rock face, which rises out of the Royal Natal high plateau. It is here that the Tugela River plunges down through a series of five cascades into the valley some 2,800ft (850m) below. The Tugela is just one of eight rivers that spring from the nearby 10,768ft (3,282m) high Mont-aux-Sources.

Record numbers of plant species

This imposing mountain massif sports a wide variety of vegetation and an impressive diversity of fauna, which have established themselves in a variety of different, and occasionally extremely rare, habitats: dark stretches of woodland, dry and exposed grassland, impenetrable bush thickets, and lush green pastures as well as the rolling hills of the high plateau, which explode into a sea of color when the flowers burst into bloom each spring.

The extraordinary variations in landscape, the climate fluctuations relative to the different altitudes, ranging from below 32° F (0° C) to 95° F (35° C), the basalt or sandstone bedrock, and the wet or dry environments contribu-

te to create a profusion of vegetation. So far, 2,153 species of plants have been recorded, 109 of which are internationally endangered species. Almost 30 percent are only indigenous to this area, a concentration of species unparalleled anywhere else in the world.

The wildlife is equally diverse: 48 different types of mammals, 299 species of birds, including numerous rarities such as the black vulture and bearded vulture, 48 different types of reptiles and 26 species of amphibians have their home here. These also include a number of endemic species, such as the gray reebok, a species of waterbuck, between 1,500-2,000 of which still roam the high plateau.

Long extinct animals have also left their mark here in places where the sandstone is visible beneath the basalt. This sandstone was formed in prehistoric times, when reptiles roamed the region and left their fossilized footprints etched forever in the ground. For tens of thousands of years, this magnificent, yet inaccessible, mountain region has been inhabited by man. Wind and water have carved numerous caves and overhangs out of the soft sandstone and it is here that the San people left one of the largest and loveliest collections of rock drawings found anywhere south of the Sahara. They are remarkably well-preserved and depict, in great detail, both the animals of their time as well as their

fellow man, thus shedding a little light on a way of life and religious beliefs that disappeared 150 years ago. Many of these caves are no longer featured on tourist maps in order to protect them from further damage by visitors.

Exotic bird life

For more than 4,000 years, the San people lived as hunters and gatherers in the sandstone caves and overhangs of the inaccessible Krakensberge. When wars started breaking out at the beginning of the nineteenth century between rival cattle-breeding tribes and crop-farming communities on the high plateau, many refugees withdrew to the mountains and began competing with the San people for living space. When the first white settlers arrived with their herds of cattle and began building plantations, the San people were unable to withstand this final onslaught and were last seen around 1880.

An elaborate network of trails provides access to the magnificent scenery of the Drakensberg, such as the Mlambonja and Mdedelelo wilderness areas with their incredible forests, an excellent area to observe the exotic bird life. The 10,480ft (3,194m) high Mount Cathkin with its basalt rock formations is also situated here. From its summit plateau, climbers can enjoy fantastic panoramic views across to Champagne Castle opposite, some 11,080ft (3,377m) in height.

GETTING THERE:
Johannesburg is South Africa's main airport; some airlines also fly to Durban. From the airport, by hire car, comfortable buses, or group taxis to the perimeter of the Park

WHERE TO STAY:
All categories of cabins, chalets, and lodges within the Park; camping sites also available

CLIMATE:
Warm, but rainy in December and January. June and July night frosts in elevated places. Best time to visit: Spring flowers in September/October

MAIN ATTRACTIONS:
Giant's Castle; tour through Royal Natal National Park, visiting the Amphitheater, Cathedral Peak, Garden Castle, and Tal Bushman's Nek

"Bourke's Luck Potholes" rock formations in the Drakensberg mountains of East Transvaal (left)

Aerial view of the Berlin Falls cliffs in the Drakensberg mountains (above, right)

View of the "Amphitheater" in Royal Natal Park, a sheer rock wall measuring 5 miles (8km) in length and 1,650ft (500m) in height (below, right)

Island of exotic plants

Unique tree ferns and orchids inhabit the misty rain forests of **RÉUNION** Island in the Indian Ocean

INDIAN
OCEAN

RÉUNION
CIRQUE DE
CILAOS

Réunion is the youngest and highest of the three Mascarene Islands. They owe their existence to the Piton des Neiges volcano, which formed two to three million years ago, rising to a height of 23,000ft (7,000m) above sea-level. Reaching a height of 10,069ft (3,069m), it is the highest mountain on the Mascarenes.

Just over one million years ago, another volcano emerged on its southeastern flank, the Piton de la Fournaise, which remains active to this day and shifts a little further southeast with every eruption.

Erosion of the mountain massif around the old, extinct volcano in the center of the island has meanwhile produced spectacular rock formations. Grouped around it and resembling steep-sided amphitheatres are three former volcanic basins, the Cirques Cilaos, Mafate, and Salazie. Each covers an area of around 40 square miles (100km²) and is composed of hills, mountains, and ridges, debris from the collapsed volcanic shield. The entire island is a protected area.

Temperate climate

Very few people in mainland France are familiar with France's southernmost Département. Even fewer are aware of its spectacular natural wonders although, admittedly, the island does not have much in the way of dream beaches. Its wildly rugged, dramatic mountains, mighty gorges, countless waterfalls, and dense jungle interior amply compensate for the shortcomings of its coastline.

Although Réunion is situated in the tropics, the climate remains relatively cool with temperatures hovering around 70° F (21° C) between April and October and 82° F (28° C) during the summer months. In the mountains, temperatures can drop as low as 54° F (12° C). The southeast

trade winds deposit a good deal of rain on the island's southern and eastern slopes during the cool season, promoting luxuriant growth in the dense, verdant rainforests that are home to numerous tree ferns and over 100 types of orchid.

The brown mountain landscape on the western side of the island receives little precipitation. Consequently, savannah plants dominate here, including palms and agaves. Like other remote islands, Réunion Island has a large number of indigenous species. Long ago, seeds carried here from Mauritius, Africa, and India by wind, rain, or birds evolved into individual species unique to the island. The mountain tamarind, a species of mimosa found primarily on the high plateaus of the caldera that can grow more than 80ft (25m) in height, is one example.

However, the island's fauna is relatively limited. Early in the seventeenth century, the first Europeans to set foot on the island hunted many animals to extinction. The first settlers encountered only two kinds of mammal, both of which have since disappeared: dugongs and bats. All the giant tortoises, which provided a welcome source of food on long sea journeys, have also disappeared. Ships' rats took care of the rest, decimating many endemic species of lizards and geckos. The ones seen today darting about on house walls were mainly introduced from Mada-

gascar and India, together with a species of chameleon from Java that is sometimes found around the Grand Étang lakes.

It was the birds that coped best with the invasion of domestic animals, colonial plants, and pests. Of the 36 indigenous bird varieties, 9 are unique to the Mascarene Islands, including the Mauritius cuckoo, the Mauritius falcon, and the cardinal with its brilliant red plumage.

Hiking into adventure

The legendary dodo, a large, flightless bird with a hooked beak, has long been extinct. It was first documented in 1598 and last seen in 1662 on two of the small islands off Mauritius.

Along the exciting trails within the three volcanic basins, you will frequently encounter huge spiders' webs, spanning up to 65ft² (6m²), with a large orange and black silk spider, a member of the nephilia family, measuring up to ten centimeters across, lying in wait for its prey right in the center. Its web is so robust that it is even capable of trapping small birds. This spider, like the rest of the wildlife on Réunion, poses no danger to humans.

The island's great beauty lies in its mountainous volcanic region and can be explored along narrow tracks and trails. The entrance to its most remote and wildest volcanic valley, the Cirque de Mafate, is not easy to find.

GETTING THERE:
Regular flights from Paris, numerous flights between Mauritius, South Africa, Madagascar, the Seychelles, the Comoro Islands and Kenya

WHERE TO STAY:
All categories of hotel, book well in advance for July and August. Some very comfortable cabin accommodation available in the hinterland.

CLIMATE:
Best time to travel is between May and October (around 21° C), the rest of the year temperatures are around 82° F (28° C) with a lot of rain and occasional tropical cyclones

MAIN ATTRACTIONS:
Point de la Table volcano nature trail. Waterfalls: Voile de la Mariée (Bride's Veil), Ravine Blanche, Ravine de Caverne, and Ravine Mazarin in the Cirques des Salazie. Trail through the Cirque de Mafate. Climb the Piton de la Fournaise

Tropical rainforest covers vast sections of the island. View of the Grand Bassin gorge and mountain chain (left)

The steep banks of the Bassin des Aigrettes (center)

The Piton de la Fournaise volcano is one of the island's highest elevations (8,235ft/2,510m). This photo shows the view across the caldera to the summit and the "Formica Leio" crater (above, right)

Réunion's forests are home to many species of chameleon (below, right)

The Aborigines' mountain

The land around AYERS ROCK and the Olga Mountains has always been a sacred place to the Aboriginal peoples

In the heart of the parched, sun-scorched Australian outback, two magnificent rock formations rise majestically out of the flat, red earth of the surrounding semi-desert. Uluru, also known as Ayers Rock, and Kata Tjuta, otherwise known as the Olga mountains, are the star attractions of Uluru-Kata Tjuta National Park in Australia's Northern Territory. The Park lies at the center of Australia's red heartland, surrounded by three deserts, the Gibson, Victoria, and Simpson. Deserts, semi-deserts, and giant sand dunes, whipped up by the ever-present wind to heights of nearly 130ft (40m), stretch in every direction as far as the eye can see.

The Park, which covers an area of 500 square miles (1,300km²), is owned by the local Aboriginals, the Pitjantjatjara and Yankunytjatjara, members of the Anangu people. The Australian Government reinstated their ownership of the land in 1985, whereupon they leased it straight back to the National Park authorities for a period of 99 years. Aboriginals have inhabited this land for around 20, 0000 years. They came originally from Indonesia before rising sea levels submerged the land links between Australia and the Molucca Islands.

Uluru and Kata Tjuta are sacred sites in Aboriginal culture and play a key role in the Aboriginal creation myth, "Dreamtime," a belief that dominates the daily lives of the Aborigine people. This spectacular desert landscape is traversed by countless so-called "dream paths," connecting all the Aboriginal sacred sites in Australia. Some places on Ayers Rock are indeed regarded as so sacred that they must not even be spoken of, let alone seen. For this reason, some of the trails are completely off limits to the approximately 600,000 visitors that make their way to this site every year.

Breathtaking kaleidoscope of color

The profusion of rock paintings in the caves and overhangs around the base of Uluru is evidence of the cultural, territorial, and economic inter-relations among the Aboriginal peoples. This rock was where they held celebrations and conducted their trading. One of the most fascinating aspects of Uluru, however, is undoubtedly the breathtaking spectacle it presents as it changes colors during the course of the day. Visitors never fail to be mesmerized by the many different natural shades of red and orange caused by the high iron content in the feldspar rock. The best time to view the Uluru is at sunrise or sunset, when the sun is low in the sky and bathes the mountain in a blaze of vermilion. The steep walls of Uluru, which measure around 29,500ft (9km) in circumference, rise abruptly from the surrounding red desert plain to a height of 1,140ft (348m), higher than the Eiffel Tower. Yet, this sandstone monolith is just the tip of a rock colossus that extends down into the earth to a depth of nearly 20,000ft (6km). It was probably formed around 600 million years ago, but geologists remain uncertain about its origins.

Deep-red sandstone domes

Many visitors find nearby Kata Tjuta, around 18 miles (30km) west of Uluru, even more impressive. This ring-shaped rock formation comprises 36 individual red-streaked sandstone domes, known as the Olgas, extending over an area of 14 square miles (35km²). Unlike Uluru, they are not crowned with a high plateau, but arch out of the plain in huge domes. The summit of Mount Olga outstrips Uluru by 650ft (200m). The fantastic, rock formations are eroded by the desert wind sweeping between the domes. Yawning chasms and caves as well as unexpected, almost lush, vegetation in the deep, damp gorges leave a lasting impression.

The Park boasts examples of all the major ecosystems found in the Australian outback. Specimens of every type of plant that can survive in this extreme climate are present in this red earth and among the sand dunes around Uluru and Kata Tjuta. The predominant form of vegetation,

however, is acacia and spinifex grass. There is even an isolated cluster of rock fig and eucalyptus. After a heavy downpour, the plains suddenly burst into a blooming carpet of color.

Mammals are relatively rare. The grass is too high, the arid plains too vast for most animals. Nevertheless, 22 species of mammal, primarily dingos, giant red kangaroo, mountain kangaroo, marsupial moles, and rabbit-like marsupials manage to eke out an existence here. Even several species introduced from Europe, such as the red fox, cats, house mice, and European rabbits seem to do well. Numerous species of reptile are also present, including the thorn devil lizard and black-headed python, as well as 8ft (2.5m) long giant monitor lizards, the largest of all Australia's lizards, which prefer to skulk in the bushes.

By virtue of its ancient Aboriginal traditions, its impressive geological features and the pristine desert and semi-desert ecosystems surrounding it, Uluru-Kata Tjuta National Park is one of the few mixed cultural and nature parks on the world heritage list.

AUSTRALIA

A bird's eye view
of the fissured slopes
of Ayers Rock,
with the Olga
Mountains in the
distance (above)

A road runs along
the base of Ayers
Rock (below, right)

A well-trodden path
leads to the summit
of Ayers Rock
(below, center)

An Aborigine working
on a wood carving
(below, left)

The Aboriginal world recorded in rock art

KAKADU NATIONAL PARK in northern Australia has saved
many animals from extinction

Kakadu
National Park   Coral Sea
AUSTRALIA
    Canberra
INDIAN OCEAN

There are very few regions that undergo so many seasonal changes over the course of a year as the Kakadu National Park in northern Australia. Situated 75 miles (120km) east of Darwin, this 7,700 square mile (20,000km²) Park extends 125 miles (200km) inland from the coast of Van Diemen Gulf. One third of it belongs to the Gagudju and Jabiluka Aborigines, who have leased it to the Australian park authorities. It is not only an outstanding natural heritage site, but also contains around 7,000 sites documenting the long history and culture of the Aborigine people.

More than 90 per cent of the annual rainfall occurs during the tropical monsoon season between November and April. Several times a day, torrential downpours batter the landscape. Violent thunderstorms unleash their fury over a bizarre landscape of cliffs and boulders, while howling tropical cyclones whip up the rivers, causing the flood waters to rise higher and higher each day and to leave large tracts of the floodplains under water. The landscape explodes into life and is suddenly carpeted with green plants, while water lilies burst into bloom on the vast expanses of water. Crocodiles are now in their element, while snakes and small lizards are forced to seek refuge on floating islands of vegetation.

Characteristic "X-ray style" art

The rainy season is followed by a period of almost no rainfall at all between May and October, with drought transforming most of the region into a desert in which temperatures frequently hit 108° F (42° C). The rivers dry up and all that remain are a few shallow freshwater puddles, the last refuge for one particular species of fish, which is specially adapted to enable it to survive the dry season.

In the east of the Park, the huge escarpment of the Arnhem Plateau, which gradually rises over a distance of 300 miles (500km) from 100–1,100ft (30–330m) in height, terminates abruptly. It is composed of a hard sandstone layer, millions of years old, overlying an older, softer rock, which has been eroded over the course of the different geological periods to create numerous caverns and rocky overhangs beneath the sandstone. Over the last 18,000 years, these rock walls have been filled with Aboriginal paintings, depicting this

people's myths and stories. There are lifelike pictures of crocodiles, long extinct Tasmanian wolves, figures wearing elaborate headdresses, and characters from Aboriginal mythology. A typical feature of these rock drawings is the "X-ray" style of art, in which they are painted, for example, with the skeletons of fish showing through. Many of these drawings are some of the oldest examples of rock and cave art in the world. Deep sinkholes and narrow crevices have formed in places where the roofs of subterranean caves have collapsed. At the bottom of these, miniature habitats have evolved, each one supporting its own uniquely individual flora and fauna. Many of the creatures that form part of these miniature ecosystems are relicts of earlier geological periods that have somehow managed to survive in these enclaves.

Lizards and vipers

A few, small, monsoon forests also manage to survive at the bottom of these ravines, even during the dry season. Sheltering deep within the caves are Australian ghost vampire bats, one of altogether 64 species of

mammal. There is a much greater diversity of reptiles, the 128 varieties including several rare species such as death adders, frilled lizards, and green and snake-necked turtles.

The hills in the southern part of the Park are, geologically speaking, much younger. Their ridges are still steep and unweathered. Between these solitary, individual rock formations are broad expanses of stone and sand. From Darwin, the gentle hills of the Koolpinyah Plains extend to the uplands of Arnhem Plateau. This stony landscape is often populated with open eucalyptus forest.

The coastal fringes are a transition zone extending some 200 square miles (500km²) between land and sea, subject to the tidal activity of Van Diemen Gulf and characterized by the wide estuaries of South and East Alligator rivers. Despite its inaccessibility, the area is one of the most significant wetland areas in the world. Seventy-five per cent of all varieties of Australian mangrove grow here, an ideal breeding-ground for fish and crocodiles, several species of turtle, rare frogs, and the internationally endangered dugong sea cow.

GETTING THERE:
Good road to Jabiru
from Darwin, along
the Arnhem Highway,
or from Katherine via
the Kakadu Highway.
Airports in Darwin,
landing strip at Jabiru

WHERE TO STAY:
Middle category
hotels and simple
accommodation
available in Jabiru,
Kakadu Resort,
and Cooinda.
Several campsites

CLIMATE:
Dry season is April/May
to September with
temperatures around
90° F (32° C). October
to December around
99° F (37° C).
Downpours
and thunderstorms.
Rainy season January
to March/April,
around 91° F (33° C)

MAIN ATTRACTIONS:
Jim Jim Waterfall
and Twin Falls, Yellow
Water Billabong.
Warradjan Aboriginal
culture center near
Cooinda. Rock drawings
at Ubirr, Nourlangie.
Nawurlandja Lookout
viewpoint

SPECIAL TIPS:
Some of the Park's
roads are flooded
during the rainy
season and there
are few gas stations

The Aborigines carved
the outlines of human
figures into soft rock
near Ubirr – these
drawings are some
of the oldest carvings
in the world (left)

View from Obiri
Rock onto the Magela
Floodplains
(above, right)

One of the premier
wildlife sightings
within the National
Park is the rare
monitor lizard
(below, right)

The beauty of the corals

The **GREAT BARRIER REEF** extends for more than 1,200 miles (2,000km) off the coast of northeast Australia

GETTING THERE:
By ship or light aircraft to the islands; most reefs accessible by boat

WHERE TO STAY:
There are 20 luxury-class island hotels and a wide range of accommodation on the mainland. Onboard ship accommodation available near Seetörns

CLIMATE:
Air temperature 75-86° F (24-30° C) in January, 64-75° F (18-24° C) in July

MAIN ATTRACTIONS:
Numerous opportunities for visiting the islands and reefs in combination with water sport activities. Flights and cruises available to more remote parts of the Great Barrier Reef. Islands: Great Keppel (hiking trails); Bedarra (rainforest); Dunk (artists' colony); Lizard and Hinchinbrook (rock paintings)

SPECIAL TIPS:
Utmost heed should be paid to warnings by tour guides and diving instructors regarding dangerous sea creatures

The largest single structure ever created by living creatures lies almost totally underwater. The full extent of its glory and its sheer size can really only be appreciated properly from space, as seen by the Space Shuttle. The Great Barrier Reef, the largest coral reef of all time, stretches over 1,200 miles (2,000km) along the flat continental shelf off Australia's northeastern coast, at a distance of 10–100 miles (16–160km) from the mainland.

The Reef is one of nature's greatest achievements and the architects of this magnificent edifice are tiny coral polyps whose finely chiseled, calcareous skeletons form the framework of the structure, "cemented" together by microscopic coral algae and moss animalcules. Reef-forming corals require sun and warmth due to their close, symbiotic relationship with zooxanthella algae, which need light to survive. The polyps waft nutrient-rich water toward the algae, which in turn ensure that the polyps have the right chemical environment to absorb the large amounts of calcium they need for healthy growth. Consequently, a coral colony always grows towards the light when the water level rises. New layers are constantly being added as each new generation of coral builds on the skeletal remains of the previous generation.

Water temperature is critical

The 2,900 coral reefs and islands, which now fall under the aegis of the 135,000 square miles (350,000km²) of protected area that is the Great Barrier Reef National Park, were all formed in this way. Seven hundred and sixty of these reefs have developed in a circular pattern, often encircling former continental islands. When the continental shelf rose slightly, it lifted 300 of them above the water level. In addition, there are 618 true continental islands, which once formed part of the Australian mainland and are now overgrown with dense rainforest.

Geologically speaking, the Great Barrier Reef is relatively young, its origins dating back a mere 500,000 years. Its present structure is only 8,000–10,000 years old. When the sea settled down to its present level 6,500 years ago, the corals stopped growing upwards. The first examples of coral reef on earth were formed 500 million years ago. The species

that populate today's reefs began their successful colonization just 250,000 years ago.

The symbiotic relationship that exists between the zooxanthella algae and the reef-building corals is extremely sensitive to environmental changes, e.g., water temperature. Conditions in the southwest Pacific are theoretically perfect as temperatures hardly vary from around 82° F (28° C) throughout the year. If the temperature does rise above 86° F (30° C) however, the brightly colored algae abandon their host, depriving the reef of its colorful splendor and leaving a white, calcareous structure in their wake. Over the past few years, global water temperatures have already risen by 1° F and some areas have already witnessed an increasing trend in temperatures exceeding the critical 86° F (30° C) threshold. Even the Great Barrier Reef has seen its algae disappear temporarily from the corals. So far, these creatures have always managed to recover and reestablish their equilibrium with the help of cold ocean currents which serve to cool down the water temperatures. The Great Barrier Reef, the greatest reef in the world, is still one of the healthiest.

Over the years, marine biologists have watched with concern as swarms of starfish occasionally besiege coral reefs. As a result of their frenzied feeding and clumsy movements, which break off pieces of coral, it is not uncommon for them to eat their way through entire reefs, destroying them in the process.

Nowadays, we know that this is simply part of the natural ecosystem of the Great Barrier Reef and that the starfish actually preserve the diversity of the reef by eating their way through the faster-growing species of coral, which would otherwise end up monopolizing these shallow waters.

400 species of coral

Coral reefs are among the most diverse ecosystems on earth. The Great Barrier Reef is no exception. More than 400 different varieties of coral have been identified on the Reef, which also supports countless other creatures. The Barrier Reef is home to altogether 1,500 species of fish, 4,000 mollusks, more than 200 types of bird — 40 of them seabirds — 20 sea snakes, and six species of turtle. There is also a large population of dugong sea cows, which are

The majority of the 2,900 coral reefs in the Great Barrier Reef lie just below the surface (main photo, above)

Only 44 of the reefs have accumulated enough sand and soil above sea level to support vegetation (below, left)

Yellow soft coral is just one of the 400 species found in this marine National Park (below, right)

Waving fronds of algae form a perfect background for the brilliant colors of the anemone fish (center, right)

very rare elsewhere, not to mention approximately 30 different species of whale, dolphin, and porpoise that regularly visit the Reef.

This amazingly diverse expanse of shallow sea also plays a key role in the history and present-day culture of the Aboriginal peoples and island dwellers of the Torres Strait. These first Australians did, after all, get here by crossing what is now the Coral Sea on foot from Indonesia, before the ocean rose and submerged the continental shelf.

Lizard and Hinchinbrook Islands and those situated around Cape Melville still boast spectacular galleries of breathtaking rock drawings, which document Aboriginal history and their links with the sea.

An aborigine paradise

FRASER ISLAND is the world's largest sand island providing a unique habitat for rare plants and bird life

GETTING THERE:
Frequent ferries and passenger ships operate daily from Hervey Bay or Inskip Point. Suitable only for four-wheel drive vehicles

WHERE TO STAY:
All categories of hotel, cabin, and holiday home; campsites of varying standards; off-site camping also available

CLIMATE:
Maritime, sub-tropical climate, 72º-82º F (22-28º C) in December, 57º-70º F (14-21º C) in July. Wettest months: January to March

ACTIVITIES AND ATTRACTIONS::
Bushwalking along forest tracks and nature trails
Central Station at Wanggoolba Creek
Stonetood shifting dune

SPECIAL TIPS:
Beware of dingoes (Australian wild dogs)
Do not bathe in the sea: there may be sharks, not to mention the extremely poisonous box jellyfish during the rainy season. Take all litter back to the mainland

Fraser Island is famed for its deep, clear lakes, one of which is Lake KcKiney (above)

Petrified sand formations are among the island's main attractions (below, left) as well as the luxuriant ferns found in Fraser Island's rainforests (below, right)

Endless white beaches that are the stuff of dreams, flanked by jagged multi-colored sandstone cliffs. Vast, enchanted rainforests surviving on ancient dunes. Crystal-clear lakes and babbling brooks winding romantically through the forest. This is Fraser Island, situated off Australia's central eastern coast.

The aborigines have always referred to it as "K'gan," or paradise. Numerous piles of shells, fish traps, encampments, and scarred trees whose bark was used to build canoes are all reminders of the fact that this island has been inhabited by the Butchella people for at least 5,000 years.

The first European settlers found the island too barren to warrant further exploration. James Cook sailed past it between 18 and 20 May 1770, but Mathew Flinders, the navigator, set foot on the beach here in 1802 although he, too, had ignored it some four years previously.

Nowadays, Fraser Island is a dream destination for nature lovers and seekers of solitude. Measuring over 80 miles (130km) in length, there is plenty of room on the island for everyone – providing they have their own four-wheel drive, as there are no roads, only rough forest tracks that you are not allowed to leave and 75-Mile-Beach on the Pacific seaboard that provides a lonely "highway" link along the beach to the northern end of the island.

Rainforest on sand

Fraser Island is the world's largest sand island, sporting the only subtropical rainforest to survive on infertile sand while also managing to provide a lush habitat for 600 different species of plants. Unusual varieties, such as the Angiopteris fern, which boasts the largest fronds of any fern, seem to prosper here. Unlike other plants, its fronds are not kept upright by tissue structure, but by high water pressure in its capillaries.

For over 700,000 years, rain has been washing sand down from the mountains of eastern Australia and into the ocean. Strong currents then carry it northwards where it accumulates in reefs. Indian Head, an imposing sandstone cliff in the north of the island, was formed in this way. From this vantage point, the view stretches far across the white beaches, the sea of dunes, and the sand hills crowned with green vegetation. Over the millennia, these have grown to heights of up to 800ft (240m) and chart the area's geographical history.

The sand along the coast can shimmer in 72 different hues. The most impressive composition occurs along a 22 mile (35km) stretch of shore, north of Happy Valley. Yet further north, beyond the wreck of the "Maheno" passenger steamer that ran aground in 1935 on its final voyage to the scrap yard, are the uniquely colored rock formations known as "The Cathedral."

Glittering amid the dense green lushness of the tropical rainforest are some 200 crystal-clear, azure-blue lakes and ponds, a tempting prospect for the would-be bather. So pure are they that only very few organisms can find any form of nutrition in them. One creature that has adapted in order to survive in these slightly acidic lakes is the endangered "acid frog," not to mention the Lake Bowarrady turtles.

The water in 40 of these lakes has the consistency of tea, however. Over the course of 300,000 years, leaves and dead plant material have accumulated on the lake beds, effectively sealing them. There are very few such lakes on the planet and Fraser Island boasts half of them.

The other crystal-clear lakes are either fed by the huge reservoir of fresh water beneath the island, or else a shifting dune has blocked off the usual soak away for rain. Clear, cool streams radiate from these lakes like arteries across the rainforest. Wanggoolba Creek, for example, has channeled out a white sandy bed for itself, winding through the dense rainforest from Central Station to the mainland side of the island.

Where the dunes are too high to sustain rainforest, vast eucalyptus forests flourish. Where the soil is even poorer, these, in turn, give way to the type of forests typically found on sandy soil, consisting primarily of kauri spruces and araucarias.

These forests and shores provide food and a haven for over 230 species of bird, as well as numerous birds of passage that stop to rest here on their journey to Siberia. Fraser Island boasts one of the largest and most varied bird populations in all Australia.

The treasures of this dream island were once very nearly lost forever: its sand, which contains valuable minerals used in some industrial processes, used to be excavated regularly, thereby depleting the dunes, and the chain saws were still droning through the forest as recently as 1991. These wounds have now healed after the northern part of the island was declared a National Park and UNESCO designated the entire island a world heritage site.

The southern fjords

MOUNT COOK and FJORDLAND
National Parks in New Zealand cover much of South Island

GETTING THERE:
Between Invercargill and Haast, Highway 6 passes all Te Wahipounamu's National Parks. Daily bus services. Airports at Invercargill and Mount Cook

WHERE TO STAY:
Mainly middle-range hotels, youth hostels, and campsites in towns along Highway 6

CLIMATE:
Cool to moderate climate. January: 66° F (19° C), rising to over 86° F (30° C) in the valleys. July: average temperatures of 34° F (1.3° C), occasionally dropping to 14° F (-10° C). Temperatures drop as the altitude increases. Westland Park is one of the wettest places on earth

MAIN ATTRACTIONS:
Hikes along well-marked trails; Mount Cook; Sutherland Falls; Kea Point (viewpoint); Hooker Valley; mountain climbing and glacier trekking; scenic flights

SPECIAL TIPS:
The National Parks are not easily accessible and only to visitors on foot. It is necessary to book several weeks in advance to walk some of the trails as only a limited number of hikers are permitted at any one time

Te Wahipounamu is a dramatically beautiful landscape of high mountains and fjords in the southwest of New Zealand. From remote beaches on the wild, jagged coastline bordering the shores of the Tasman Sea to the grandeur of the rugged, glacier-clad mountains of the Southern Alps, the two National Parks preserve a unique, almost untouched, natural landscape with a large diversity of habitats. The scenery has been shaped by various periods of glaciations spanning hundreds of thousands of years.

Steep, forested slopes plunge into deep, impenetrable gorges. Dense rainforests occupy the low-lying areas and the coastal region is studded with an abundance of tranquil, shimmering lakes and inlets. It is a land of dramatic contrasts and its 10,000 square miles (26,000km²) have now been designated a world heritage site, encompassing not only Westland, Mount Cook, Fjordland, and Mount Aspiring National Parks, but also 36 additional conservation areas in southwestern New Zealand.

This nature park is situated in one of the most seismically active regions of the world. Southeast New Zealand lies precisely above the spot where the Pacific and Indo-Australian plates collide. The resulting mountains are the product of five million years of geological movements combined with the effects of the glaciers that have carved out deep valleys between the mountains. Westland and Mount Cook National Parks together boast

28 of the 29 peaks in New Zealand that exceed 9,900ft (3,000) meters. At 12,350ft (3,764m), Mount Cook is New Zealand's highest mountain. The force of the breakers, which have rolled in unchecked from the Southern Ocean since prehistoric times, has created some dramatic coastal scenery with steep, bizarrely shaped cliffs, innumerable rocky outcrops, and sheer rock walls.

Three-feet-high tussock grasslands
The most spectacular coastal scenery was created as a result of land being thrust up from the sea and forming numerous terraces, tiered one above the other. The lowest level supports mixed woodland, while the middle band is dominated by mountain beech and yew. Approaching

2,000ft (600m), the terrain becomes shrub landscape.

The rich diversity of habitats, ranging from rainforest to grasslands, shrub land, and broad-leaved woodland is due largely to the dramatic differences in altitude and temperature between east and west. Colorful flower meadows carpet the mountaintops between the tree level and snow line.

Large mountain daisies and Mount Cook lilies, the largest buttercup in the world, grow in the shelter of the three-feet-high tussock grass. Its remote location has spared Te Wahipounamu any significant human interference and preserved it as a key habitat for many indigenous species. Around 50,000 fur seals now congregate in colonies along the coastline. These mammals were once

hunted so ruthlessly by Europeans that by the end of the nineteenth century, the species had almost been wiped out.

The bird life here is also outstanding. The National Park is home to a large proportion of New Zealand's forest birds with many of the 170 varieties exclusive to this region.

The one and only mountain parrot

Above the tree line, the kea can be found hopping among the tussocks of grass, apparently finding the effort of flying against the blustery mountain winds too arduous to contemplate. These crow-sized birds with their dull, olive-green plumage are the only mountain parrot to be found anywhere in the world. They are extremely curious and will rummage

through people's belongings at campsites, even having been known to make off with small items of equipment such as cameras.

The flightless Takahe is a rare and endangered species of rail with blue-green foliage and a red, curved bill. The Park's coastline is also the sole habitat of the 20in (50cm) tall Victoria penguin with between 1,000 and 2,000 breeding pairs occupying the coastal cliffs. In contrast to the rest of New Zealand, the numerous lakes and fjords in this region are a veritable paradise for fish. Seventeen species occur here, many of which are rarely found elsewhere in New Zealand, for example the giant Kokopu, a species of pike popular with anglers that is frequently found in Te Wahipounamu's rivers and lakes.

The picturesque Lake Pukakai lies at the foot of 12,350ft (3,764m) high Mount Cook, New Zealand's tallest mountain (above)

The twin peaks of Mount Tasman and Mount Cook dominate the mountain scenery of South Island (below, left)

PHOTO CREDITS

p. 4/5 Bilderberg/Michael Ende; p. 8/9 above picture-alliance/dpa/Scanfoto Thingvold, below left picture-alliance/dpa/Paul van Gaalen, above left Bilderberg/Wolfgang Fuchs, below right picture-alliance/dpa/Winfried Wisniewski; p. 10/11 above left Schapowalow/Larkins, above right Schapowalow/Furhmann, below left Schapowalow/Kölsch, below center Schapowalow/Wolf, below right Schapowalow/Aspect; p. 12/13 all Schapowalow/Novak; p. 14/15 above Schapowalow/Dr. Harten, below left Schapowalow/Heaton, below center Schapowalow/Lossen, below right Schapowalow/Messerschmidt; p. 16/17 above Schapowalow/Kirsch, below Schapowalow/Heaton, p. 18/19 above Schapowalow/Atlantide (GC), below left Schapowalow/v.d. Hecken, below, center Schapowalow/Fuhrmann, below right Schapowalow/Sander; p. 20/21 above Schapowalow/Neuner, below left Schapowalow Atlantide (GC), below center Schapowalow/Atlantide (GC), below right Schapowalow/Atlantide (GC); p. 22/23 all Schapowalow/Wood Buffalo National Park; p. 24/25 above Schapowalow/Heaton, below Schapowalow/Scholz; p. 26/27 left Schapowalow/Schulke, above right Schapowalow/Peters, below right Schapowalow/Peters; p. 28-29 all Schapowalow/Huber; p. 30/31 above Schapowalow/Atlantide (GC), below Schapowalow/Beckert; p. 32/33 all Schapowalow/Huber; p. 34/35 above left Schapowalow/Tolkmitt, above center Schapowalow/Tolkmitt, above right Schapowalow/Tolkmitt, below right Schapowalow/Ziegler; p. 36/37 all Arne Nicolaisen; p. 40/41 all Arne Nicolaisen; p. 42/43 above right Schapowalow/Atlantide (MB), below left Schapowalow/Dörig, below center Schapowalow/ Dörig; p. 44/45 above right picture-alliance/dpa/F. Hoogervorst, below left picture-alliance/dpa/Raimundo Valentim, below right picture-alliance/dpa/F. Hoogervorst; p. 46/47 all Bilderberg/Michael Ende; p. 48/49 all Bilderberg/Michael Ende; p. 50/51 all Schapowalow/Atlantide (GC); p. 52/53 above right Schapowalow/art of nature, below left Schapowalow/K. Scholz, below right Schapowalow/K. Scholz; p. 54/55 above Schapowalow/Bernutz, below left Schapowalow/Rosenfeld, below right Schapowalow/Huber; p. 56/57 above right Schapowalow/Novak, below left Schapowalow/art of nature, below right Schapowalow/K. Scholz; p. 58-59 above right Schapowalow/Komine, below left Schapowalow/Landschack, below right Schapowalow/Schröder; p. 60/61 above right Schapowalow/Heaton, below left Schapowalow/JBE, below right Schapowalow/Heaton; p. 62/63 all Bilderberg/Dinodia; p. 64/65 above right picture-alliance/dpa/Str, below left picture-alliance/dpa/Harish Tyagi, below right Schapowalow/Rocksien; p. 66/67 above Schapowalow/Stepan, below right picture-alliance/dpa/Christian Mikutta; p. 68-69 all Schapowalow/Huber; p. 70/71 left picture-alliance/Okapia KG/Hans Reinhard, right picture-alliance/dpa/Zhou Kang; p. 72-73 above Schapowalow/Huber, below left Schapowalow/Atlantide (MB), below right Schapowalow/Atlantide (MB); p. 74/75 left picture-alliance/dpa/Panasia, right picture-alliance/dpa/Tomonori Otsuka; p. 76/77 all Bilderberg/Milan Horacek; p. 78/79 above Schapowalow/Moser, below Schapowalow/Huber; p. 80/81 above Schapowalow/Atlantide (SA), above right Schapowalow/Atlantide (SA), below right Schapowalow/Sander; p. 82/83 Schapowalow/Reichelt; p. 84/85 all Schapowalow/Behrendt; p. 86/87 above right Schapowalow/JBE, below left Schapowalow/Reichelt, below right Schapowalow/Scholz; p. 88/89 above right Schapowalow/Nebe, below left Schapowalow/Ponzio, below center Schapowalw/Huber, below right Schapowalow/Nebe; p. 90/91 all Bilderberg/Klaus Bossemeyer; p. 92/93 above right Schapowalow/Gierig, below left Schapowalow/Fahn, below center Schapowalow/Gierig, below right picture-alliance/dpa/Jesper Sandström; p. 94/95 above left picture-alliance/dpa/Mauri Rautkari, above right picture-alliance/dpa/Hannu Vallas, below right picture-alliance/dpa/Mauri Rautkari; p. 96/97 above right Schapowalow/Thiele, below left Schapowalow/Pratt-Pries, below right Schapowalow/Thiele; p. 98/99 above left Schapowalow/Pratt-Pries, above right Schapowalow/K. Scholz, below right Schapowalow/Brooke; p. 100/101 Schapowalow/Aspect, below center Schapowalow/Patt-Pries, below right Schapowalow/Aspect; p. 102/103 left Schapowalow/Gierig, above right Schapowalow/Gierig, center right Schapowalow/Aspect, below right Schapowalow/Aspect; p. 104/105 above right Schapowalow/Nebe, below left Schapowalow/Koserowsky, below right Schapowalow/Backhaus; p. 106/107 above left Schapowalow/Dr. Nowak, below right Schapowalow/Rakebrand; p. 108/109 left Schapowalow/Huber, right Schapowalow/Busert; p. 110/111 above Schapowalow/art of nature, below Schapowalow/Huber; p. 112/113 above left Schapowalow/Weißer, above right Schapowalow/Böker, below right Schapowalow/De Vree; p. 114/115 all Schapowalow/Pratt-Pries; p. 116/117 all Schapowalow/Atlantide (GC); p. 118/119 above left Schapowalow/Pratt-Pries, above right Schapowalow/Pratt-Pries, below left Schapowalow/Fuhrmann, below right Schapowalow/Pratt-Pries; p. 120/121 all Schapowalow/Pratt-Pries; p. 122/123 below right Schapowalow/Messerschmidt, above right Schapowalow/De Vree, center right Schapowalow/Huber, below right Schapowalow/Mader; p. 124/125 above right Schapowalow/Kirsch, below left Schapowalow/Geiersperger, above right Schapowalow/Mader; p. 126/127 above right picture-alliance/ZB/Matthias Hiekel, below left picture-alliance/gms/Sächsische Schweiz Tourist Association/Frank Richter, below left picture-alliance/ZB/Matthias Hiekel; p. 128/129 above left picture-alliance/gms/Czech Central Tourist Association, above right picture-alliance/ZB/Transit/Christian Nowak, below left picture-alliance/dpa/CTK Saskia Bergova, below right picture-alliance/dpa/CTK Saskia Bergova; p. 130/131 above left picture-alliance/Polska Agencja Interpress, above right picture-alliance/dpa/Göbel, below right picture-alliance/dpa/Polska Agencja Interpress; p. 132/133 above left picture-alliance/dpa/Dick Klees, below left picture-alliance/dpa/Sari Gustaffson, right picture-alliance/dpa/RIA Novosti; p. 134/135 below left Schapowalow/Scholz, above right Schapowalow/Huber, below right Schapowalow/Huber; p. 136/137 all picture-alliance/dpa/RIA Novosti; p. 138/139 all Schapowalow/Lensch; p. 140/141 above left Schapowalow/Nebe, above right Schapowalow/Huber, below right Schapowalow/Johansson; p. 142/143 left Schapowalow/Dr. Novak, above center Schapowalow/Atlantide (GC), above right Schapowalow/Dr. Novak, below right Schapowalow/Huber; p. 144/145 above Schapowalow/Huber, below Schapowalow/Bodo Müller; p. 146/147 above right Schapowalow/Schröder, below right Schapowalow/Doormann; p. 148/149 above right Schapowalow/Nebe, below left Schapowalow/K. Scholz, below right Schapowalow/Nebe; p. 150/151 all Schapowalow/Thiele; p. 152/153 above left Schapowalow/Atlantide (SA), below right Schapowalow/Cora; p. 154/155 all Schapowalow/Atlantide (MB); p. 156/157 all Schapowalow/Atlantide (GC); 158/159 above left Schapowalow/Gessler, above right Schapowalow/Thiele, below right Schapowalow/Gessler; p. 160/161 links Schapowalow/Thiele, above center Schapowalow/Thiele, above right, below center Schapowalow/Ambild; p. 162/163 above Bilderberg/Klaus-D. Francke, below Schapowalow/Klee; p. 164/165 all Schapowalow/JBE; p. 166/167 above right Schapowalow/Atlantide (SA), below left Schapowalow/Atlantide(SA), below center Schapowalow/Atlantide (SA), below right Schapowalow/Doormann; p. 168/169 all Schapowalow/Atlantide (GC); p. 170/171 all Schapowalow/Atlantide (GC); p. 172/173 all Schapowalow/Scholz; p. 174/175 above right Schapowalow/Huber, below left Schapowalow/Huber, below right Schapowalow/Fahn, p. 176/177 above right Schapowalow/Atlantide (SA), below left Schapowalow/Aspect, below center Schapowalow/Nebbia, below right Schapowalow/Nebbia; p. 178/179 above right Schapowalow/Aspect, below left Schapowalow/Atlantide (SA), below right Schapowalow/Nebbia; p. 180/181 above Schapowalow/Atlantide (SA), below Schapowalow/Huber; p. 182/183 Schapowalow/Wende; p. 184/185 above right Schapowalow/Thiele, below left Schapowalow/Huber, below right Schapowalow/Atlantide (GC); p. 186/187 above Schapowalow/Thiele, below Schapowalow/Pratt-Pries; p. 188/189 all Schapowalow/Pratt-Pries; p. 190-191 above left Schapowalow/Jean, above right Schapowalow/Sperber, center right Schapowalow/K. Scholz, below right Schapowalow/Nacivet; p. 192/193 above right Schapowalow/Ebel, below left Schapowalow Maetschke, below right Schapowalow/Huber; p. 194/195 all Schapowalow/Huber; p. 196/197 left Schapowalow/Röhrbein, below center Schapowalow/Atlantide (MB), above right Schapowalow/Huber, below right Schapowalow/Atlantide (MB); p. 198/199 above right Schapowalow/Heaton, below left Schapowalow/JBE, below center Schapowalow /Heaton, below right Schapowalow/JBE; p. 200/201 left Schapowalow/v. Rennings, above right Schapowalow/Sander, below right Schapowalow/Heaton; p. 202/203 below left Schapowalow/Heaton, above right Schapowalow/Heaton, center right Schapowalow/Kägi; p. 204/205 all Schapowalow/Neuner; p. 206/207 above Schapowalow/Neuner, below Schapowalow/Heaton

IMPRINT

© 2004 REBO International b.v. Lisse, The Netherlands

Published and edited by: Dr. Manfred Leier
Text: Hanns-Joachim Neubert / ScienceCom (all text apart from pages 108 – 111 and 126 – 127)
Winfried Maaß (Pages 108 – 111 and 126 – 127)
Research: Dr. Onno Groß, Axel Grychta, Vera Stadie
Graphics: BartosKersten Printmediendesign, Hamburg
Photo editing: Stefanie Braun / Photoagentur Schapowalow
Proofreading: Edwine Bollmann
Documentation: Dr. Onno Groß
Copy-editing: Onne Behrends
Editorial technology: Bollmann & Rieprich, Hamburg
Production: HVK Hamburger Verlagskontor GmbH, Hamburg
English translation: Susan Ghanouni for First Edition Translations Ltd., Cambridge, England
Typesetting: A. R. Garamond s.r.o., Prague, The Czech Republic

ISBN 90 366 1577 1